TREVOR BRENNAN

Heart and Soul

With Gerry Thornley

Gerry Thornley has been rugby correspondent of The Irish Times since 1997.
He is a frequent contributor and rugby analyst on television and radio.
He lives in Sandyford in County Dublin with his wife, Una,
and three children, Dylan, Evan and Shana.
This is his first book.

RED ROCK PRESS | FIRST FOR SPORT

Running out onto the pitch for the Toulouse v Leinster encounter in the 2006 Heineken Cup quarter-final. Defeat at the hands of his former team was devastating.

"We could beat the hell out of each other for 80 minutes and it was forgotten as soon as the match was over. We'd be the first two at the bar. I suppose he reminded me of myself."
PETER CLOHESSY
Former Munster and Irish prop.

"He was a great team man, probably one of the best team men you could ever get."
NOEL McQUILKIN
Former Bective Rangers coach.

"He was the type of guy that you'd have followed out over the trenches in World War I."
BRENT POPE
Former player and St Mary's coach. Now an author and rugby analyst.

"One of the worst liars I have ever met."
DENIS HICKIE
St Mary's, Leinster and Ireland teammate.

"Extraordinary, fearless and totally committed."
MATT WILLIAMS
Former coach of New South Wales Waratahs, Leinster and Scotland.

"I got on really well with him, and I found him to be a great person — a real genuine person. There was no shit about him."
PETER STRINGER
Irish scrum-half.

"An indispensable, unquestioned and deeply loved element in our team."
GUY NOVÈS
Toulouse coach and former French international.

"Mad as a hatter."
HARRY WILLIAMS
Former Ulster and Bective coach.

AUTHOR'S ACKNOWLEDGMENTS

This was, by some distance, the hardest project I've ever undertaken and, quite simply, wouldn't have been possible without the considerable help of many people. Uppermost amongst these were my mother, Petria, who made an invaluable contribution to the manuscript, and my sister Yseult, for hours and hours of painstaking transcribing.

To my sports editor at *The Irish Times*, Malachy Logan, for his encouragement and advice all along the way.

To ERC commercial manager, Diarmaid Murphy, who came up with the idea of Trevor's 'Toulouse Diary' in *The Irish Times*.

Thanks to my publisher and driving force, Stephen Ryan, for the initial kick up the derriere that was required, and thereafter was a joy to deal with throughout.

So many people helped in checking and re-checking facts. Ronnie Brennan who verified innumerable dates, times, and places. Likewise, Donal Lenihan very generously took the time to dust off all his old manager's notes from 1998 and 1999.

Thanks too to all Trevor's former teammates and coaches who, so very generously, gave of their time.

To Trevor, whose time, effort and willingness to recall the details and episodes from his life was remarkable. I enjoyed every minute of our time working on this project.

To Trevor's wife Paula and their children. Thanks for your hospitality in Toulouse.

To the many friends and colleagues who listened and offered advice.

Most of all – for the intrusions into family time over two holidays and in between times – to Una, Dylan, Evan and Shana.

Gerry Thornley
September 2007

Trevor Brennan, playing for St Mary's in 1999, takes on the best that Garryowen has to offer.

1981-1991

Begins career with Leixlip club Barnhall as far as Leinster Junior League.

1992

Joins Bective Rangers.

1997

Joins St Mary's.

1999-2000

Captains St Mary's to victory in the AIB League.

St Mary's is the only Leinster club ever to win the title.

2001-02

Plays one season with Barnhall in AIB League Division Two.

1997-2002

Plays with Leinster.

2002-2007

Joins Toulouse and becomes a key player for the French side
over the next five seasons.

1998

v South Africa. Makes debut for Ireland as second-half replacement for Victor
Costello in 37-13 defeat in Bloemfontein.

2ND Cap

v South Africa. As replacement for Victor Costello in 33-0 defeat in Pretoria.

3RD Cap

v France. As replacement for Victor Costello in 10-9 defeat in Five Nations
Championship. Lansdowne Road, 1999.

4TH Cap

v Scotland. As replacement for Andy Ward after 65 minutes in
30-13 defeat in Five Nations Championship. Murrayfield, 1999.

5TH Cap

v Italy. Plays full 80 minutes and named Man of the Match in 39-30 victory. Not a
Five Nations game. Lansdowne Road, 1999.

6TH Cap

v Australia. After missing first test in Brisbane through injury, starts in
32-26 defeat to Australia in Perth, 1999.

7TH Cap

v Argentina in World Cup warm-up. Starts in Ireland's 32-24 win.
Replaced by Eric Miller after 59 minutes. Lansdowne Road, 1999.

8TH Cap

v USA. Starts opening World Cup match in Ireland's 53-8 win.
Replaced by Eric Miller after 59 minutes. Lansdowne Road, 1999.

9TH Cap

v Australia. Starts fourth test in a row in 23-3 defeat
to eventual champions Australia. Lansdowne Road, 1999.

10TH Cap

v England. A 48th minute replacement for Dion O'Cuinneagain in Ireland's 50-18
defeat in Six Nations Championship. Twickenham, 2000.

Dropped for the following 44-22 win over Scotland and misses next 13 Irish tests.

11TH Cap

v Wales. As 58th minute replacement for Mick Galwey in 36-6 win over
Wales. Cardiff, 2001.

12TH Cap

v England. As 67th minute replacement for Mick Galwey in 20-14 Six Nations
Championship win. Lansdowne Road, 2001.

13TH Cap

v Samoa. A half-time replacement for
Eric Miller in 35-8 win. Lansdowne Road, 2001.

2003

Wins Heineken Cup medal with Toulouse, starting in
22-17 win over Perpignan at Lansdowne Road.

2004

On losing Toulouse team in final of Heineken Cup to
Wasps (27-20) at Twickenham.

2005

Wins second Heineken Cup medal, starting 18-12 win in final over
Stade Francais in Murrayfield.

2007

Announces his retirement from the game.

TREVOR BRENNAN
HEART AND SOUL

First published 2007

RED ROCK PRESS
Glengyle
Claremont Road
Howth
Dublin 13
Ireland

redrockpress@eircom.net

This edition published 2007

© TREVOR BRENNAN and GERRY THORNLEY

The moral right of the authors has been asserted.

A catalogue record for this book is available from the British Library.

ISBN 978-0-9548653-5-1

COPY EDITING AND INDEX: **MARK GILLEECE**
PRINTING: **J H HAYNES, SPARKFORD, SOMERSET**
PRINTING LIAISON: **HUGH STANCLIFFE**
COVER PHOTOGRAPH: **DAVID RODGERS** (GETTY IMAGES)
BACK PAGE: **LORRAINE O'SULLIVAN** (INPHO)
AUTHOR PHOTOGRAPH: **THE IRISH TIMES**
ALL OTHER PHOTOGRAPHS: **INPHO PHOTOGRAPHY/BRENNAN FAMILY**

WWW.REDROCKPRESS.IE

Coming off the Lansdowne Road pitch after his 13th and final cap for Ireland, against Samoa in 2001.

FOREWORD

To Paula, whose love and support has kept me afloat
while storms have raged about me.

To my children, Daniel, Joshua and Bobby.

To my father Rory, mother Iris, and brothers Ronnie and Errol —
family and friends in equal measure.

And to Damien.

We think of you every day.

And miss you every day.

*

My Ma and Da were great storytellers. As a family we often sat around the kitchen table listening to them or to the many people who came through our house in Leixlip. I've been very lucky and privileged to have met so many interesting people in life and to have listened to their stories.

Now I get the chance to tell mine. I feel like I'm doing what I did on the pitch; putting my neck on the line. And I'm a lot more nervous doing it here than I ever was in the heat of a game.

The idea for the book began to take shape four years ago when I began collaborating with Gerry Thornley for my columns in *The Irish Times*. Those columns began shortly after I left Ireland for France, and recorded both my professional rugby and family life here in Toulouse.

The reaction to the columns was fantastic. And if I heard the line – "you should go and write a book," – once, I heard it a thousand times.

Doing the columns was one thing; pulling the many threads of my life together

for this book was another, and I thank Gerry enormously for his help, patience and the craic we had while doing it.

It was quite a tough task not least because I wasn't sure there was enough in my life to justify a book.

But as we talked and recalled various events and incidents over my playing career, I thought "why not?"

That "why not?" approach pretty much reflects how I've lived my life whether trying to achieve my dream of playing for Ireland or winning Heineken Cup medals.

Someone once said to me that my story of coming from 'the wrong side of the rugby tracks' was remarkable and that how I managed to re-start my career after it looked dead and buried, was inspirational.

I'd never make that claim myself. But if my story – that of a very ordinary man trying to get the best out of himself – helps anyone achieve their goals, then that will do me just fine.

Many things have been written about me in the course of my rugby career. Some good – some bad. This is an attempt to set the record straight. I'm not as bad as some think – but I'm certainly not as perfect as my children believe I am.

I hope that I've got everything pretty much right in this book and I hope that I have given everyone a fair crack of the whip. You can't go through a career in professional rugby without upsetting some people. But at least I hope that I've been fair.

Like anyone, I've made a lot of mistakes along the way. Some of those mistakes have been particularly hard to live with. But I am determined to learn from them – particularly for my children.

I want to instil in them the belief that you can fulfil your dreams if you work hard and commit to whatever path in life you choose.

I loved my life in rugby, the doors it opened and the countries I visited; but most of all I enjoyed making so many friends and acquaintances along the way.

So to my former team-mates, adversaries, coaches, referees, pals, supporters and fellow travellers in the world of rugby, I sincerely hope that you enjoy the story (so far) of my life.

Merci encore

Trevor Brennan
September 2007

PROLOGUE

AFTERMATH

JE REGRETTE

I can still go along with them (the team), but it's not quite the same. I haven't earned it. You feel as if you're in the way. It's not that they make me feel that way; it's me making myself feel that way. The week after I was banned for life, Guy Novès told me "you can come here any time you want, you can train here whenever you want; you're still part of this team."

I didn't expect a life ban, but I did expect a year or two. I regret going into that stand. I regret hitting that Ulster fan. There isn't a day I don't think about it.

Maybe if I had warmed up with the rest of the subs instead of on my own ... even if the fitness coach had accompanied me I'd have been talking with him and not heard the chants ... maybe if I had warmed up at the other end of the pitch ... maybe if I had just jumped over the wall and shaken his hand...

Saturday, May 7th, 2007.
TODAY'S A MATCH DAY, EXCEPT THAT I'M NOT PLAYING. THIS IS HOW IT WILL BE from now on. I don't like going to matches as a spectator. The visit of Bayonne to Stade Ernest-Wallon is our second last home match of the season. It should have been my second last home match too, but my career has been ended by suspension.

All players are bad spectators. We're not good watchers. I'd rather have a few pints with friends in a pub and get a text message with the result. Even when I was injured I had to wear the club's suit, go to the match and attend the post-match sponsors' marquee. That was part of the job. It's a light grey, pin-striped suit with a pink Stade Toulousain crest; a nice suit, but it's still a suit.

My weekends used to be very different. Even for home matches in le Championnat, I'd meet the lads in the club the day before, have a light team run, go to the team hotel and maybe watch a video of the opposition. I don't miss that. It could be the third or fourth video session of the week. We'd be cracking up. After the team meal, the evening was our own. Most lads played some poker whereas I opted to read a book or watch television in my room.

I was usually one of the first down to breakfast along with the coaches and management. I never liked lying in bed all morning. I preferred to have a chat, read the papers and go back to bed for a nap. Today's kick-off is at 6.30pm, so the lads would have had their line-out practice or a light stretch in the hotel grounds around 3.00pm, and be meeting again in the next half-hour, at about 5.00pm.

It's a long day; a 3.00pm kick-off is better. But it's not the worst. Some games kick-off at 8.30 or 9.00pm. After icing whatever knocks you invariably took, it could be past midnight by the time you emerge from the ground. You're in no form to hit the town then. Tonight though, the lads will probably have a meal together afterwards.

The club have been good to me since my suspension, supporting me and keeping me involved. The manager rang me yesterday and said "if you're not doing anything come along to the meal afterwards. We'd love to see you." Two weeks ago, after the Six Nations, they went into camp in St Cyprien for four days and asked me along, but I'd made plans to return to Ireland.

I have been banned from playing rugby for the rest of my life, but I still use the club's gym three or four times a week. I still have the same locker I've had for the last five years, number 69. Soixante-neuf. Last week we were handed the new Stade Toulouse tracksuit and t-shirts. The bagman told me "You mightn't be playing but you're still part of the team and part of our thoughts."

Nike and Puma have been my boot sponsors and I'd built up a collection of about ten pairs. Last Monday week I looked at them and thought "I'll never be wearing these again." So I put the boots in a big box and handed it to Daniel Renard.

He spends the whole day cleaning our dressing-rooms and laundering our gear. Sometimes twice in one day. Even on days off, if I go to the gym, Daniel would be there working anyway. He's paid a salary but when I asked him why he does it, he said because he loves it, the players and the club. He's been part of the furniture since long before I joined.

I handed him the box. "Give them to any of the young guys on the Espoirs (Toulouse's under-19s) who have size 13 feet." Yea, size 13. I needed planning permission to wear them! I'm always giving away my gear but I've never had too many takers for the boots. When looking for gear, mates ask me "Could you not get me Freddy Michalak's?" Any time Danny, my son, comes with me to the club he goes straight for the locker of Jean-Baptiste Élissalde, our scrum-half. The same size feet: 42. The same size clothes: small man's.

That moment, knowing I'd never wear those boots again, brought a lump to my throat.

I've already been asked by Golden Oldies teams to play for them. But even if my appeal reduces the life ban, and I'm allowed to play charity matches one day, my professional rugby career is over.

Maybe it's a blessing in disguise. I've taken thousands of knocks because of the way I play. I'm 33, but I'm a high impact, high mileage 33-year-old. The body was starting to feel the effects, and who knows, I might have ended up crippled if I'd continued to play.

I'll have problems climbing out of bed, and my back will always trouble me. If it's a cold day, my hands kill me. I'd say I have arthritis, which dates back to peeling potatoes in freezing cold buckets of water in the chipper.

It's all been worth it. Not for the win bonuses or the salaries. I've played rugby since 1982. My career has spanned the amateur as well as the professional era. I played because I love rugby, I love the camaraderie, the fun I've had and the friends I've made.

The under-age trips to Jed-Forest with Barnhall, my old club in Ireland where I began my rugby career, were as good as the Irish tours to South Africa and Australia. More than anything I loved the feeling that came with winning. You trained with your mates on wet and windy Tuesday and Thursday nights. With Barnhall in Parsonstown. With Bective in the aptly named Glenamuck. Or St Mary's in Templeville Road. All season long.

We all did that, most coming straight from college or work. Like me, those team-mates could have found something else to do.

If rugby had remained amateur, and I'd been asked to play for either my club or my country, I would gladly have continued to play the game. For the feeling of pride I had, for making my family and friends proud of me, wearing that jersey, and winning an All-Ireland League or a Heineken Cup or a test match for Ireland.

There's no better feeling than having something tangible at the end of a season, to win a final in, say, Lansdowne Road, where I've been lucky enough to win a few. The first thing you want to do is hug and kiss a team-mate. But the second thing you want to do, and I know other players feel the same, is to look to the stands; for your family, for your friends. I always knew where they were and I always tried to make eye contact. Because they suffer as much as you when you lose, you want to see your own happiness and joy in their faces when you win.

None of it would have been possible without their support. I just think of my father, my brothers, uncles and friends who have followed me throughout my entire career, the expense they've incurred on flights, hotels and spending money.

And they'll experience the whole range of emotions, just as I will today. I'll live through every kick-off, line-out and scrum; I'll feel every tackle even though I'll be sitting in the stand. They're still my team-mates, and I regard Stade Toulouse as more than a club. They're very much a family. I'm not thinking just of the coaches and the 22 players.

It's everyone, from the guy who cleans the dressing-room, to the groundsman who cuts the grass and marks the pitch, to the girls in the ticket office or the caterers in the canteen, as much as the backroom staff or the players who have been injured.

Everyone is equal. No-one goes around with their heads up their arses. Everyone's part of the family and I believe 'Stade' achieve what they achieve because of that. So today I'll go through the same emotions that I've made my family and friends go through. It's payback time, in a way.

'Stade' have been my saviours. My career with Leinster and Ireland had hit a cul-de-sac. But Toulouse gave me five years that I could never have expected. I would never have played for Ireland again anyway. Although not playing for Ireland in the last five years, when I've played my best rugby, is hard to come to terms with. I'll always be a Leinster man. The big games, the wins, the drinks in Kielys, the camaraderie were among the best days.

But the last year was the most frustrating. Even if I played my heart out, I felt I was banging my head against a brick wall trying to get back into the Irish team.

By the end of the 2001-02 season I went home one night to Paula, then my partner and now my wife, and said "Whatever else happens next, I'm finished with Leinster". I didn't know what would happen next, but I ended up with what I believe to be the best club in the world, for five fantastic years. And so the best was kept to last, even if wasn't reflected in a 14th Irish cap.

I've never had any major injuries, and I intend to keep fit. There was a time when it took me 24 hours to recover from games. Just 'a rub' on the Sunday and be right as rain on the Monday. But in the last two years it was the Wednesday before I felt like that. I don't know whether you'd call it cheating but in those last two years I didn't do too many of the physical sessions on Monday or Tuesday.

Not that the lads in Toulouse were having that. "Ah la la, he's back. He trains on Wednesday and Thursday, does the team run on Friday and he plays!" They were a little jealous, and I'd play along, as if I were the cute Irishman, but I was genuinely feeling sore. I was managing my body in the last two years; I *had* become a little cuter.

It's like the discipline. Discipline would be the main aspect of my game I would change if I could turn back the clock. Lately, I tried to stop myself from always jumping in to defend a team-mate. If I was to be honest, right up to the end, I was often my own worst enemy.

Then again, if you look at Alan Quinlan or Lawrence Dallaglio, or Roy Keane or countless others, you know that some sportsmen have to play on the edge. And, with that, come the penalties, the yellow cards, the occasional red one and the suspensions. But take that 'edge' away, and just like them, I wouldn't have been half the player I was.

It's now two hours to kick-off. From my office on the first floor of the bar which I own in Toulouse called De Danu, I can see the bridge on the Canal du Midi. Further up the canal is like a crossroads, branching off in different directions. It used to be the main transport system. The A62 road from the motorway passes over this bridge, and hence any motorists coming to Toulouse from Barcelona, Narbonne, Aude or Carcassonne have to pass my bar.

I've been clever enough in preparing myself for this day. We weren't spoilt kids. I haven't frittered away money on toys for men. I bought my first house for £45,000, in Leixlip, when I was 21. We always understood the value of a pound. I've never had a pension scheme; instead I learned the importance of bricks and mortar over the years.

When I worked for Sammy Macari in his chipper in Leixlip, his motto was 'Pennies make pounds, pounds make hundreds, hundreds make thousands'. At the end of the night I'd see him picking up coins off the ground, and he was a wealthy man. He always told me: "Property. Property. Bricks and mortar."

He used to ask me to read the Irish papers to him, and he bought property all over the country. At 16 I tried to obtain a loan from a local estate agent. You could probably buy a house in Leixlip for £18-20,000 at the time.

If I'd had a crystal ball I'd have bought ten houses. When I was given my first IRFU contract, I didn't believe in flash car stereos or plasma screens. Rather than a top of the range mobile phone, I had a ready-to-go, top-up phone which was usually out of credit.

I wasn't mean. I'd be first up to the bar. But working 70 or 80 hours a week in a fish-and-chip shop, on a building site or the Springfield Hotel taught me not to blow money.

I made mistakes too; bad investments, stocks and shares that have lost money. All part of life's swings and roundabouts.

Yannick Bru is also retiring at the end of this season. He is a financial consultant who looks after investments for rugby and soccer players in France. They buy the equivalent of section 23 properties here with nine or eleven year tax free leases. I see a market in Ireland now for people who might want to invest in French properties, especially with more direct flights between the two countries.

As much as I like De Danu, I'm not sure I could work behind a bar full-time. Throwing people out and coming home at 3.00am or 4.00am in the morning doesn't appeal to me. We have a good staff. We're lucky in that we employ Irish students or bilingual French students, but I served my time behind a counter in my younger days.

Rugby will, I hope, be less than half my life, but it's been such a huge part of it. It can never be replaced and the suddenness of the end hasn't helped.

Paula, asked one day: "What kind of day are you having? Are you having a good day or a bad day?"

I say "What do you mean?"

"Well I see you're not yourself today?"

"Yeah. It's really bad today."

She understands when I need some time to myself. She knows me better than anyone. But there's nothing that can replace that buzz. Going out for a drink or a game of golf is no substitute. When you're 100% fit, in your full health and you've trained all week, everything revolves around match day. Stade Toulouse have a lap of honour after every home win. Then there's the feeling in the dressing-room, and making plans for that night.

I can still go along with them, but it's not quite the same. I haven't earned it. You feel as if you're in the way. It's not that they make me feel that way; it's me making myself feel that way.

The week after I was banned for life, Guy Novès told me "You can come here any time you want, you can train here whenever you want; you're still part of this team."

I didn't expect a life ban, but I did expect a year or two. I regret going into that stand. I regret hitting that Ulster fan. There isn't a day I don't think about it.

"Maybe if I had warmed up with the rest of the subs instead of on my own ... maybe if the fitness coach had accompanied me I'd have been talking with him and not heard the chant ... maybe if I had warmed up at the other end of the pitch... maybe if I had just jumped over the wall and shaken his hand..."

So many 'what ifs'. Unfortunately we all make mistakes in our lives. Don't get me wrong, that wasn't my first mistake. But it has been the most costly.

It hurt me financially as well. I'd been offered a two-year deal with Montauban, only 30 kilometres away, on similar terms to those which I was on with Toulouse. I could also have returned to Ireland where I had offers to be a player-coach at club level.

Aside from all of that, the fallout from that moment of madness became something of a circus.

I wish I could have rung him the next day and apologised. More than anything, as a professional sportsman, I should have just walked away.

Toulouse come into today's match having beaten Montpellier, Castres, Clermont and Narbonne, three of them with bonus points, to move into third place with three games to go. Newspaper reports of our demise, notably in *Midi Olympique* back in November, have proved premature, and journalists from that rugby paper have been cold-shouldered a little.

I'm taking Jarlath Daly, a former player and president of Barnhall, and his wife Marie to today's match. There's scarcely ever a home game without some visitor from Leixlip. The traffic is a curse. On a sunny evening, the day before polling day in the Presidential race between Nicolas Sarkozy and Ségolène Royal, all roads seem to lead to le Stade Ernest-Wallon.

I take a u-turn from a normally quiet back route and head for the motorway, but the tailback from three exit roads to the ground has caused gridlock so I carry on and try another way. This works, though I have to abandon the sponsored Peugeot in a car park despite the objections of the attendant. As one of the newspaper headings said of me recently 'More French than the French'. I joke to Jarlath and Marie.

I take my seat in the third row of the area behind our dug-out reserved for injured or former players, club officials etc. It fills up in the five minutes before kick-off. Franck Belot, the lock I replaced at Toulouse and heavily involved with the French players union Provale, informed me that all the clubs have signed the petition supporting the appeal against my life ban, as have thousands of individuals.

He tells me to call into his office and collect them for my solicitor. Didier Lacroix, an ex-Toulouse player whom I played with, and against, is there and Clément Poitrenaud greets me in the customary French way with a 'bisou' – a kiss on both cheeks – and takes his seat two rows in front of me.

"What's wrong with you?" I ask him.

"J'ai un entorse de cheville. Pas de sérieux." (I've a sprained ankle. Nothing serious.)

"Pas de mental?" (It's not just in your head?), I chide him. He laughs. He knows I'd play with my ankle hanging off.

A minute to kick-off. In the dressing-room, we'd be having our last huddle now. We have seven internationals on the replacements' bench in front of us. The first out is Jean-Baptiste Élissalde. Guy Novès, the coach, is next out and gives him an affectionate pat on the back of his neck. Yannick Bru, Salvatore Perugini, Grégory Lamboley, Thierry Dusautoir, the biggest hitter in France, Freddy Michalak and Xavi Garbajosa join Jean-Baptiste. And this is the bench!

Autograph hunters move around us. Some of our supporters are so devoted it's scary. One fella standing beside us with glasses and Toulouse tattoos is at every training session, never mind every match, and hangs around outside when we're having our meals. Another woman, beside him, has an old Ford Escort plastered in Stade Toulouse stickers and badges. Even her dog has a mini Toulouse jersey. Scary.

Another fellow, a huge Stade Toulouse crest tattooed on his upper arm, is looking to have his photograph taken with one of the lads. I couldn't imagine too many Leinster fans chanting "Allez Les Bleus" with the 'harp' tattooed on their arms.

The pitch looks like a work of art, as if it's been painted green with white stripes. It's nearly a 19,500 sell-out. Within a minute, right in front of our dug-out, our scrum-half Valentin Courrent flips an offload over his right shoulder which Fabien Pelous runs onto. Soon the chants start up.

"Tou-lou-sain. Tou-lou-sain."

"Levez-vous, qui ne sont pas Toulousain."

"Stand up those men who are not Toulouse men."

That's what I miss the most. You might think we don't hear the crowd on the pitch, but believe me we do.

The boys are on fire. Guy Novès, typically, is moving around like a coiled spring. From his bench to squatting, hunched down on his toes, on the edge of his 'zone'. You see other coaches up in the back of the stand, rigged with modern technology, radioing down to the bench. That's not Guy. He is always talking to the boys; he's in the touch judges' faces; he constantly points out mistakes.

Both brass bands play non-stop, and in the right corner opposite us are 'les petit Toulousains.' All children under 12 are given free entry to the ground. Parents simply sign them in and collect them afterwards. They are supervised and learn the Toulouse songs. After half an hour, it's they who start a Mexican Wave. The club sees them as the future supporters, and possibly players, of Toulouse.

The left corner opposite us is light blue. Bayonne have about 1,500 here. "Un convoi exceptionnel".

Bayonne score their fourth try in the 76th minute. Although Toulouse are winning well, they celebrate as if they'd won the World Cup. That bonus try keeps them a point above the relegation line. The Basque anthem rings around the ground and suddenly you're aware that there's about 2,000 of them here. It lasts about 20 seconds.

Incredibly, Freddy Michalak shapes to kick-off towards our forwards but instead flicks the ball with the outside of his left boot ten metres up the middle of the pitch, gathers it and zig-zags past a couple of players. Only Yannick Nyanga is alive to what Freddy is doing, and takes the pass to score in the corner.

Freddy is off to South Africa for a year, but will likely return afterwards. He just needs a break. He's been here since he was a kid. He had his hair cut short the other day and it prompted a half a page in the paper. If I get my hair cut I'm lucky if the missus notices.

We win 47-28 and I head into the dressing-room. In the corridor, the players come past. I give Freddy a kiss. Fabien stops and asks if I miss it.

"Yeah, when I see you out there fighting Fabien, I wish I was out there fighting with you."

He laughs. "Oui, je sais que c'est difficile Trevor." "Yes, I know it's difficult."

I tell him that it's good to see him back playing the full 80 minutes after his injury problems. "You're earning your few bob now. Your gravy train is over."

Inside the dressing-room the first player I meet is Freddy and we high five. I chat with William Servat, Jean Bouilhou, Clément Poitrenaud and Patricio Albacete. They all seem delighted to see me, and that makes me happy. We slag Garbajosa for trying to push their winger into touch five metres from the touchline, and failing badly.

"Bon match Garbo."

"Merci. Merci."

"Good try, but you let in a soft one there. Don't envy you the video session on Monday," I say. "I'll be glad to miss that one, Garbo." The lads enjoyed that.

Guy gives me a kiss. "For you I always have a kiss." He shakes hands with everyone else, as he used to do with me for four and a half years. He's kissed me only since I was banned. That's partly due to the distance he has to keep while it's a coach-player relationship. I'll probably get to know him better now.

I meet Jarlath and Marie in le Brasserie, the club's Michelin starred restaurant. Every table is taken and plasma screens are showing Brive v Clermont. One grey-flecked, bearded supporter with long hair approaches us with a copy of the glossy, hard-back history of Stade that marks the club's centenary this year. He drives four-and-a-half hours from Haute-Loire in the Auvergne, south of Montferrand, 400 miles away, to every home game. He opens the book at the page with my biog and asks for my autograph. The heading above my picture reads: Un pur guerrier, "A pure warrior." I'm happy with that.

I walk across the car park to the marquee where the sponsors meet the players, but the players have already slipped away. I lose count of the number of kids and adults who want autographs or pose for photographs. It's warmer, more affectionate than normal.

"Hope your appeal goes well."

"Thanks for what you brought to Toulouse."

"Thanks for your fighting spirit."

"We wish you the best of luck."

"It shouldn't have ended this way."

"It's not right."

If more players had still been around, I probably wouldn't have been in such demand. But this is usually the way. I love it. I'd have stayed there for an hour signing autographs. Instead, I take Jarlath and Marie to Le Cinecita, where the chic people of Toulouse eat. A cool restaurant which becomes a night club as the evening wears on. We're taken through the dimly lit restaurant and a table is set up near the front bar counter under a big screen showing Fashion TV.

My team-mate Patricio is at another table with his brother. We sign off the night by calling into De Danu.

It's been a long day. The boys played well. They looked at ease. Maybe it's because I'm not there! But this season I played 13 matches in Le Championnat and six in the Heineken Cup, so I still feel part of it.

For the moment.

CHAPTER 1

SPENT YOUTH

MY MA

If we were ever in trouble, she would never take somebody else's word without asking us "Did it happen that way, did you do that?" I suppose she was a big worrier as well and we gave her plenty of reason to be, whether it was working late, partying late or getting into the odd scrap.

BEHIND THE CHIP SHOP COUNTER

"My job was to take the order and cook the burgers. "Who's next?" I'd ask. "Cod and chips." Next? "Snackbox and a can of coke." Next? I always remember one fella in particular. With about 50 people in the chipper, a big, stout man — easily 20 stone — said in his thick country accent: "Two bags of chips, a sausage in batter, a spring roll, a quarter pounder and a half chicken. And I'll have a large bottle of diet coke; I'm on a diet." The place was in stitches.

"WHAT'S MY NAME?"

"Johnny T," I answered.

Johnny slapped me on the head, and asked me again.

"What's my name?"

"Johnny T."

Another slap on the head.

"For the last time Trev, if the cops catch any of us, you don't know anyone's name here. Okay?"

"Yeah, yeah, yeah," I say.

Johnny was one of the older guys I sometimes hung around with. I was the youngest in the group, by about five or six years. They were veterans, and they reckoned if anyone was going to be caught, it would be me. We were crossing the field to the The Spud Farm, a 'shop' where the exchange of money wasn't always necessary.

The UCD Horticultural Research Station, locally called St Catherine's, was also known as The Spud Farm, though it didn't just have spuds. We saw it as an extension of our rear gardens as it ran alongside the green next to our houses in the Glendale estate. UCD students served their time and studied there, learning about fruit and veg. They grew every sort of vegetable – potatoes, onions, cabbage, carrots, as well as fruit: strawberries, apples, raspberries, pears and plums. You name it, they grew it, though most of their produce went to waste – boxes and boxes of stuff just left there, either to rot or be stolen.

Horses, sheep and cattle grazed there on thousands of acres, so it really felt like living in the country. This was the Leixlip I grew up in. The Spud Farm was our back garden, the Rye River was our swimming pool while St Catherine's Park – or what was known locally as King Harman's Wood – was our playground. It was the same for all kids growing up in Leixlip in the '70s, '80s and early '90s.

From the age of seven to 12, we spent our summers this way. You usually woke up at first light to the sound of the birds singing. For the rest of the day, you never knew what time it was; just that it was daylight. I have great memories of growing up there, playing in the hay barn, chasing horses around the field. With so much to do in the fresh air, if the weather was any way fine, our mother would let us leave the house at eight in the morning and not worry if we didn't come home until five or six in the evening.

Everyone knew everyone, and all the neighbours looked out for each other's kids. Now if your kids are out of sight for five minutes you have a panic attack. There weren't too many panic attacks in our house as I suppose the mother was only too glad to see the back of us sometimes.

Mornings were usually spent kicking a ball in the field at the side of our house – soccer or kicking a ball from hand to hand. For me, as a youngster, it was more likely to be round-shaped, and a Gaelic one at that, rather than oval. I played there with my father, my brothers and my neighbourhood friends.

Decisions on what to do or where to go were made according to the weather. If the sun was splitting the heavens, we headed off in our shorts to the Rye River, where most of us learnt to swim, and not with instructors. It was the school of sink or swim. After being thrown in by older boys, my first stroke was the doggy paddle. If the weather was not so warm, we usually went into the King Harman's Wood.

Wet and windy days were normally spent in front of the television watching

Little House on the Prairie, Anything Goes or *Little Rascals*. Alternatively it would be fighting with the brothers or coming down the stairs on a cardboard box.

The Rye River was our water park with no admission fees. There we could do whatever we wanted. Most of the attractions were boy-made, as opposed to man-made, with the exception of the weir. When it was built, it held a certain fear factor. It was a concrete shelf, at a slant, which in effect created a split level river so as to regulate its flow. This dam was built beside the horse stables where a nursing home now stands. For a seven or eight-year-old who was not a particularly good swimmer, this weir required some balls, especially if it had rained the night before and the river was swollen.

We'd dive off it and be carried along with the current before climbing the banks and walking back to the weir to repeat the process. We'd slide off that weir on car or tractor tyre tubes; or anything we could find that could be constructed into a raft. Further down, a tree hung over the water, ideal for tying a rope, with a stick at the end of it, to one of the branches. We could swing off the rope into the deeper end of the river where we'd built our own dam with timber and rocks. This helped to raise the level, and we'd dive into six-to-eight feet of water.

Thinking back, it was crazy, but you just did it for the adrenaline rush. The older lads always had a fire going on the banks where we could warm ourselves after our swim, and sometimes they drank a few cans of beer. The younger ones were despatched to collect timber for the fire. That was how we were accepted.

King Harman's Wood was a totally different story. You might be taking your life in your hands when you headed down there to play because it wasn't 'our' territory. It belonged to the lads from St Mary's Park. Ours was two estates away and we had to go through the park and down the old hill to reach the forest. We'd always try to muster six or seven lads for these excursions behind enemy lines; the Kenny brothers, the Kelly brothers, the Byrne brothers, the Murphy brothers, the Giltrap brothers and the Gilfoyle brothers. All were big families, and usually older than us. But by God it was worth the risk, because there was so much to do there.

It was the private estate of the King-Harmans, a family who owned a couple of hundred acres of forest. A gate house stood at the road entering the woods, and at the top of the hill was a big mansion which included separate living quarters for the staff. It was a dark place. The sun never seemed to penetrate the tall trees and bushes making it a perfect place to play.

Several trees had swings, all of them built by the lads from St Mary's Park. We played Cowboys and Indians, and army games. In our imaginations, we were Sylvester Stallone's Rambo or Arnie Schwarzenegger's Commando. I remember watching the film *First Blood,* with Stallone on the run in a forest. He made his own bows, had his knife and compass; everything he needed to survive. In my little head, back then, I was John Rambo.

That was until the hard nuts from the St Mary's estate arrived on the scene. Then I was little Trevor Brennan again. Some of them were about 14 or 15, and I, a mere seven or eight. Punishment for being on their territory could be Man Hunt, when they gave you a one-minute start to run for your life. If caught, you were usually tied to a tree and simply left there, or else made to sing. If they were unhappy with either the tune or the lyrics, you were given a few slaps with sticks, or had your head punched. Nothing really serious, but enough to let you know they weren't pleased.

Any wonder I'm never shy about sing-songs today. Yet we kept going back. We loved the excitement and the thrill of it. "They're coming! Run." We'd go there early in the morning, when they were still in bed, to have a couple of hours' play before they arrived. Even then, I was probably caught once a week.

Leixlip wasn't what it is today. There were no big factories, no Intels or Hewlett Packards, but it seemed a vibrant village. It had a few pubs and one hotel, the Springfield, with its night club, Ninjas, all owned by the Hannigans; the exceptions were a pub, then The Captain's Inn (now The Three Sisters) owned by Jackie McNamee, the Salmon Leap (owned by John Nolan) and Sammy Macari's chip shop. The Springfield gave many a young person a job, and that was where I met my wife Paula, when she worked as a waitress and I was a barman.

The main employers were Irish Meat Packers. Fellas came from all over Ireland to work in the IMP, and the local Barnhall Rugby Club was set up in 1969 by employees of IMP. After IMP closed down, trustees of Barnhall raised funds and some members made voluntary contributions of £500 – some even donated £1,000 – to buy the 14 and a half acres and establish the club. In the first days of the club, the players changed literally in the slaughter houses.

Before they made a suburb of my village, we had Hayden's Clothes Factory, which made boiler suits, Brown's, which made all kinds of coats; the John Swan Supermarket (now the Courtyard Hotel); Carroll's Meats, John Paul's clothes shop (where we bought our school uniforms); Pat McCabe's (where we bought our shoes and runners); the ESB; an AIB branch; John Hynes' Hardware Shop (now a bookies), and a chemist at the top of the village. All these small businesses, save for Bernie Owens Menswear, have closed their doors.

Back then families lived in Leixlip village. Few now do. There are five or six auctioneers, three or four bookies and several banks. Village life is no more. Trips to Dublin were rare when I was growing up, because Leixlip had it all. Only in exceptional circumstances, such as communion, confirmation, buying some furniture (always Langan's in Capel Street) or clothes – Michael Guiney's was a family favourite – we'd hop off the '66' at the top of Abbey Street, do our bit of shopping, then hit the arcades while waiting for the bus back to the sticks.

The inhabitants of Leixlip fell into two categories; the ones who had lived in Leixlip all their lives or the country people, mainly from the west, who came to work in the village or in Dublin. In this category, I include my own mother, who came from Mullingar.

Leixlip probably doesn't have good memories for many of those who passed through. No less than Kinnegad, Maynooth and all the villages on the Dublin-Galway road which were yet to be bypassed, Leixlip was a bottleneck which could take an hour to navigate, especially at weekends. If Galway or Mayo, for example, were involved in a big Croke Park match, the village would be buzzing. They were always good for business. Cars and buses stopped for supporters to have a drink or a feed. I worked in Sammy's chipper and on those days it was black with supporters and alive with banter.

My job was to take the order and cook the burgers. "Who's next?" I'd ask. "Cod and chips." Next? "Snackbox and a can of coke." Next? I always remember one fella in particular. With about 50 people in the chipper, a big, stout man – easily 20 stone – said in his thick country accent "Two bags of chips, a sausage in batter, a spring roll, a quarter pounder and a half chicken. And I'll have a large bottle of diet coke; I'm on a diet." The place was in stitches.

Things have changed in the village I loved so well. The Rye River, our old swimming pool, is polluted beyond belief. You wouldn't put your dog in there now, never mind your kids. The air smells of sewage. It's shocking.

Our old playground, St Catherine's Park, is now a privately-owned hotel. The King Harman's old mansion has been refurbished and extended. The Spud Farm has been closed down and barred up for the last 15 or 20 years. The corn fields which led to it have been converted into a park with pathways and football pitches. And Leixlip is no longer a bottleneck, thanks to the bypass.

Intel employs about 5,000 and Hewlett Packard about 3,000. Leixlip never saw that coming. There are now five or six hotels and a similar number of estate agents. Many locals own two or three houses, which they rent out. There are big supermarkets at either end of the town and two churches instead of one. Whereas we used to walk two miles to school every morning from Confey to Scoil Bhride in St Mary's, now there's another primary school in Confey. At the top of the town, there were four estates: Glendale, Avondale, Riverdale and St Mary's Park. Now there's also Glendale Meadows part one and two, Newtown, River Forest and Woodside. These were our playgrounds. Today, virtually every blade of grass has been covered in concrete.

When we lived on the hill, there was one shop, Jack O'Neill's; a portakabin where everyone purchased their bits and pieces. And there was Mr Landy's mobile van shop which resembled an old transit van and had the distinctive chimes to go with it. For anyone who has seen the film *Man About Dog*, with the guy up north who drove around in a shop van, that was Mr Landy. He visited our estate two or three times a week, parked at the bottom of the cul-de-sac, opened the back of the van and the queue formed for the tea bags, sugar and groceries. The bread man left your loaf at the door, the milkman your milk and eggs. There were no supermarkets in Leixlip. If people wanted to do a weekly shop they made the trek to a supermarket in Lucan.

There's no need for milkmen any more, nor for door-to-door bread delivery men. Mr Landy's van no longer chimes. SuperValu have built a supermarket at each end of the town. Jack O'Neill's shop remains, but he's been joined by a hardware shop, a chemist, a chip shop, a bookies.

The areas of land in front of the shops where kids used to play football have become apartments. That appears to be typical of the urban growth in towns and villages throughout Ireland, usually sacrificing green areas for kids to play on in the process.

And we're not talking 100 years ago, just 20. Children's quality of life, or certainly their outdoor way of life, has virtually vanished. It's not just Leixlip. Many towns and villages in Ireland have suffered similarly in the name of progress. It's an awful shame.

As kids, we used to travel to Mullingar most weekends to visit our grandparents. A two-hour trip. It seemed to be in a different country. You'd need passports, a map and a compass! Though only 45 kilometres away, the traffic congestion could trap you in Maynooth, Kilcock, Kinnegad or Enfield; or all of them. Today you can reach it in 30 minutes.

Mullingar has become a commuter town for people working in Dublin and has grown massively; 60-odd pubs are proof of that. No doubt Leixlip and Mullingar are typical products of the Celtic Tiger. Developers, despite making staggering profits over the last decade, have plonked huge estates in the middle of nowhere. There appears to be no obligation on them to provide infrastructure in the form of proper roads, recreational facilities, playgrounds and sports facilities for kids.

It might have been excusable in the '60s and '70s when there was no money about – but there's no excuse for what's happened over the last decade.

Sports associations have partially filled that void. Where before there was one GAA club, St Mary's, now Confey has its own club. Though the local dividing line was always there, there are now, more than ever, two communities within one town. We were 'The Hillers', those at the other end of the town were 'The Far Enders'. Many a battle took place between these rival communities, and probably still does.

"Where are you from?"

"Far Ender." Boomph.

"Where are you from?"

"The Hill." Boomph.

By the time I was 16 or 17 and working behind the bar, many of my old tormentors in the forest had emigrated to America or England for work, and when they returned they'd come into the bar and order drinks from me.

"How's it going? Give us two pints there and a whiskey and coke. Where are you from?"

"Ah, I'm from up the hill."

"What's your name?

"Trevor Brennan."

"You're Trevor Brennan, that little bollix who played in our woods. I'm terribly sorry. Jaysus – the f****** size of you."

I always remember one of the lads saying "Jaysus, my father was right, small apples do grow big. Terrible sorry. Apologies. Will you have a drink yourself?"

"No problem," I said. "It's alright."

They were all characters. No more slaps on the head. But they never beat me to a pulp. It was more or less a game to them too.

Spent Youth: Part II

TREVOR BRENNAN. BORN SEPTEMBER 22ND, 1973 IN THE COOMBE HOSPITAL IN Dublin. My parents, Rory and Iris, had just returned from Canada, with my older brother Ronnie, and had bought a house in Leixlip. Ronnie was one and a half years older, and below me would come Errol, three and a half years younger, and Damien, nine years younger.

I lived in that house until I was 21-years-old and it holds many good memories, mixed with a few bad ones, as is normal in any family. A three-bedroom, semi-detached house at the end of the road in the Glendale estate. It sits next to a green maintained mainly by the council and occasionally by neighbours.

In the midst of this village life there was the Brennan family. Don't be deceived by Iris being named after a flower – she is anything but delicate and sweet. She is always right, even when she is wrong. You can never win an argument with Iris. She is outgoing and friendly to most, but if you get in her way, she'll let you know.

When a neighbour from across the road called Sarah moved into our estate 30 years ago, not long after us, my mother christened her Sheila. It didn't matter how many times that woman came into our house and said "Listen, my name is Sarah."

"No it's not, it's Sheila," my mother would say, as she does to this day.

Sarah was a wonderful neighbour, who had six kids herself – two boys and four girls. She would bring over home made apple tarts and buns to our house two or three times a week. We loved to see her coming. It was heaven. The tarts and the buns had just come out of her oven, and were still warm. Then there was her home made brown bread and jam.

I loved those days. We'd all sit around with a cup of tea, a slice of tart and a few hot buns. She also did running repairs to our frequently damaged clothes. Even when Paul Dean gave me a mix of 20 jerseys to give to friends and family for the AIL final with St Mary's in 2000, Sarah redesigned one of the jerseys to fit my son – little Danny.

Iris was a very loving mother, always worrying about us. She kept the whole family together over the years. Her own mother's name actually *was* Sheila and her father's name was Georgie. She had two brothers – Georgie and Joe – and a sister, Rita. She came to Dublin to work in the canteen in the James Connolly Memorial Hospital, Blanchardstown. She met my father Rory at a dance in Dunboyne.

I suppose you could describe my mother as a housewife. With four boys, she couldn't really work outside the home. But I doubt any housewife ever did more in the home. I'd say she also looked after more children in more families than anyone else in Leixlip, as well as double and triple jobbing.

Back then in Leixlip, as in other parts of Ireland, many homes needed a second income, which could be earned only in Dublin. So, my mother combined a local child-minding service with rearing her own four. The house was always full. It was extraordinary. The bionic woman is what we called her back then. Even now, my ma just has super energy although the workload she took on over the years has taken some toll.

Iris Brennan (nee McMahon) was the local manpower agent. Prior to the advent of specialised recruitment agencies, Iris was the unofficial recruitment officer for the hotel industry in Leixlip. She organised jobs in the Springfield Hotel which was, in Leixlip, the only place where anyone under 18 could work. She also arranged employment for people in the Ryevale Tavern, The Middle Shop – all owned by Paddy Hannigan – and babysitting jobs. Everybody in Leixlip knew her, or at least knew of her. And if the Springfield Hotel was full they'd suggest Iris Brennan's house.

We were almost a B&B. We'd have people from every county in the country, from Donegal to Kerry, staying in our house. Most of them stayed Monday to Friday, but sometimes for the weekends, as the work demanded. Bricklayers, carpenters, roofers etc. They might be married men or kids themselves.

The mother sometimes had six or eight lads in our house; the kitchen being the only room without beds or mattresses. When we returned from school in the evening we were never too sure whether the bed would be the same one as the night before. She always seemed to be shuffling beds around, asking us to bring mattresses upstairs and downstairs, or to move beds, chairs and couches.

She spent her days minding kids and preparing dinners for us and whatever lads were staying in the house.

At night Iris would make school lunches for myself and my brothers and pack lunches for the builders. I don't know, looking back, whether she really had to do all of that work. She still minds a few kids to this day, but her B&B days are over.

For any fund-raising, such as selling raffle tickets, Iris would be the first to lend a hand. If somebody in the community died, she was the first to help out. She and a few friends would get together to raise funds. It could be to pay for a headstone, a funeral or something else needed at the time. She would often be in the home of the bereaved family, making sandwiches and tea.

Iris is an absolute character, and anyone who knows her will tell you so. She just loves the craic. My mother is the sort of woman who wouldn't sit in the house on a weekend night watching *The Late Late Show*. She has a few good friends who she'd usually meet up with for a pizza or a Chinese, and then would normally finish their night off in the Confey GAA club or the River Forest Hotel.

She loves having a few pints with us, more so than the da. "Eh lads, are you going for a few pints?"

Wherever I was, whoever I was with, she'd meet us there and would mix with anybody or any group; me and my friends, or the brothers and their friends. It wouldn't matter to her or to them if she was the only woman in the group. She is usually the life and soul of a party, and loves singing, even though she hasn't a note in her head.

She was strict. She had to be; we were mad. She'd always say "Youz would break iron, you'd break iron." And we would break iron. But we never broke her.

My parents are big strong people. My mother is not a small woman and I suppose we get the height and the strength from both of them. She is a country woman and we get that bit of hardness from her. My father was always a hard worker too, and all that rubs off on you. We all inherited a strong work ethic from them.

She always stood by her kids, and did everything for us. If we were ever in trouble, she would never take somebody else's word without asking us "Did it happen that way, did you do that?" I suppose she was a big worrier as well and we gave her plenty of reason to be, whether it was working late, partying late or getting into the odd scrap.

Then thrown into all of that, was the loss of my brother, Damien, in 1995 to meningitis. That changed both our parents. For a mother to lose a 13-year-old son is obviously very traumatic. I think she started drinking and smoking more. Even to this day, she tells us to live every day as if it's your last.

"Listen lads, life is no dress rehearsal. You don't get any second chances."

She's right, and I try to live like that. Because, as she says, you don't get any second chances. And when you're gone, you're gone, and that's it. Her whole attitude to life, about making the most of it and taking your chances, has rubbed off on all of us. I believe I've taken my chances in life, but I mightn't have if it wasn't for my parents.

We never wanted for anything and always seemed to make ends meet; we had stereos, televisions and bikes. Looking back on those days, you'd think it was never easy. But actually, we didn't realise how good we had it.

At night I remember us going to the farm with groups of friends who always seemed to gather in our house. On the way back from the farm, when everything was put away, we'd all gather in the kitchen. We'd sit around the table, drink tea and tell stories. What happened that night, a bit of craic, ghosts, banshees, people dying, fairy rings.

My father worked as a CIE bus driver for 18 years. He was based in the Coyningham Road garage. At Christmas time the father would always ring CIE and report sick, or take his holidays then. We would make holly wreaths, and it was always damned hard work. You had to cut down holly, bring it home with the hay, cable or wire for making the rings. When you had gathered all the bits and pieces, then the real work started.

You made the round rings, put the hay around the wire with string, put the

ı more string, and then made the ribbons. We made
in' things, and we sold them door to door while my father
ts in Moore Street or wherever. That was the Christmas
hat was why myself and the brothers used to get a new bike
aleigh Choppers were the big thing back then.

ıe Christmas when, aged about eight or nine, I took the holly
wreath money and went on a bit of a spending spree. All of a sudden I had about
20 new friends for three or four hours. A shopkeeper who knew the mother collared
me and rang her to come and get me – and whatever was left of the money. By
that stage most of it was gone and I was given a good slap for my troubles. But well
deserved.

Although he was christened Michael, everyone calls my dad Rory and I've
always known him as Rory. I only discovered the reason for this a few years ago.
Apparently his grandmother, granny Hughes, christened him Rory because he was
always roaring!

My da is a big man and back then he had a beard. Most of our fuel for that
open range fire was delivered coal. But sometimes it'd be wood from the trees he'd
cut down that we helped drag home. He'd chop them up with his axe. He had
huge hands and unnatural strength. In my eyes, he was a giant and I always looked
on him as Grizzly Adams. In the flesh. My da.

When people ask me who were my inspiration or childhood sports heroes, I
always answered "my dad". Most kids look up to their fathers, and I was no exception.

Rory had hands like shovels, and seemed to be happiest when he was putting
those hands to something. Whether it was chopping wood, making holly wreaths,
cutting the grass, cleaning the house, washing the car, tidying or ironing and
hoovering, he was always busy.

He was a hard grafter, no doubt about it. He's from Blanchardstown, one of
five boys and a girl. He was a butcher by trade, serving his time with T.P. O'Reilly's
on Main Street Blanchardstown and in a couple of abattoirs on the North Circular
Road and Grand Canal Street, before moving to Canada and then returning home
to work with CIE. In his younger days as a butcher he handed over most of his
wages to his mother and kept a bit for himself. That's just the way it was, and any
time we had jobs we did the same. When they married, they honeymooned in
Toronto and decided to stay there for a couple of years, where he worked in nickel
mines.

In his CIE days, he might start a shift at 5.00am and be back at 2.00 or 3.00pm that day. He was an imposing man, who commanded respect. He used to say that his mother and father kept pigs and they were cleaner than us because of the mess we usually made. Like most fathers, at times he had to be strict, and now that I've become a father, I've done it myself. I've usually felt a terrible sense of guilt afterwards, and I'm sure, like most fathers I was harder on the first – Danny. By comparison, the other little fella, Josh, has been let off lightly.

He wasn't the sort of man who'd demand that his dinner be on the table, though it was often made for him. If not, he'd make it himself, or go out and cut the grass first. He'd have no problem cutting half the field, or washing dishes and ironing clothes. He was very house proud. The house had to be kept fairly spotless when he was around. "Feet up there lads," he'd say, the hoover purring around the place as you tried to watch *Football Focus* or *The Superstars*. If it wasn't the hoover he'd be bringing around trays of sandwiches and biscuits. And to this day he's forever running around the house with a hoover, cleaning his car, cutting the grass or doing the ironing – something my mother is not too fond of.

Sadly, the farm – which had supplied all the vegetables for the dinners cooked in our house for years – was closed down and Glendale Meadows was built in its place. For a ten-year-old, his brothers and his mates, this was another source of things to do. We'd drive dumpers and tractors, and use the half-built houses as playgrounds.

The builders on the site helped my father with our extension in 1990; a new kitchen, a new bedroom, a new toilet and shower, and two more bedrooms upstairs. It was an expensive job, which was overseen by the foreman on a local site, who also stayed in our house. For the first time I had a bedroom all to myself. All that building in the area was also another source of income for the father and mother.

The mother is a big, forceful lady – and one to be reckoned with. She has her own view of the world. Although when it came to my rugby career, she took a back seat. I'd say she was uncomfortable with my whole career.

She invariably saw me return from matches with black eyes, cuts or something broken or dislocated. Like all mothers she'd look after me when I was sick or injured. She'd bring me my meals or whatever tablet or medication I needed while I sat in front of the fire and watched television. It was no wonder she never liked to watch me play. She would go out to the garden (or anywhere, for that matter) to avoid watching a match.

In the latter stages of my career, Ronnie brought her to his house for lunch and to watch a Heineken Cup game. But she went out for a walk around Phoenix Park

– apparently singing carols to herself – hoping that we'd won and I wouldn't be injured or sent-off. And that's generally how she'd spend her time if I was playing a game.

Even when I returned to Barnhall, just up the road, she'd still spend the whole time in the bar. She was too nervous to watch me play. The only advice she ever gave me was "keep your hands in your pockets." In other words, don't punch anybody.

The only Irish match she ever attended was the Ireland-Australia game at Lansdowne Road in the 1999 World Cup, and she was late. So she was blamed afterwards for everything that went wrong that day. "It was all your fault ma." The family constantly slag her or wind her up with some outrageous tales, even to this day.

"Did you hear Trevor bought a hotel?"

"Did you hear Trevor bought a yacht?"

"Did you hear Ronnie has bought a bit of land and built ten houses?"

She's one of the most gullible people you could meet, so the next time she'd meet me, she'd say something out of the blue, like:

"Thanks for telling me?"

"Huh? What do you mean?" I'd answer.

"Thanks for telling me?" she'd repeat, indignantly.

"Tell you what?"

"I had to hear from someone up in the pub that you bought a hotel?"

"What pub? Who told you?"

"Ronnie and Errol. I don't want to say it, but they told me you bought a hotel. Is there any truth in that?"

"Yea, right ma," I'd say, but no matter how much I'd try to tell her otherwise, she'd take some convincing.

"And where do you get the money?" she'd ask. "And I've nothing." "Oh woe is me." "I need a new cooker," she'd hint, or "My washing machine is on the blink and you have all that money."

Iris used to cook a big Sunday dinner for the family. In latter years, however, there was no family there to eat it, because all of us would invariably be off playing rugby. So, fed up, she stopped. She didn't drive but the da went to every match under the sun, be it rugby or Gaelic or athletics. He was always chasing around after the lads. If not to one of mine or Ronnie's rugby matches, then to Errol's races. He ran the 800m, 1500m and cross country for Leixlip Athletic Club, and later on, Donore Harriers.

Finally, sick of this, Iris announced "I have to get out of the house. I have to learn how to drive. I want a car and I want to know how to drive." I was about 18 or 19 at the time, and I helped her buy a little Mini one weekend. I drove it back and parked it in the driveway where there was room for just one car, and that was my da's. And as mad a driver as he is, I don't think he ever got a scratch on his car. They were usually big cars, like an old Ford Cortina, a Datsun Sunny or an Audi, which he polished regularly.

But this little Mini took pride of place in the driveway for a few days, and such was the communication policy in the house that she didn't bother telling him. Eventually the da asked "Who owns that f****** car in the driveway?"

"It's mine," said Iris, but he didn't believe her, presuming it belonged to one of the builders staying there. When it had been there for over a week, and nobody actually living in the house had taken it out, he still didn't believe it was hers.

Some days I took her out to the green at the side of our house, and she drove it around in circles in first gear, and also forward and back, until one day I said to her "Jaysus ma, I think you're ready to get out on the road." We went down to Glendale Meadows. "We're going to go from second gear to third gear here. Here's the clutch, you press that down, and here's the gear stick and this is where you move it to."

Next minute I saw a car coming towards us and we were bearing across the road – she was changing into third gear with both hands and I had to grab the wheel to avoid her first crash. She had the personality for driving, because she didn't care who was in front of, or behind her. It was the ma, the car and road, and no-one else mattered.

She was so courageous that after only a week's lessons, she drove the car herself with a friend, Rose Farrell, beside her. She decided to drive to Lucan, further than she'd ever been. She stopped at a set of lights at the bottom of the Captain's Hill; the lights went green, then they went red again, then green, then red again, and Iris couldn't start the car. But she got a fit of laughter, as did her friend, and they couldn't get it together to move the car.

A couple of years ago, she passed her driving test in Mullingar. Fair play to you ma!

I suppose I have much of her personality, along with the work ethic from both of them – and the short fuse from the da. Education came second to the work ethic. All the boys learnt to have jobs from age 14 onwards. We learnt to understand the value of money from a very early age; we even bought our own clothes.

None of us ever thinks something will simply be given to us.

We were given free rein to go out and enjoy ourselves. We played hard too. Maybe that's what made us brothers so close. We were given our independence and always looked out for each other. That's just the way we were then, and the way we are now. We'd all, however, be quite emotional lads. When we're angry, sad or happy, you know it.

RONNIE BRENNAN
BROTHER

"Trevor as a player has excelled in the sport ever since he was a kid playing at Barnhall. He won player of the year at various levels all the way up through the ranks. I always knew he would make it as a serious player because his dedication to training was extraordinary – even at a young age,.

Personally I am extremely proud of him and I believe what he has achieved playing and living in France will not be matched by any other Irish player for a very long time. The one thing that annoys me is that a lot of Irish rugby followers will never really know how much Trevor was respected, loved and admired as a rugby player by all the people of Toulouse and the south of France.

I have followed his career closely since he went to France and the way he integrated into the community and learned the language was just sheer class. Who would ever think Trevor Brennan could be fluent in French! His record of achievements in rugby have been incredible. I honestly believe he had a lot to offer the Irish rugby team at the peak of his career, but that is now something we will never actually know.

You would have to travel a long way to meet a man like him. He is funny, witty, generous and extremely loyal to his family and friends. Over the years I have seen Trevor going out of his way to help total strangers, and seen many things of true goodness that are just typical of his nature.

To me he is a great brother but most of all a great friend. I will leave you with one story about Trevor. In the week of the Toulouse-Leinster Heineken Cup quarter-final I spoke to him throughout the week and he kept saying how hard it would be to play against old team-mates like Denis Hickie, Shane Horgan, Reggie Corrigan and Gordon D'Arcy.

He dreaded that game because of the bond he had with Leinster, which is still close to his heart. After they lost to Leinster, the family and a couple of close friends brought Trevor to a small quiet bar in Toulouse as he could not face the masses for a while. I have to say I'd never seen him look as bad. I tried to reassure him that it was only a game and he'd get over it. He turned to me and said "Never again."

I asked what he meant and he said that in the run up to that game, even on the day of the game, Trev had spent so much time organising tickets and accommodation for Leinster fans that he totally lost focus on the game. Another example of Trevor the generous man. This time being too generous for his own good.

As we say in Barnhall, form is temporary but class is eternal. And by God, Trevor Brennan has plenty of class.

CHAPTER 2

CONFESSIONS OF A MILKMAN

MY DA, THE DRIVER

The father mainly did the driving, with us at the rear of the open-backed lorry. We loaded our crates from each side of a road. Two pints, one pint, one litre, fresh butter, yoghurt; you'd have it all in your head. You'd get your crate ready while you were on the back of the lorry as the da drove. Mind you, he drove like a lunatic. They used to call him Mad Max when he was driving the buses.

GROWING UP QUICKLY

I was 16 when I left the chip shop to work in the Springfield Hotel. I did various jobs; cleaning ballrooms or kitchens, barman, bouncer, car park attendant. I did any job they wanted me to and that was a real learning experience. It was then that my real drinking days kicked off. You work with chefs and barmen, and on your nights off you'd go to Ninjas Nite Club and have a few pints.

I CONSIDER GROWING UP IN MY HOUSE AS MY FIRST JOB. THERE WAS NO SUCH thing as pocket money in our house. We'd be told "Cut the garden and we'll give you a pound or two." When my dad bought our first petrol lawnmower, I remember him saying "Right lads, you can take it out on Saturday and ask a few of the neighbours if they want their grass cut." We were getting two or three pounds for mowing front and back gardens, 20 odd years ago.

My first proper job, as I consider it anyway, was at the age of eight or nine, delivering milk on weekend mornings with my brother Ronnie. We worked on a milk round covering Leixlip and Lucan. My brother and I went out at three or four in the morning to deliver milk for four or five hours. At the end of our shift we were given milk, yoghurt and butter for the house, plus two or three quid. Sometimes, when the owner was let down during the week, we'd get a knock on our door at 2.00 or 3.00am to give a dig out. When we returned home we had breakfast, put on our uniforms and went off to school on the back of the lorry. I wasn't always bright-eyed during my classes. When the business was sold we were temporarily unemployed.

After that I did everything from raspberry to strawberry picking, turkey plucking one Christmas, all sorts of Mickey Mouse jobs. The raspberry picking was on the Dunboyne farm of Sean Boylan, long-time manager of Meath and Ireland's most famous herbalist. They were short-term summer jobs within walking distance of Leixlip, where he now grows all his herbs.

I was 11 when I took two weeks off school to pluck turkeys. We were collected in the early hours of the morning outside the church, put in the back of a van and driven to a large shed full of turkeys where we spent the day plucking and slaughtering. At 60p a bird it was hard work and not very rewarding.

I was Ronnie's shadow. We got the same clothes, the same bikes; you name it, we got it. Ronnie was known as 'The Backbreaker' in our house, as myself and my younger brother Errol would wrestle him. This would always finish off with the heel of his foot in our backs, usually leading to tears and something broken in the house as we'd let fly with whatever was in throwing distance.

When I was about 12 my older brother left school at 14 and served his time as a butcher in Noel Carroll Meats in Leixlip. We played a lot of sport and I did everything Ronnie did. Or at least I thought I did, until I noticed he was vanishing on Saturdays with a friend of his called 'Gitzer' (Gareth Fitzpatrick).

One Saturday morning, I asked the mother where he was and she told me he had gone off to play rugby. I followed him the next Saturday and ended at number 2, Ryevale Lawns.

This, as it transpired, was the home of my first rugby coach, Paul Deering.

Ronnie was surprised to see me waiting in the coach's car. Like all older brothers with a younger brother hanging out of them, he wanted to do something on his own. We had a few words – him wondering how I got there and asking if I'd followed him. Paul came out and said "C'mon now lads, stop the fighting." And off we went to Barnhall.

Had it been a BMX club or a karate club, I'd have done it too. It just happened to be rugby. If it weren't for him, I might never have picked up a rugby ball. I've no idea why he took it up...except perhaps to get away from me. Which would be ironic. There was never any history of rugby in our family, just Gaelic football, hurling and, in my father's case, athletics. His brother, Colm Brennan, played hurling for Dublin, and won a minor All-Ireland in '68, and his sister, Marie Brennan, won All-Ireland camogie medals for Dublin.

Growing up in Leixlip I played Gaelic football and hurling, I captained the schools' soccer team and I boxed when I was 12 or 13. Rugby was always my best game. By comparison, there was a lot of skill involved in soccer, and a fair degree of skill in Gaelic too. Rugby, for me, was pick the ball up and run straight. I progressed quicker in rugby because although I was a streak of misery at first, I was big and strong for my age and in my teens I began to do weights and bulk up.

Barnhall RFC in Leixlip, where I started playing, was a simple club, just a wooden shack, with three changing rooms, showers and toilets. The minute I started, I loved it. As well as being a great sport, it was a great way for me to release energy and aggression. I think the year was 1982. Even though I was two years younger, I always played with the brother. Whatever team he was on, I wanted to be on. If it was under-10s and I was eight, so be it. And so it was – all the way up through the under-age ranks in Barnhall to 18s. I suppose it helped that I was a big lad for my age.

I've great memories of those ten years. We won a lot of cups and trophies. The first, which I considered a big thing, was the McGowan Cup for under-14s. The final was played on the main pitch at Lansdowne Road. We changed in the Lansdowne clubhouse on the back pitch. Playing on the same field as our international rugby team was a huge experience for us, remembering all of the greats – current and past – who had played there.

We won the match. Paul Deering had organised drinks and a meal for us in the Springfield Hotel. I had a few lemonades and crisps, and a bit of craic with the lads, but I couldn't stay for too long – I had to go to work in the local chip shop later that evening, to peel a few bags of spuds.

I had started working in Macari's chip shop in Leixlip when I was 12 years old. I had spent the summer asking people for odd jobs and doing bits and pieces. Ronnie, who was now serving his time in Noel Carroll Meats in Leixlip, said he'd heard there was a job in Sammy's Takeaway, aka Macari's, in the village.

I went and spoke to Peter Macari, son of the owner, and boss at the time. He started me off peeling spuds. I hadn't a clue, of course. I was given a potato peeler and was told to put the spuds into the machine. When they came out I'd put them into a big stainless steel bath of water and when chips were needed into the chip-slicing machine they'd go.

He brought me into a shed with about 150, four-stone bags of spuds and explained "Today is Monday, so peel four. Tomorrow and Wednesday, it's four. Thursday it'll start to get busy, so peel eight. Then Friday it's ten, Saturday 15 and back to ten on Sunday."

It soon became second nature and I'd fly through it. I'd have my system; fill the bath with water, shift the bags to the kitchen, and get the machine ready.

Saturday was the busiest day. It would take me three hours to get through the workload. The machine would remove all the skins. It had a turntable on the inside with a sandpaper effect and a hose. It would churn them out, peeled and cleaned, into the sink and I had to take out the eyes. There was another machine for cutting them into chips, and then another bath of water.

I still have the scars where I nearly chopped off my finger cutting chickens, and burns where I scalded myself with chip pans.

I copped on soon enough that you didn't have to take the eyes out of every single spud. Once they were chipped and put in a deep fat fryer that would be that. No-one coming in half pissed at 1.00am was going to examine the chips. It was my first big job. Every Friday I picked up an envelope with £30 inside – and £30 to a 12-year-old was magic in those days.

It was an income. I used to give the mother £20 and keep £10 for myself. At that age you didn't need much more. I handed up a few bob and Ronnie handed up a few bob. My brother Errol, the next in line, was going through what I went through at this stage – lawnmower duty.

Seven days a week for three years, I peeled spuds, cut fish and cut chickens. I worked every day during the summer and then two or three hours every day after school. And I worked around my rugby training.

I went to Scoil Bhride in Leixlip. No such thing as rugby – all Gaelic football and hurling. There wasn't even soccer. The head gamesmaster, a fella called Donal Fallon, was a Gaelic football and hurling fanatic. He couldn't understand how I could play that foreign sport.

A few times, he tried getting the ma and da to persuade me to play Gaelic football. He'd seen how dangerous I could be with a hurley in my hands; and I don't mean to the sliothar. He was passionate about Gaelic football, history, and Ireland.

He was as Irish as they come. A great influence and a great motivator. But he eventually copped on that I wasn't going to change my ways. I'd still play the Gaelic football and the hurling when I could fit it in – say on a Monday after school or on a Wednesday when we had matches. But come Saturday morning it was rugby and that was that.

After school, he sometimes brought lads to the GAA club or off on trips, and was always organising matches for us. We had our own Gaelic pitch in the school and played matches among ourselves as well as against other teams.

I was a good Gaelic midfielder and had some trials for Kildare under-18s; but that was it. Fallo kept many lads out of trouble thanks to the time he put in during and after school. He's still a teacher there.

He seemed to be about 40, but looking back he was probably a good deal younger. The last time I met Donal Fallon was in the GAA club, where I often go for a few drinks when I'm back in Leixlip. He was singing in a band that plays traditional music in a couple of the local pubs.

To this day he calls me 'The Refrigerator', because of the way I played football. I had some truly great teachers in Mrs Brennan and Mrs Ahern, but with everything that was going on in my life, I was just too busy for school.

All my primary school years were in Scoil Bhride, which was up what they called 'the far end' of Leixlip. There was no primary school where we lived, but as the population of Leixlip expanded, it split in two and the younger brothers ended up in the new school, Scoil San Carlo, at Captain's Hill.

My older brother Ronnie went to Coláiste Ciaráin, a secondary school beside Scoil Bhride, but Confey College had opened nearby in time for my stint in secondary school.

When I started off there it was just two or three pre-fabs in the grounds of the primary school. The 40 or so students had to walk to Coláiste Ciaráin for subjects like woodwork. That walk along the river was one of the highlights of the day; a breath of fresh air. We were like prisoners allowed out of their cells.

I was in third year when they put in more pre-fabs and later got their own site at the end of River Forest. Again it was all pre-fabs, but more established as a school. It was only after I'd left that a proper building was put in place.

A lot of our teachers were young student teachers who went out for a few pints at the weekend. They knew I'd be working at the weekends and they'd see me in the chip shop. I did that for four years, and then started as a barman in the Ryevale Tavern. Sometimes I also helped as a doorman in Ninjas Nite Club, both of which were part of the Springfield Hotel.

I don't know who looked more surprised, me or my teachers, as I'd be letting them in. Sometimes I'd ask the lads to tell my teachers they couldn't come in because they were wearing runners or the wrong clothes. Then I'd appear and say "Ah, they're alright, let them in."

They'd be fairly taken aback. "Trevor?" A 16-year-old student letting them into a night club.

For me, when the bell rang at 4.00pm *whoosh*, onto the bike, fly home, get the grub into you as quick as you could, on the bike again, speed back down the village, get the apron and the wellies on, load the spuds, peel them, work for three or four hours, get dinner there – your fish and chips or your snack box – go home that night, do whatever bit of homework you had, go to bed and then school the next morning.

But when I started working at weekends and nights, getting home at three or four in the morning – particularly on a Sunday morning – it came to the stage where Mondays didn't exist for me. Like the song says *I Don't Like Mondays*. I didn't go to school on Mondays; instead I slept off the weekend's work. The parents were pretty good about that. They didn't mind as long as I was working.

One day in fifth year the headmaster at the time, Mr Travers, called me into his office. "We've noticed that you haven't been in on a Monday for 20 weeks and if you want to sit the Leaving you will have to do a bit more work."

So they kept me back. He knew I was working and they were happy enough. I wasn't one of those lads who hung around walls. They knew I was going straight to work, and then straight home after. They knew the only reason I wasn't in on a Monday was because I was asleep all day.

In fairness to him, he cut me a deal. They'd keep me back for an hour after school on Tuesdays and Wednesdays for a bit of extra study, and let me sit the Leaving. So I did that and I got it – just.

I did almost four years in the chip shop and it was both a great experience and an eye-opener. It was a good way to grow up very quickly. You'd see people coming in there at all hours of the night. You'd see fights, and you'd see real characters. Fellas arm-wrestling on the counter. There was always banter and you'd be on first name terms with everyone in the town. During the day I couldn't walk up the town without saluting someone.

I was 16 when I left the chip shop to work in the Springfield Hotel. I did various jobs; cleaning ballrooms or kitchens, barman, bouncer, car park attendant. I did any job they wanted me to. That too was a real learning experience. It was then that my real drinking days kicked off. You work with chefs and barman, and on your nights off you'd go to Ninjas Nite Club and have a few pints. Or after work we might stay back for a few pints in the staff room to watch a Mike Tyson fight.

I suppose you grow up a lot quicker when you work. I look at fellas coming straight from school into professional rugby and wonder if they realise how good they have it. When I got my first rugby contract it meant I could retire from work!

That was a great summer, 1990. I left school and I started going out with Paula Kennedy. I'd known Paula from my years working in Sammy's chip shop; sometimes she would come in with her friend after the pubs closed. I took a fancy to her even then. I would have been 15 or so. Then we lost touch for a while. When I went to work in the Springfield at 16, Paula came to work there as a waitress and we became friends.

Ironically, it was when we both went to the Springfield as guests at a 21st birthday party for a neighbour, Eddie Casey, that things began to take off. I was there with my family and my mother would have known Paula better. She came over to our table for a chat. She was home only a month or so from a trip to Australia. She looked fantastic and that was my opportunity.

Typical of her own drive and ambition, Paula balanced studying with all manner of jobs in the Springfield, in the cloakroom, as a waitress, and in the disco, to put herself through college. She worked with handicapped kids, with blind kids – in Ireland and in Romania – and eventually became a family therapist.

My family always liked her. She got on well with my mother, father, and my brothers. And I always got on really well with her family. Her mother and father have always welcomed me warmly into the family home.

We just hit it off and eventually we did everything, backwards. We bought our first house together in '96, Daniel was born in '98, we had Joshy in 2001 and then came to France and married in 2003.

I went on my first ever sun holiday in the summer of 1990. Errol was also working as a barman in the Springfield Hotel and we went with two other barmen, Matt and Don O'Reilly, to Ibiza.

Most summers, we were foisted off to the grannies, or rented a house 'in the country', as we did in Courtown one year. We played on the beach all day and in the evenings amused ourselves by tilting the machines in the arcades for a few pennies.

An exception was the summer of 1986 when my grandmother Mary and aunt Marie took me, Ronnie and our cousins to Pontins in England. They had one chalet, and myself, Ronnie and my grandmother had another. Not a clever idea. We went wild.

We got drunk – for the first time – watched England being beaten by Argentina on the big screen in the disco where, in the company of boxers from Crumlin, we also saw Barry McGuigan get beaten in the Las Vegas heat ... and had a few first-time experiences with girls.

I think that was my last holiday until Ibiza in 1990, with me, the oldest of four boys aged 14 to 18. I paid £450 for my brother as best I can remember.

It was during the 1990 World Cup in Italy. I had intended to go there because of the Italian connections in the chipper and because Irish fans were clearly having so much 'craic'. But a friend let me down so I ended up going to Ibiza instead. We arrived at about 1.00 in the morning, threw the bags in the hotel and hit the town. Ibiza had everything – as we were to find out.

Our first port of call was Sergeant Peppers; I'll never forget that name. We were delighted that the doorman let us in. The lads hit the dance floor straight away and I hit the bar for two beers and two cokes. The barmen were firing water pistols at each other as I shouted my order. Next minute, Village People's *YMCA* came on, and everyone began to dance and sing along.

A big German bodybuilder, about seven feet tall, asked me to dance. I said no and kept on trying to get the barman's attention. But the German bodybuilder wasn't taking no for an answer and started pulling me towards the dancefloor. Then it clicked. There weren't too many girls around, except for a few cross-dressers, and those that were, were kissing each other in the background.

It was like the scene from *Police Academy* set in the Blue Oyster. I made my way to the lads to tell them we were leaving. They were having a ball, jumping around the dance floor.

I said "Listen lads, walk quickly towards the door. I'll keep the Village People at bay."

The lads sprinted across the dance floor to the door and I followed suit. On the way I out I said to the doorman "Jaysus, you never told us this was a gay club."

He said "Ladies' night tomorrow lads," and laughed.

After that we tracked down a good old reliable Irish bar and had a great time singing *We're All Part of Jackie's Army* and *Olé, Olé, Olé* until the early hours.

The lads went home and I woke up the next morning on a bench minus my wallet and the new trainers I'd bought for the holiday. Luckily I'd brought just enough money for the night; the rest was back in the hotel. When I returned, the lads were sunning themselves by the pool. It was one of those apartment blocks where everybody knew one another after a few days.

The Republic of Ireland's performance at Italia '90 added to the holiday atmosphere. During the day, we played seven-a-side football against the Brits, and at night there were many renditions of *Ooh Aah Paul McGrath, We're All Part of Jackie's Army* and *Molly Malone* in Irish bars.

We had a ball. When I came back I settled down. I started working on the building sites – £40 a day – six days a week. I maintained the door work at weekends and saved most of the money as I didn't go out much. When I did I usually went to the Ryevale Tavern, great craic with live bands.

But I wanted more. I was 18 and I wanted to work for myself. Reading the

Evening Herald one night – looking for something for Errol and myself – I noticed an advertisement about a milk round for sale in Castleknock. A good area, not too far from Leixlip. And I had a couple of thousand saved.

I had been earning IR£130 a week from as far back in the summer months when I was 12. For a young fella that was a lot of money; give your mother £30 and stick a hundred in the bank. Taking into account the jobs as a doorman, barman and the rest, I had my couple of thousand saved when the milk round came up.

I suppose we didn't realise what we were letting ourselves in for. My da had taken his early redundancy from the CIE. Driving a bus had been a hard job, especially on his route: the '78', in Ballyfermot. He was going in and out from town ten times a day, with a last run at 12.00 or 12.30 at night, and many a dodgy character to contend with.

The final straw for him was when he and his conductor, Tom Corrigan, were attacked by a group of lads. Corrigan was as hard as nails and they managed to fight off the attackers. But the attack left them shaken. Not long after, CIE announced that they wanted to introduce the one-man bus. The incident had happened when my da was working on a two-man bus; imagine a one-man bus doing the same route? You'd have no chance at all, whatever you had with two.

We went to the Woodchester Bank. With uncle George "The Rottweiler" as guarantor, we got a loan. I think we paid about £35,000 for the round and we bought a lorry which cost us another £15,000. So we had a loan of about £50,000.

All of a sudden here we were in business. an 18-year-old and his 16-year-old brother. School wasn't for Errol either as he had left after the Inter Cert.

We worked out of Premier Dairies in Finglas. We'd leave the house around 1.45am every morning to be there between 2.00 and 2.30am. We'd load up our crates and set off for Castleknock. We were usually first out of and first back into the dairy. We'd sprint around the place. Fastest Milkmen in the West, they used to call us. We did our round of over 600 houses in about five hours.

The da mainly did the driving, with us at the rear of the open-backed lorry. We loaded our crates from each side of a road. Two pints, one pint, one litre, fresh butter, yoghurt; you'd have it all in your head. You'd get your crate ready while you were on the back of the lorry as the da drove. Mind you, he drove like a lunatic. They used to call him Mad Max when he was driving the buses. He was a headcase. He'd go to the top of the road at speed, screech to a halt and wake up everybody in Castle-knock.

My father was the sort of fella who'd lock the gates and put out the bins. He was more than a milkman. He'd do a few houses at the top, while we did the rest of the road before joining him. He was always barking at us "C'mon lads, c'mon."

And I'd tell him "Calm down, calm down, you'll have a heart attack."

That year I left Barnhall to join Bective Rangers, and the rugby started to take off. The milk round was a great way to keep fit, but at 19 I was asked to go to New Zealand for four months. Noel McQuilkin, a New Zealander coaching Bective at the time, sounded me out. I consulted my family on whether I should accept the offer. Even though I had the milk round for only a year they said, "No you can't turn it down. Go."

My da worked every hour under the sun to accommodate me being away for four months. As did Errol. It remained a family business for another two years, although Erroll often said "All you ever do is count the money."

I suppose they all believed in me, that I could achieve something in rugby. My days as a milkman were over.

PAUL DEERING
BRENNAN'S COACH AT BARNHALL UNDER-8'S, 10'S, 12'S AND 16'S.

"I more or less picked up Trevor and Ronnie off the street and brought them to Barnhall. Even playing for the under-10s he stood out – though he couldn't catch a ball to save his life. I always had to bring his birth cert with me because opposition coaches would query his eligibility.

He really blossomed with the Under-14s. John Cody did a great job with him. He also played under-16 rugby that same year. We knew when he was 12 that he had real potential and at under-16 he was absolutely remarkable.

He's had a great career and I'm so fond of the guy. He was great on the pitch. He had a short little fuse, but he wasn't a dirty player. All the way up through the system he was a hard player.

He's full of the spirit of life, he's great with other people and has time for everybody. There's no airs or graces about Trevor Brennan – he can mix in any company and he calls a spade a shovel. He's done himself and Barnhall proud. "

CHAPTER 3

THE BARNHALL BRUISER

THE NEW ZEALAND RUGBY CULTURE

They worked hard, they drank hard and they played hard. And rugby was like a religion. Everybody talked about it. There were rugby ads on TV constantly. "If you get injured, go to this hospital," or "See this doctor." Ads for the All Blacks. Watties beans. Marmite. "Zinzan Brooke eats marmite with his toast." Every time you turned on the television you were confronted by All Blacks. They were legends.

SECONDS AWAY...

We fought solidly for five minutes. Now five minutes solid is a long time, non-stop. No-one tried to break it up because it was Joe Veitayaki. We did everything as we rolled around on the ground for five minutes. When we were finished, we looked as if we'd gone 12 rounds with Mike Tyson.

WHEN I JOINED BARNHALL THEY HAD TWO PITCHES, AND BAD ONES AT THAT. The 'pavilion' was a wooden shack, about 100 square metres, with three changing rooms and a couple of showers which – depending on their mood – could be cold or hot.

Training there two nights a week, with a match at the weekends made for enduring friendships. It helped that we had a good team and won our fair share of matches at under-age level. We had the Leech and Burke brothers, Peter Smyth, Derek Halpin, Warwick Bowden, Basil Kelly, Keith Brennan, Jack and Joe Looby, Brian and Douglas Clancy, Aengus Waters, Kenny Charles and of course the Brennans: Trevor and Ronnie. A real tight-knit community club.

We had good forwards and backs who trained hard and got results for the club.

Our senior team wasn't setting the world on fire at the time. But as a young fella you didn't give a damn if the club was in Division Six. The fun, the craic, and the friendships, were all that mattered.

Because I insisted on playing on the same team as Ronnie, they were all about two years older than me. These were the fellas who introduced me to drinking, to clubs or bars, and to discos. It quickened my education, on and off the pitch. Hardened me quicker too, I suppose.

Most of these players had made the first team by the time I left; my brother Ronnie, the Looby brothers, the Clancys played somewhere along the line, the Burkes, Keith Brennan, Kenny Charles. An awful lot came through from under-age to that first team.

We won a Leinster Under-18 Cup at Lansdowne Road against Carlow. It seemed as if the whole of Leixlip had invaded the old grounds, but I remember the night more vividly. We visited a few pubs around the town, filling the Cup with drink. We stopped at Macari's – home to happy memories – and filled it with chips. Sammy went out back for some of his home-made wine and filled the greasy cup again, before we headed to the Springfield Hotel, finishing in Ninjas Nite Club.

The celebrations didn't stop there. The following night we rented a minibus. We started in Celbridge – as a couple of the guys were from there – and finished in the Ambassador Hotel.

The club was forever organising trips away. Scotland was a popular jaunt. One particular trip to Jed-Forest we met in the club at 10.00pm, drank solidly until about 2.00 or 3.00am and then back onto the bus for the Larne-Stranraer ferry.

As the self-service breakfast on the ferry was still closed, our lads invaded the kitchen for cereals or fruit; anything we could get our hands on. When the staff opened their kitchen an hour into the trip, security was called.

These were our first weekends away, and lads got up to the usual antics when away from home for the first time; meeting girls and having the craic.

A Friday evening match cleared the weekend ahead, even if we got knocked out. We'd get the bus up from 'Jed' on a Saturday to see Scotland v Ireland internationals at Murrayfield, have a few pints in Edinburgh, return to 'Jed' for another night there, and then get the boat back on the Monday.

1991, was a World Cup year, so we went back to Jed-Forest for the World Cup pool game between Scotland and Ireland.

I'd played for Leinster Youths at 17 in 1990 while I was with Barnhall, and won my first Irish Youths cap in 1992 – which was a big deal for the club. There was only one Youths International each season then, against Scotland. We lost 4-0 in the

Galway Sportsground. That night in Galway I had a few drinks with the brother and another one or two of the Barnhall lads, Paddy Ennis and Peter Smyth. We were playing a final in Seapoint the next day for the club's under-18s. The next morning we jumped in a crappy old Fiat that Paddy's grandfather had left him when he died, drove the car back to Dublin at lunatic speeds, got togged out and played. Only for Barnhall.

The coach John Cody, and his assistant Danny Slevin, thanked me for coming back. I played the full match for them and we won the bleedin' thing. I caught a ball five metres out from the line – back when there was no lifting – and we drove it over for the decisive try.

I had great times at Barnhall and leaving was a wrench. It was a junior club in the third division of the Junior League. I was 18 at the time and everyone in Leixlip advised me that in order to further myself as a rugby player, I needed to join a senior club.

Teams like Terenure, Clontarf and Blackrock had approached me, and I thought, "These guys aren't approaching me for nothing. These guys have scouts." In 1992 the AIL was only two seasons old, but it was all there was. There were only three interprovincials, no Heineken Cup or Celtic League. The big Limerick clubs were drawing huge crowds of 10,000 or more and sometimes there'd be 15 internationals or so playing in a Division One game.

Why did I choose Bective Rangers in the third division? Because they came highly recommended by a man who I believed wouldn't put me wrong: Paul Deering. He knew Bective's Joe Nolan and assured me that Joe would look after me, which he did – along with another Bective stalwart Frank Smyth.

And I suppose I had a thing about clubs linked to what I saw as private schools. Whenever we played clubs or schools like Blackrock or Terenure, it always seemed to me that they felt they were better than us. To be honest, they probably were.

Bective came recommended; it was a club for fellas from the country who came to Dublin to work. There were also a few D4 heads like Ben Kealy, Maurice Mortell and Peter McNamara, but they were bloody good D4 heads. No shite about them and they joined in the craic.

But most of them were country lads, the Pat Bolgers, the Phil Lawlors, Geoff McCaffrey from Naas. Guys with similar backgrounds to myself who had played for junior clubs and were either scouted or had found Bective for themselves. It was a bit like going from one big family, in Barnhall, to another.

I had always been a number eight. My game was all about ball carrying and big hits. When I left Barnhall I became a number six. Noel McQuilkin, the coach at

Bective when I joined, was a hard man. A dour Kiwi, but a damned good coach. He reinvented me as a number six and my career took off. Phil Lawlor , who was both the club and the Leinster number eight, had made the Irish team and was at the peak of his career. As a young fella there was no way I was going to take his place. I thought second row was the only place for me, but McQuilkin reckoned I'd make it as a number six.

I'd gone to Bective to play for the under-19s, but I never actually did. The Bective seniors went on a tour to Scotland to play Glasgow in a friendly on the weekend of an international. Phil Lawlor was the Irish number eight, Brian Rigney and Brian Cusack were in the Irish A team, Tony Casey was with the Irish Army, and as a few others were also unavailable a couple of us were given our chance, including me.

I made an impression and McQuilkin liked what he saw, so much so that he brought me straight into the squad when we returned to Dublin. On the weekend of the Wales-Ireland game we had another friendly against Cardiff on the Cardiff Arms Park back pitch.

It was a very physical game. Derwyn Jones, the 6' 10" second-row now part of the Ospreys' coaching staff, became involved in a fight with Mike Carswell, our South African flanker. Needless to say, I got stuck in along with him. T. Brennan was there to help and that seemed to go down well. More people were talking about me in the club. "Who's this new 19-year-old throwing himself about?"

Later that season, when Ireland played England, Northampton came over for a match in Donnybrook. Buck Shelford was the number eight for Northampton and – in no time – who ended up rolling around the pitch with him but myself.

Life at Bective took off for me after that. Frankie Smyth, another sound fella, was then at Bective. He and Joe Nolan looked after the younger players and were very shrewd operators.

They saw me as this poor 19-year-old kid from Barnhall. I don't know how they did it, but for that trip to Glasgow, Ray McKenna and a few of the club's sponsors banded together and gave me £200 sterling as spending money. "Have a few pints son. Enjoy yourself."

They thought I was like the college boys; without a bean. I had a few bob but I kept the mouth shut and took the money. They wouldn't even let me buy them a pint when we got over there.

Frankie always threw me what he called 'petrol money', £150 or so every two or three weeks. I actually was spending a fair bit on petrol, driving up from Leixlip to Bective or their training ground in Glenamuck. Every now and then he'd say "Give your mum and dad a ring and we'll go out for a meal."

He'd always pick up the tab. I don't know whether it was Bective or him paying for it, but there was a massive appreciation there. Here was someone not just looking after me but looking after the family.

On one occasion when we were playing Sligo away he said "Tell Paula to come down and we'll put her up in a room for the night – but don't tell any of the boys." Obviously I wasn't the only one he was doing this for, but he clearly saw a bit of potential in me as well.

I was 19 stone then, two stone heavier than I am now, and I was mobile; perhaps in part because of the milk round. That's when they gave me the nickname Horsebox – because I ate like a horse. Since turning professional I've trimmed down. Nowadays you can't eat what you used to eat and get away with it.

Bective was good for me, with wonderful members, some of whom I am still in touch with. In 1995 we went to Boston on a ten-day trip, which was funded through race nights, raffles etc. I think the da had as good a time as I did. We played three matches and won them all, in between some serious bonding.

Bective organised my truck driving licence. The club paid for all the driving lessons in Naas and lined me up for a job in the Fire Brigade – for which you needed a licence. But I cracked a vertebra in my first year with Bective so the job with the fire brigade never materialised.

They arranged a job for me with Tayto through Ben Kealy, another stalwart of the club, but that lasted a week. At the time, I still had the milk round, but the da, my brother and their helpers could manage without me.

Bective gave me a few quid every now and then in expenses, like most clubs did at the time, and it was a good incentive to play well. The name Trevor Brennan was starting to get noticed.

At the end of my first season McQuilkin asked me if I fancied four months in New Zealand as he knew a team that were looking for a hooker and a number eight. To play club rugby in New Zealand sounded like too good an opportunity for a 19-year-old to turn down. They would cover the cost of the flights and provide us with jobs. In 1993 rugby wasn't professional, but New Zealand rugby was years ahead of anywhere else.

But it was also my first year on the milk round. As it would be a four month trip during the off-season – effectively the Irish summer – I asked my family what they thought about McQuilkin's offer.

The da, who was always very supportive of me and my rugby career, said "Listen, we'll manage somehow. You go and take the opportunity." He took on two helpers to cover for me.

My team-mate Peter McNamara – who's brother, John, owned Shamrock Rovers at the time – would be the hooker to my number eight. At the end of the season, we headed off to New Zealand.

We were to play for Taumarunui, near Rotarua and Taupo in the north island. We played against the other club sides in the King Country province, who played the big sides like Auckland and Canterbury. We had two or three All Blacks trialists and one All Black, Dean 'Hacksaw' Anglesea.

It was my first long trip abroad. Taumarunui is a small town in the sticks. The people there were very welcoming. We were met in Auckland by two players and taken on a four hour drive to Taumarunui. We were put up in the club president's home, a big house in the hills. Alan Hizcock was the president and we couldn't have asked for nicer hosts.

They had two children and his wife Elaine was both a lovely woman and a fantastic cook. They organised various jobs and a car for us. The club was like a professional outfit even before rugby was professional. Taumarunui was a junior club in New Zealand but the standard of rugby was like the AIL back home.

Alan had a collection of rugby books, mainly concentrating on New Zealand, and gave me one about back-rowers, dating back from the 1920s to the present day. One story stood out for me. It concerned a flanker called Maurice Brownlie, who travelled with a touring All Blacks' squad by boat.

His finger became affected by gangrene. The doctor told him that the only way he could play the next day against England was to have his finger amputated. He paused for a minute, and then said "Take it off."

My time there was an education – I'd always thought I was up to playing rugby at senior level in Ireland just because I was big and strong. The rugby was tough. Every match, every week, was a dogfight. I'd never seen or experienced rucking like it. It was club rugby. There were no cameras and you had referees not so much protecting you, as telling you that you were on the wrong side and warning that you were about to get a shoeing.

I vividly remember one match in which I really rolled over on the wrong side. The referee said "Give him the boot, get him out of there. Keep the ball going." I was looking up thinking "Oh my God, if he's telling them to do that, what chance have I got?" So you hardened up. You gave it and you took it. And more times you took it.

It would never happen in Ireland. If someone stood on you like that it'd be a yellow or red card. Every week you'd have one or even two black eyes. But New Zealand made me a better player, especially in a physical sense. And it taught me how to look after myself. I returned from New Zealand a beast. I'd put on two stone, mostly through eating – Mrs Hizcock fed us only too well. I practically ate weights as well.

They taught you how to scrummage, how to ruck and especially how to maul properly – by being tight and staying together. To me a maul was go in, and hit a man, turn and someone will come and rip the ball. As a unit we could get eight men in a maul and drive it 20 to 30 metres. That was a big part of their game.

Their rucking game was, to an extent, basically stamping. Every time the ball went to ground, someone got stamped or raked. In Ireland, if it was visible and the scrum-half can get it out, no-one put a boot in. But over there, boots went flying everywhere.

In one of my first matches, against a team called Puipui I gave a guy called Paul Mitchell a good rucking. By this stage I'd learned to ruck like the locals. You do after a few weeks. You had no choice.

Before the game my new team-mates had been talking about a fella called Joeli Veitayaki, who ended up having a season at Ulster later in his career. "Just be careful today, he's a really tough player."

I'd cut Mitchell fairly badly on the side of the ear and I recall running from the ruck one minute, and the next minute, BANG. Even though I was still on my feet I was seeing double everywhere, but I could make out the unmistakable figure of Joe Veitayaki running past me. For a moment I thought about the lads' warning. But then ignored it.

I ran after him, jumped on his back and we went over toward the touch-line. We fought solidly for five minutes. Now five minutes solid is a long time, non-stop. No-one tried to break it up because it was Joe Veitayaki. We did everything as we rolled around the ground for five minutes. When we were finished, we looked as if we'd both gone 12 rounds with Mike Tyson.

After the match, we were kept apart in the clubhouse. This was in my first month there, and I suppose it earned me some respect. It probably sounds funny, but from there on that's the way it felt, although the matches didn't get any easier.

I said to Peter "Look, if we've come all this way together we've got to stick together." Another match, another fight. All that separated the players from the crowd was a wire fence on stakes and in the midst of this fight, suddenly a bunch of Maori supporters pulled me over the fence. They put the boot in along with a few punches. I woke up in the dressing-room and looked at Peter "You bastard, where were you?"

He laughed. "You're mad."

I had my nose reconstructed there after taking a knee full in the face when making a tackle. The bridge just collapsed and I was brought to Auckland for the operation. In one of my last games in NZ, I also broke my ribs.

Another treat was seeing a couple of All Blacks' tests, and provincial games in North Harbour, Otago and Auckland. En route to the All Blacks' games, we'd stop at a drive-thru off-licence and load up cases of DB and Lion Red. In some of the smaller villages horses were tied up outside the local pubs. No cars. It was like a Western. You sat in the corner in your Ireland Youths tracksuit having your bottle of DB, observing the local Maoris covered in tattoos, thinking "I'd better not cross any of these fellas."

Playing with Taumarunui exposed us to a different culture. Wins were celebrated with drinking sessions and boat races. The club had a long table where two teams lined up opposite each other. At the end of the table there were two kegs with taps, and two guys pulled the pints. You downed your glass and perched it on your head before the team-mate next to you could start his, and so on. Up and down the line five times. In other words, whichever team finished off five glasses per man was the winner. Another keg or two might be downed before the night was out.

They worked hard, they drank hard and they played hard. And rugby was like a religion. Everybody talked about it. There were rugby ads on TV constantly. "If you get injured, go to this hospital," or "See this doctor." Ads for the All Blacks. Watties beans. Marmite. "Zinzan Brooke eats marmite with his toast." Every time you turned on the television you were confronted by All Blacks. They were legends. To this day I've never seen an international team with such an aura or presence, and their public expect them to win every match. Their history demands it.

Most of the guys we played with were farmers, cattle dealers, sheep shearers or scrub cutters – all hard, physical, rural labour. We had a stint as scrub cutters – cutting hedges on the side of a mountain with a chain-saw. We also had stints fencing, digging holes, cutting logs etc. It was all manual labour and I loved it.

They had thousands of sheep and we'd go into a huge shed where there might be as many as 50 men shearing. Most of the guys were Maoris whose families lived on the farm. We didn't work every day, only on days we weren't training, but after a long day's 'wool pressing', we drank a few beers with them.

Having got to know me better, they eventually relented and allowed me to try my hand at shearing. You're supposed to run the blade up the sheep's belly to shear the wool but I inadvertently killed the poor fella. It was the only one I attempted. He was one unlucky sheep. So they came to the conclusion that I was better employed pressing wool. They were right.

The British and Irish Lions were on tour there that year and I managed to see two of their matches. In Hamilton, for the second match, myself, Macker and an English guy called Justin (who played in the second-row for Taumarunui) stayed in a hostel and ended in the same night club as some of the Lions. It was there I met Nick Popplewell and Mick Galwey. I also bought Dewi Morris a beer and later on he bought me one back. I haven't a clue what we chatted about. Rugby, I presume.

It was an enriching, varied four months in New Zealand. We skied in Taupo, bungee jumped, went white water rafting, sampled the natural spas in Rotarua, played golf, cut trees and chopped logs. By the end of it, through Noel McQuilkin, we met the legend that is Colin Meads and various other All Blacks. And the normal stuff a 19-year-old might get up to when away for four months on the other side of the world: drink, rugby, women.

However, myself and Macker weren't finished yet. We decided that we needed a holiday, and Hawaii was on the way home. We booked the two-week trip through a local travel agent in Taumarunui. But, arriving at the check-in desk in Auckland came the question:

"Where are your visas?"

"What visas?"

Apparently you needed a holiday visa for Hawaii. We hadn't been told about this by the travel agents. We drove to a travel agent in Auckland who gave us a few options, one of which was a trip to Fiji.

"When?" we asked.

"In two hours' time there's a plane leaving," she said.

We looked at each other. It had to be a quick decision. We said we'd take it. On arrival in Fiji, the first thing we noticed was the poverty. Shanty towns lined the road from the airport to the port. Shacks everywhere, and then you were suddenly struck by the sight of a Sheraton Hotel with armed bodyguards, marble hallways and an 18-hole golf course. Further on people sold anything and everything on the side of the road; fruit, vegetables, clothes, newspapers and things they'd made themselves.

At the port we were met by some locals and headed to our port of call for the first six days, Beachcomber Island. We travelled on a boat with a net attached to its side. People took turns diving in, to be dragged along by the net, or to swim with dolphins.

At first sight the island was like something out of a film; in the middle of the ocean with 30 private huts and a big hall that could sleep about 80 lads. And that's where we stayed.

Met by more locals at the dock, we weren't allowed carry our bags. We were greeted with flowers, music and a big feast, like a scene from *Mutiny on the Bounty*.

We discovered that most of the men working on the island loved rugby and played it in the evenings on the beach. Myself and Macker and a few English who were holidaying there played touch rugby with them. I did a running commentary based around Waisale Serevi, the little Sevens genius then at his peak. "Serevi shows the ball, jinks one way, jinks the other, goes into the sea, comes back out of the sea..." And we seemed to be playing with dozens of Serevis.

We wore runners but they were barefoot. It was a proper sandy beach, with shells and stones. I didn't understand how they could run on it, but their feet had obviously hardened over the years.

All of them worked on the island. One guy had a job in the scuba diving club, another had a speedboat and looked after the water-skiing, another did the paragliding, and another worked in the bar. We did a few deals with them, and gave them all our rugby gear in exchange for free scuba-diving, water-skiing and the like, and a few drinks here and there. We promised to send them a full set of Bective kit when we got home but we never got around to that.

We were entertained in the bar every night by different groups brought over by boat from the mainland. One night we were taken back to a hut by some workers who lived on the island and were introduced to a local drink called cava. This is made from cava tree roots, which are ground and then mixed with water.

It looked like dirty rotten muddy water in a basin, and we took turns drinking it from a half-coconut. It was like a visit to the dentist, except that having numbed your mouth, the cava then had a similar effect through your whole body.

To be honest it wasn't very pleasant, too much like an anaesthetic. I remember having to crawl from the hut with Macker, both of us on our hands and knees. We couldn't speak to each other. It was about an hour before we could talk again. We went to the bar and at closing time bought a couple of beers which we drank at the natural jacuzzi next to the sea.

They were six eventful, free and easy days. On returning to the mainland we were advised not to go to the nearest corner bar, but instead to the Sheraton, as it was safer. So we jumped into a taxi to the Sheraton every night. One night myself and Pete searched for a restaurant in the hotel but ended up in a reception room which was hosting a wedding. It was self-service, so we helped ourselves, sat down at a table and spoke to a few people, managing to pass ourselves off as guests before returning to the bar for happy hour. This consisted of ordering whatever you wanted and then playing heads or tails with the barman. If you called it right you didn't pay. If you called it wrong, you paid. That was our last night in Fiji.

My playing weight before I went to New Zealand was 16-and-a-half to 17 stone. On my return I was 18-and-a-half stone, and I wouldn't say it was all muscle. I still felt fit and a lot stronger – while a few weeks on the milk round soon got rid of the excess weight. It wasn't easy getting back into the swing of things, the early morning starts and swapping a New Zealand winter for an Irish one.

One of the first things I did was contact Paula. We met for a few drinks and it was as though I had never been away, with both of us sliding back into our relationship with ease.

My first Bective game in the '92-93 season was away to Greystones. It was a lovely sunny Saturday afternoon in Wicklow. Paula came to watch. They had a good pack, with Nick Popplewell, the Rigney brothers and John 'Spud' Murphy.

At one stage in the game, Brian Rigney fell over on our side of the ball at a ruck and was preventing it from coming back. I gave him a hell of a shoeing. It was on his back, and no different from what I'd been doing (and getting) week-in and week-out for the previous five months in New Zealand.

For a moment or two, players just looked at me, obviously thinking "Who is this lunatic?" before someone hit me. All hell broke loose and the two packs began killing each other. I exchanged punches with one of their props whilst he and one or two others went off for stitches. I had to leave the pitch as well. It was the first red card of my career.

Paula slipped off and waited in the car. She told me later that spectators were calling me everything under the sun; an animal, a knacker, a dirty bastard. She said I had made contact with his head and that was why everyone went mad.

I was given a six-week suspension. Louis Magee, who was involved with the first team at the time, came to the hearing in the Leinster Branch and reckoned I was lucky; it could have been a lot longer.

They took into consideration my time in New Zealand, where Louis explained they had a completely different approach to rucking. That I had been trying to ruck Rigney on the body, and hadn't meant to touch his head.

I served my suspension, stayed out of trouble for the rest of the season and my form went well. We missed out on promotion to the first division by a point that season and again the next.

The 1995-96 season had been my first year training with Leinster under Ciaran Callan and Jim Glennon. Leinster were training on the back pitch in Old Belvedere where Bective were playing Blackrock the same evening in the Floodlit Cup. At the time it was a big competition, one match a week every Tuesday in front of good-sized crowds.

Mike Brewer, the former All Black, was on the Blackrock team. He picked off the base of a scrum and came 'round my side. I was playing wing-forward and I tackled him. He didn't like it. He let me know this with a quick punch, which was followed by about six from myself. While the referee was pulling what I think were two yellow cards out of his pocket, Mike threw another punch over his shoulder – so I let fly again. When it was all over, we were both given red cards. We went off the pitch, he escorted by someone from Blackrock while I was accompanied by Ed Martin, our backs' coach then. The two of us continued to abuse each other.

People piled into the corridor as we made our way to the changing rooms. We traded some more words as we waited for someone to open the doors. There was another stand-off.

As the Blackrock punters screamed abuse at me, The Fanatic (also known as my da) pushed his way through the crowd to stand by my side and hurl abuse back at them. I was all right with the da by my side. Whenever he kicked off it was time to clear the room. So I knew there would be no problem if trouble flared again. It didn't, thank God.

It seemed as if my 'incidents' were now being highlighted a bit more. I didn't care really – maybe it was because my adversaries were usually high profile. At the time, Rigney was an international, and Brewer – aside from being a former All Black – was working alongside Brian Ashton as an Irish forwards' coach. Much was made of our three-week bans.

I suppose I did have a bit of a reputation as a hard man and a firebrand. Growing up I had been in fights, I had been beaten up, I'd given out a few myself, I'd done doorwork, worked in chip shops, I'd had my fair share of rows; I'd always had an aggressive streak. Yet I still reckon my 'rep' is a bit of myth. Sometimes one incident can be highlighted and then it's 'give a dog a bad name'.

If five papers on a Sunday write the same thing about a player, that tag will stick, whether that player has a bad day for place-kicking, missed tackles or dropped balls.

I don't think I was in any more rows than some others.

These were hard men, and at that time there were more hard men around. That's the way the game was.

NOEL MCQUILKIN
FORMER BECTIVE RANGERS COACH.

"When I first met him he was probably the greenest player you'd ever meet in your life; 100% enthusiasm. He would die for the club. Trevor was very basic in those early days, but then he learnt very quickly. He would pick things up and, if you asked him to do something, he would then go out and do it to the best of his ability.

He was a great team man, probably one of the best team men you could ever get. Possibly too much of a team man. Trevor sort of looked after everyone. If there was a bit of 'how's your father?' and Trevor wasn't involved, he'd go and help his team-mate out. I think that came right through his rugby career – even for Ireland.

Trevor came out here to New Zealand to a little town in King Country called Taumarunui, the local stock agent employed him and Trevor played rugby for them, and he was loved. Everyone loved him. Even then, when he was raw, he would try to do anything. I know they had a sub-Union match one day, and Trevor sort of took on the whole team, and ended up staying with us for the rest of that night. He was quite a sick boy. I think he had a few broken ribs and a broken nose, but it didn't worry him in the least.

But then when he went back to Ireland, he knew what it was all about. He didn't try to do everything himself, he became more of a team man and I think New Zealand improved that part of his game. After three or four years of application and dedication, Trevor became a forward to be reckoned with.

A great family man, and from a good family too.

As far as taking the ball up Trevor had one fault, he'd want to take it up himself all day. He wanted to do all the work, and he was a workhorse, but very quick off the mark and very quick over 20 metres. People don't realise that. He was as quick as you'd get and a bloody ferocious tackler. If he hit you, you knew you'd been hit.

As a person, he was as honest as the day is long. He came from humble beginnings to become a wealthy professional rugby player. He deserved every penny of it. If you wanted a guy in your team for loyalty, Trevor would probably be one of the first guys you'd have. A great trainer, always gave his best, and so proud to be an Irishman. That was his ambition, to play for Ireland, and he did that, and did it very well.

He's one of the fellas Ireland could be proud of."

CHAPTER 4

REQUIEM FOR DAMIEN

MY BABY BROTHER

I remember his birthdays. I remember him starting to date girls. I remember how bright he was, how good he was in school and how mannerly he was. How he enjoyed life, how he made us all smile and laugh, and how he loved sport.

As for rugby, I've no doubt that he had more skill than I ever had. He was bigger and stronger than I was at his age and I know if he were still alive he'd have been a professional rugby player. The first name on most team sheets. And we would surely have played together.

But as my da says, the man above had other plans for Damien. That's just something we all have to live with.

THERE WERE FOUR BOYS IN OUR FAMILY. RONNIE, THE OLDEST, WAS BORN IN Canada in January 1971. I was born in September 1973. Errol was third, born in February 1976. And then came Damien. He was born on July 26th, 1982. He was the baby of the family, and we all loved him.

Damien was a real character – a great character – friendly and well mannered. He loved school. He was particularly good at history and geography, and was brilliant with numbers. Like all of us, he was a hard worker. He cut gardens at weekends and sometimes helped out on the milk round. We did so much together and all my memories of him are happy ones.

Damien was a good Gaelic footballer and hurler, but when it came to rugby, he was exceptional. This isn't a rose-tinted, big brother view. He really was. Being both very big and strong for his age, he followed myself and Ronnie to Barnhall. Sometimes, when asked along by coaches Kevin Corcoran and Seamus Cummins, I used to help out his under-age teams in Barnhall before their matches.

For me it was more fun than playing, showing them how to clear out rucks, how to maul and how to tackle. Damien loved it when I helped coach his team. Any time he had a big match, he'd ask me to give a dig out. If he was proud of me, I was even prouder of him. He captained the team and they won everything; the Kettle Cup, the O'Daly Cup, the All-Ireland under-12s, the Pat Lawlor Trophy. Let's just say he'd done it all for his age.

Bective played Old Belvedere on September 5th, 1995; a date I'll never forget. Afterwards, I was in the dressing-room when one of the lads said two gardaí were waiting for me outside. A few jokes were made as to why they might be looking for me; parking tickets, no tax on the car – the usual banter. When I went outside to meet them, they told me that my brother Damien was very sick in hospital.

"Where's your father?" they asked me. I said he was up in the bar. They told me to get him immediately.

Still in my dirty rugby gear, I ran upstairs to the bar in Belvo. When I couldn't see him, I stood in the middle of the crowd and started screaming for him. The place fell silent. He appeared, asking "What's wrong?" I said "Damien is in hospital and the police are here to take us there."

I remember what followed as if it were yesterday. We all got into the garda car and they flew through the traffic – with the sirens going and me still in my rugby gear. I kept asking them "What's happened? Is he alright?"

I knew from what they weren't saying that it was bad news. I kept asking the father "When you left the house this morning was he alright?" He said that Damien had been sick a few times during the night and he had left him with my brother Errol that morning, thinking it was a stomach bug or something like that.

We screeched into the grounds of Crumlin Hospital to be met by Ronnie and Errol. Errol was crying, saying "He's gone." At this stage we were in the hospital corridors with the gardaí, nurses and doctors. I screamed "Where's he gone? What do you mean?"

Errol answered "He's dead."

"What do you mean he's dead? What happened?"

I began to hit the walls and the doors. The brothers were hanging out of me. When they managed to calm me a little, I remember talking with one of them about my dad; why he just stood there, with his hands on his mouth, and didn't say a word. We were waiting for him to explode but he didn't.

He was in complete shock. It's an image I'll never forget.

More people began to arrive. We were allocated a room where aunts, uncles and friends gathered with us. Errol was in an awful state. He and his girlfriend at the time, Nicola, had been with Damien that morning when he became very sick.

The doctor came in and explained that Damien had died from meningitis. I'd never heard of it. He explained to us what it was and that they'd done everything they could to try and save him. Later he asked if we wanted to see him, but warned that it would not be the same Damien we'd known and loved.

I remember looking at him laid out on a table.

The doctor was right. His skin was black and blue. I kissed him and whispered that I was sorry I hadn't been there for him. I felt guilty. I wished I could talk to him one more time. I had an image from the night before, Friday September 4th. It had been his first day in secondary school and that night I had dinner in the ma's.

I told him to clear the table and wash up. He told me to get stuffed, to do it myself, but in the end he did it after some abuse from me. That was the last time I saw him alive. I learned, like I've never learned before or since, that in life you never know what's around the corner.

Our mother arrived later from Mullingar, where she'd been visiting her own mother Sheila, who was unwell. I know now, because she has told me since, how terrible it was for her. She got a call to come home a.s.a.p., and get to Crumlin Hospital. She'd been driving only a few months and had to go to Leixlip to find someone who could direct her to Crumlin. She said she knew it was bad; she just got that feeling. I suppose a mother does. When mam arrived, everyone was crying. When I look back on it now, with kids myself, I understand better what she must have gone through. I also know she's never been the same since that day.

Paula arrived with Frankie Smyth and Ray McKenna, two of the Bective stalwarts who were there for you when you most needed them. Paula had been at the match earlier and the lads had looked after her. They had assured her it would be alright. One of them drove Paula to the hospital, with the other following in his own.

We left the hospital later that evening. I drove away with Paula and remember arriving at the house with neighbours there and cars everywhere. During the next few days we all turned into robots. The neighbours were fantastic, making tea and sandwiches.

All the local clubs, the whole community, were incredibly supportive. The mother didn't want any alcohol in the house as she didn't want us drinking.

Everybody was so helpful in the days that followed. Soon they had to return gradually to their own lives. That's the way life is, and I found the months after, when no one was around, very hard. When we did drink it was 'mental'; usually ending in tears, fighting with each other or with anyone else.

Damien, nickname 'Did' was born in St James's Hospital on the 26th of July 1982. He died on September 5th, 1995, aged 13. What can I or anyone else say about him? For us he was a little brother, and we'd do anything for him. He was just a kid that everybody liked.

I remember his birthdays. I remember him starting to date girls. I remember how bright he was, how good he was in school and how mannerly he was. How he enjoyed life, how he made us all smile and laugh, and how he loved sport.

As for rugby, I've no doubt that he had more skill than I ever had. He was bigger and stronger than I was at his age and I know if he were still alive he'd have been a professional rugby player. The first name on most team sheets. And we would surely have played together. But as my da says, the man above had other plans for Damien. And that's just something we all have to live with.

I really believe he's looking after us all from that big blue sky they call heaven. I know when times have been difficult over the years, and when I've felt down or needed to go that extra bit in sport or life, I'd ask Damien for help. I usually got it. I always carry a picture of him, and for the last few years in Toulouse, I've always had one of him on my locker.

In October 1995, just a month after Damien died, I had a bad accident. I was involved in a head-on collision with a garda van. Driving down the Nangor Road on my way to deliver some bags for a customer in Bawnogue. I had a green light. A truck was turning right up to Neilstown. The next thing: Bang. The garda van had broken the lights on their way to a robbery. The car was mangled. I wasn't wearing a seat belt. I hit the windscreen but I was still holding onto the steering wheel because I had gripped it so hard.

Before I knew it, the car was surrounded. People were asking "Are you all-right?"

All I could say was "I had the green light. I had the green light."

"Yea, yea," someone said. "Don't move. An ambulance is on the way."

I felt paralysed. It transpired that I had sustained only trapped nerves but I didn't know that at the time. On my way to the hospital I was thinking to myself "This is the last thing the mother needs. One son dead and the other paralysed a month later." At St James's Hospital the nurses cut off my clothes and took x-rays and scans. I was okay; just a few stitches here and there, and a busted ankle. I didn't play again for a few months and missed out on an opportunity of playing for Leinster.

Some months later when we were all having dinner at home, the mother returned from a visit to a clairvoyant. The car accident had come up during their 'session' along with various other subjects. My mother told me the clairvoyant had said Damien had stood in front of the car. It freaked me out. I didn't want to believe it but she continued with what the clairvoyant told her. There wasn't a dry eye in the room. Later, we went out for a few pints to 'still the head'. That was our way of coping at the time.

Damien's death affected us all and we dealt with it in our different ways. As for me, every time I had a few drinks I became very emotional. I could be out with friends or family, break down in tears all of a sudden, and then apologise for doing so.

I've lost many friends and family members over the years. I've even seen friends take their own lives; fellas I've played rugby with or went to school with. My grand-fathers both died when I was relatively young, whereas my grandmothers lived longer. I have more vivid memories of them as they didn't pass away until a few years ago.

Granny Brennan and Granny McMahon were two remarkable women. They gave a lot to society, and left me with many good childhood memories. Every second or third weekend, all the family would meet Granny McMahon, my mother's mum, in their Mullingar family home.

Once they passed away, that all stopped. When the grandmother in a family passes away that is inevitably the case. My da was one of six boys and one girl. As kids, that's where we met uncles George, Colm, Vivien, Paul with exception of uncle Kevin, who was living in Canada.

Granny Brennan, who lived in Blanchardstown, worked with elderly people for the Vincent de Paul, and Granny McMahon wrote a book herself. I miss them both. But the death of Damien affected me like no other, and still does.

Sometimes, lying in bed, I'd leave the curtains open so that the streetlights would light up the room. I'd ask Damien to appear to me or give me some kind of sign, to tell me he was okay; to say "everything is alright, Trev". And then I'd cry myself to sleep.

I remember leaving the Ryevale pub in Leixlip one night when the rain was lashing down and the wind was blowing furiously. I became more and more upset that my brother was all alone up there in Confey Graveyard. I ran up the village, up the Captain's Hill, and didn't stop until I reached the graveyard. I made my way to his grave and just fell to my knees. I kissed the picture on his headstone and told him I was here for him. I began to curse the skies above "Why? Why? Why him? Why us? Why did You do this to us? What did we do to deserve this? He was only 13-years-old! He was just starting his life. Why not take someone else who had lived their life?"

Later I made my way to my parents' house in Glendale. I tiptoed in the back door, changed out of my wet clothes and put on the kettle to make a cup of tea. Then my mother appeared and we sat there together, in the kitchen, drinking pots of tea. We talked for ages about Damien, one of those get-everything-off-your-chest conversations.

After Damien's death I had no desire to play rugby for quite a while. But Bective were very good to me and arranged a job through Ray McKenna. He was much more than an alickadoo and often gave jobs in his packaging company to players. Ray was fairly flexible so long as I did the work, and this gave me time to train. This was when I broke into the Leinster squad. I could knock off at 3 or 4.00pm to go training, while leaving my brother and father in charge of the milk round.

A couple of months after his death, we sold the milk round. No-one had the heart to do it anymore, to get up at 2.00 in the morning to deliver milk in the dark, the cold and the rain. It isn't good for the soul. The father found it hard getting up in the morning because he was still grieving, as the brothers were too.

Damien used to help us out at weekends and collecting money owed to us on Thursday and Friday evenings. To be honest, there were just too many memories. So we sold it and moved on to other things.

Errol, who was 18 at the time, moved to Ballyshannon in Donegal for two years. He was working in a bar called Creevy Pier just beside the Smugglers' Creek – a landmark pub in the county. We made various trips up and down to him. I think he was badly affected by the loss of Damien but you couldn't really tell, as Errol is very quiet in general. He never really talked about it either. When he returned to Dublin, he served his time as a painter and decorator. Now he has his own business, A and E Décor, along with his friend Andy.

I continued working for Ray as a sales rep, selling packaging, for another two years. He was a great boss and looked after me well. As he did all his employees. On top of your pay, he always gave you extra cash at Christmas and for summer holidays.

There were some 'headers' in the job and we sold everywhere, Tallaght, Clondalkin, Walkinstown, with trips to Wexford, Sligo, Wicklow and elsewhere.

When I was recovering from my car accident, Ray told me to take a break and gave me his apartment in Spain for two weeks. That was typical of his generosity.

I stayed with Bective for another two years, and trained with Leinster on a part-time contract in the 1996-97 season. The following year I was given a full-time contract worth IR£15,000. My professional rugby career was up and running. Life moved on, as it does, and I owe a lot to Bective.

But I owe even more to Damien. Nickname 'Did'. A legend.

CHAPTER 5

ACE OF CLUBS

ON LAYING DOWN THE LAW AS ST MARY'S CAPTAIN

I also introduced little court sessions after every home game which lasted between half an hour and an hour. We'd pick judges like Ray McIlreavy, Conor McGuinness and Denis Hickie. Fellas would be pulled up for things they had done in training or in matches. They weren't major, end-of-tour court sessions. They usually consisted of players having to down pints or, for the more serious offences, a cocktail of spirits.

ON THREATENING TO KILL GEORGE HOOK

....on the Monday we ended up in Brady's in Dunboyne. It had been an absolutely shite game — as George Hook had more or less said in describing it as the worst AIL final ever. And while he may have been right I took exception to his comments. On the lash in Brady's, someone rang him, started giving him stick, and then handed the phone to me. Full of drink I threatened to kill him.

WHEN DAMIEN DIED I WANTED TO EMIGRATE. RONNIE AND MYSELF CONSIDERED travelling to Canada for a fresh start. But Phil Lawlor and a few other Bective people sat me down and encouraged me to stay, that I had a future in rugby and should stick with it. My dad also told me that Damien wouldn't have wanted me to run away from everything and pack in the game. Rugby kept me in Ireland.

I'd always have wondered how much I might have achieved. At least I won't die wondering. By playing for Ireland, I reached the top and I can look back without regrets. In the end, I got to see the world through rugby.

If I hadn't become a professional rugby player, I might have been a bricklayer or a builder; something like that.

I'm still not sure what road I might have taken but I do know that, in many ways, rugby saved my life. I played every sport until I was 18. Then began to break into the Leinster scene. Thereafter there was always enough recognition to encourage me: the Irish Youths, the Leinster under-21s, one cap for the Irish under-21s against Wales and the one cap for the Irish As against England in Richmond.

There were good rugby people in Bective. None better than Ray and Frankie Smyth – who lived, breathed, ate, slept and drank Bective Rangers. They brought young fellows through from the under-19s to the senior team, recruited players from around the country, coached and generally acted as confidants and Mr Fixits for anybody who needed help.

In Bective there was a good 'crew'; the Trout, Muscles, the Guller, the Butcher, the Badger, the Body, Out of Africa, The Squirel and the Phantom, also known as Terry Buckley, Finbarr O'Regan, Brian Conway, Brendan Phelan, Paddy Freeman, Paul Regan, Brian O'Halloran, Eddie Bryan and John Paul Regan.

There was also Ben Kealy Snr, aka 'Flipper', Paddy 'Butch' Costello and Padraig 'Butch' Power, Frankie 'Cozzy' Costello and Declan 'Shanty' Shalloe and all the other Shalloes, Des McDonnell, the most laidback man in Ireland, Mick 'Sweat' Doyle, and garda Gerry Quinn, aka 'The Officer'.

There were good players too. In addition to Phil and Macker there was Maurice Mortell, Stephen 'Monty' Montgomery, Craig Whelan, Shane Buckley, Jeff McCaffrey, Johnny Carvill, Ben Kealy Jnr, Pat Bolger, and Brian Cusack.

Dr Tim O'Flanagan got me through many a match. There were times I'd never have made it onto the pitch without him. Then there's Johnny O'Hagen, one-time Irish cricketer, Shelbourne footballer and Bective winger. 'Haygo' was then the Bective kitman, and is now doing the same job for Leinster. I spent five fabulous years with the Rangers, full of laughs and brilliant memories.

In some ways too, they were ahead of their time, especially in the way Frankie enlisted the help of Dr Liam Hennessy, now the IRFU's National Fitness Director. In the mid-90s, Bective were doing bleep tests in pre-season training long before most teams. Liam was years ahead of the posse in terms of preparation, diet and aerobic fitness.

In my first season there, Bective won promotion from Division Three and spent four seasons knocking on the door to the first division. This was when it was smaller than it is now and harder to get into. After we missed out on promotion by one place in 1995-96, Noel McQuilkin moved on to Greystones. Harry Williams stepped in to replace him. Harry would go on to lead Ulster to the Heineken Cup in 1999.

It was the same again the following year when we finished third, a point behind Dolphin, after losing a last-day decider to Clontarf.

At the end of the 1996-97 season, I decided that if I were ever to progress, and have any chance of playing for Leinster or Ireland, I had to play at the highest club level. That was division one of the AIB All-Ireland League.

After our own games with Bective we'd go into the club house and watch Shannon playing Cork Con, or Garryowen against Young Munster, or whatever. In those days RTE used to give the AIL significant coverage on a Saturday afternoon, and the results and round-the-country highlights package had the clubhouses crammed.

We used to get crowds of a few hundred. But if St Mary's played Shannon, each team had at least half a dozen internationals, and they might get 7,000 or so spectators. Hard to believe, but club rugby was the heartbeat of the game in Ireland back then.

By contrast, all the provinces had going for them were the interprovincial or European Cup matches; there was no Celtic League, the interpros didn't have the same intensity or profile of the big club rivalries and even the European Cup hadn't really taken off.

There weren't that many provincial games to go around, and certainly nothing like the opportunities there are for fringe players if you wanted to make a name for yourself, and if, like me, your Under-21 days were behind you, the All-Ireland League was your only means of breaking into the provincial set-up – and then the Irish A/Ireland scene.

I'd spent two years on the fringes of the Leinster squad and five with Bective. They'd been good to me and had exposed me to a higher level of rugby, with better players and coaches. They'd even sorted me out with jobs. But it was time to move on. I was ambitious and in all honesty, I should probably have done it two years earlier.

Who knows, I might have had more of a run for Leinster – and maybe Ireland that bit sooner.

Before the end of that season, I'd met with different clubs; Garryowen, Clontarf and St Mary's. I thought seriously about Garryowen and declaring for Munster, but that would have meant commuting from Dublin to Limerick, so I let it go. Clontarf offered me a few bob in expenses and a job, but they didn't have many big-name players at that point. Although they've since become the biggest club in Leinster.

St Mary's was the most interesting club in Dublin as they had several Leinster players and a few internationals I'd trained with at Leinster over the previous couple of seasons. I had a meeting with Steve Jameson, their captain, and someone from their executive in the Montrose Hotel one evening to discuss a move to their club.

They said they would be happy to have me on board, that their aim was to win the All-Ireland League.

They told me about the club's history, past and current internationals, including Lions; Johnny Moloney, Ciaran Fitzgerald, Tom Grace, Rodney O'Donnell, Paul Dean, Shay Deering, Tony Ward, Denis Hickie, Malcolm O'Kelly, Victor Costello among others. They sold the club well and I was impressed. They told me that if I played for them, I'd have a better chance of playing for Leinster and Ireland. And, to be honest, they were right.

At that stage most clubs in Ireland were paying a few bob in expenses to any player who, in their view, was worth it. Once they confirmed I'd be granted that status, the deal was done.

My mind made up to join St Mary's, I received a phone call out of the blue from a member of a leading club in Leinster.

"Would you be interested in coming to join us?"

"No, I've already made my mind up to join St Mary's."

But he wasn't taking no for an answer. He told me about other players they were signing, the squad they were trying to build and how I would fit into it. I was pretty shocked when I heard the figures involved.

"My biggest worry," I said to him, "is how do I know you are who you say you are? How do I know this is genuine?"

He even offered to meet me that day and would hand over the signing on fee there and then. This was only the start of the professional era, and players were already on contracts from the previous year, but this was the equivalent of nearly a year's salary 'repping'. A ridiculous amount of money to pay a club player. The offer went up. It was the deposit on a decent house.

But I turned it down. I'd made a commitment to join St Mary's and decided to honour it. Although I had a few sleepless nights afterwards.

St Mary's had a pre-season training camp in Galway in the summer of 1997, which was as much a bonding exercise as anything else. We had three meals a day, plenty to drink and a good laugh. Although I knew several of the players through Leinster sessions, I was still adapting to my new team-mates and adjusting to my new club.

Early one evening in our hotel, I saw some of the lads going in and out of a room. The laughter inside was so loud I had to investigate. It was like walking into a sauna, smoke everywhere.

"How are ye lads, what's the story?" I said. That just made them laugh more. They were almost rolling around the floor. No answer.

"Anyone going for a pint later lads?" I asked. More laughter. I don't know whether it was my accent, but they couldn't stop laughing. It took me a while to catch up, but later that night five or six of us split of from the rest of the squad and found a snug in a little pub in Eyre Square.

My 'entrance' into that hotel room was still good for a laugh, so much so, that the pints were just sitting there for a while. Eventually we all got a bit thirsty and didn't move from that little snug for the night. It was my welcoming night to the club and showed me that these lads were just ordinary Joe Soaps like myself.

My first game with my new club was away to Wanderers. It was a bit strange driving into the Wanderers' clubhouse and introducing myself to a few of the lads and the coaches. We won the game well and afterwards, in the dressing-room, the coach Steve Hennessy told me it was the tradition for new arrivals to sing a song. I didn't need to be asked twice. I sang two verses of *Dublin In The Rare 'Oul Times*, which went down well. It had become the Leinster song the season before and would now become the St Mary's song. We would sing only two verses, otherwise you'd be there all night.

It proved to be the start of a good run with a good club, and we got to the semi-finals of the AIL. We lost 28-21 to Shannon in Thomond Park where they were unbeatable. On the morning of one away game against Galwegians we read about the three new caps from our team whom Brian Ashton had named for the upcoming game against the All Blacks, John McWeeney, Kevin Nowlan and Conor McGuinness.

As usual we stocked up a few beers for the train journey. Everyone chipped in a fiver with the club adding a few quid. Some of the best laughs of my career were on these trips, especially if we won. Some played cards and drank, some just drank, and some sang songs and drank. I was always in the last group and was occasionally the worse for wear when we hit Dublin.

We usually ended the night in a club. Everyone wore their blazers; they were a licence to gain entry into night clubs or the wine bars in Leeson Street. We'd invariably run into players from other clubs, also in their blazers. They would also have come back from other trips in Limerick, Cork, Belfast or wherever. Legs and Buck Whaleys were particularly popular haunts. We were like a community with our own social circle, from internationals to provincial and club players of all ages. I feel sorry for young players coming into the club game now as there doesn't appear to be anything like the same social scene or camaraderie.

In my second year with St Mary's, we again lost in the semi-finals, 20-17 away to Garryowen in Dooradoyle. This was despite being 17-3 ahead against 14 men at half-time. You couldn't help but feel sorry for Steve Jameson in particular. It was his last year and he'd given so much to the club.

If you were one of the first to arrive in the evening for training in Templeville Road, you'd see Jemo's car there. He was a rep like myself at the time, and he might have spent the day driving all over the country before stopping in Walkinstown or somewhere nearby so he could catch a few Zs in his car before anyone else arrived.

Jemo had been there for all the near misses by St Mary's. He played in that famous league decider against Young Munster at Lansdowne Road. He'd played for Leinster, though never for Ireland. Nobody typified the club's obsession about winning an AIL more than Jemo. But for him it wasn't to be. He hung up his boots at the end of that season.

It was a club full of talent and there were players who didn't receive the recognition at provincial level that they deserved. Indeed, Conor McGuinness went to Connacht as a means of making the Irish team. As Victor Costello and Barry 'Bomber' Browne had done before, Mark McHugh also took the Connacht route. As would Mark Reilly and Conor McPhillips.

Others were probably good enough to have done the same, like Ian Bloomer and Gareth Gannon – brave beyond belief and a fabulous little footballer who had to retire prematurely. His midfield partner, Ray McIlreavy, was also fearless. There was Frank Fitzgerald and Craig Fitzpatrick, who I always knew as Bundy and there was Slasher....

Before the AIL final against Lansdowne, I was reading the match programme in the dressing-room and said out loud to the lads "Who's yer man Kelvin McNamee. They've made a misprint in the programme."

There was silence as players looked at me. Slasher leant across and said "Trevor, that's me." I only ever knew him as Slasher.

The following summer, 1999, the incoming president of St Mary's, Brendan Spring, arranged to meet me in the Springfield Hotel. He told me he'd like me to be captain, and he'd put my name forward if I agreed. I said I'd love to do it but felt there were other guys in the club who'd come through the feeder school (St Mary's College) and who had given more time to the club than myself, like Denis Hickie for example.

But Brendan was adamant that he put my name forward as he thought I'd bring the best out of the boys. So I agreed, but on a few conditions. Compared to Barnhall and Bective, I felt St Mary's lacked the after-match buzz. I told him that I wanted the club to put on a bit of music to keep the supporters there, and provide food. Both teams were always fed but I was suggesting sandwiches, cocktail sausages, chicken wings etc for the supporters.

I, for example, would bring family and friends from Leixlip, others would bring supporters from Newbridge, Naas or wherever. So rather than send them home early, create an environment for them to remain in the club on a Saturday evening. Make it more of a family club – which is what I was used to. He agreed. I also told him that, unlike previous captains, I didn't want to be involved in selection. That was the coach's decision and I'd back whoever the coach picked.

As it transpired, that was to be Brent Pope. In another change, Steve Hennessy and Hugh Maguire were replaced. I felt for them. They were two former St Mary's players who gave everything to the club, and more or less voluntarily. Losing that game to Garryowen was a huge blow to the club, but it wasn't their fault we lost both semis. It was due more to our stupid mistakes in the second-half, which led to a penalty count something like 11-1 against us.

Being captain had its perks, such as having a free bar for team mates, opponents and friends. I ran amok, to be honest. A free bar? Half of Leixlip would drink Templeville Road dry, and not all of them had a keen interest in rugby. I'm sure there were a few meetings behind closed doors to discuss my tab.

I also introduced little court sessions after every home game which lasted between half an hour and an hour. We'd pick judges like Ray McIlreavy, Conor McGuinness and Denis Hickie. Fellas would be pulled up for things they had done in training or in matches. They weren't major, end-of-tour court sessions. They usually consisted of players having to down pints or, for the more serious offences, a cocktail of spirits.

The manager would be running up and down the spiral staircase in Templeville Road with trays of beer. It gave us time to have a laugh amongst ourselves and we usually emerged in good spirits to rejoin everyone else in the bar.

The stars, like Malcolm, Victor, Conor, Denis and co. were absolutely brilliant. But there were times when they might have trained twice that day with Leinster and didn't see the need for training with their club that same evening. Myself, I felt that was bollox and asked them all to train unless they were injured. In fairness they did.

The Celtic League was a year away so that was the last year when provincial players and internationals played regularly for their clubs. I was training with Leinster also, but I thought at times some of them mightn't be pulling their weight. Nowadays, while every player is still associated nominally with a club, in reality he won't have put on the jersey for four or five years.

The games with Shannon really stood out. There were days we played them when there could be half a dozen or more internationals on each team. They'd have the likes of Marcus Horan, John Hayes, Mick Galwey, Alan Quinlan, Eddie Halvey and Anthony Foley. Mary's would have Emmet Byrne, Mal, myself, Victor, Conor McGuinness, Denis, John McWeeney and Kevin Nowlan. You'd fill Thomond Park or Templeville Road. You couldn't get into the place. It's one man and a dog now.

The biggest thing in Ireland now is Tag Rugby. It's nonsense rugby. Any eejit can play it. Fellas are dislocating their fingers left, right and centre. No-one is learning to tackle. This is the new craze. Mary's on a Tuesday or Wednesday is packed to the hilt for Tag Rugby and barbecues. It's the same in Barnhall.

We qualified for the top four play-offs the third year in a row – the least a squad of our ability should achieve – but for the first time earned a home semi-final, against Ballymena. I didn't finish the game as I was knocked out but the club made our first final. Victor Costello sealed the win with a wonderful try off the base of a scrum about 30 metres out.

The AIL had been dominated by the Munster clubs, but we played Lansdowne in the final. Lansdowne were reduced to 14 men with the sin-binning of my future Toulouse team-mate Aidan McCullen for standing on me. We kicked to the corner, rolled a maul and Victor broke off it to score the decisive try. He was a match-winner for us that season and at club level he really stood out, like he did in his school days with Blackrock College. Our victory made us the first club from Leinster to win the AIL.

In celebration I'd say we nearly drank Dublin dry. We went to the races in Punchestown the following day and on the Monday we ended up in Brady's in Dunboyne. It had been an absolutely shite game – as George Hook had more or less said in describing it as the worst AIL final ever.

And while he may have been right I took exception to his comments. On the lash in Brady's someone rang him, started giving him stick, and then handed the phone to me. Full of drink I threatened to kill him.

After mentioning it in his autobiography, *Time Added On*, without reference to me, George was asked about the incident in an interview with Pat Kenny. "I can't say Pat, but let's just say it was no Peter Stringer."

Thanks George. But now the truth is out. It was me what done it!

Sorry George. I didn't mean it. *Really.*

We had a big dinner in the Berkeley Court Hotel. As captain, I felt it shouldn't be just the 22 fellas on final duty who received a medal, everyone who played throughout the season should also have one.

But the IRFU only presented 22 and the club weren't in a position to do this. So I bought whiskey jugs for everyone who I thought had helped us win that year.

I think I offered Jemo my medal that night but, of course, he wouldn't take it.

I spent one more year in St Mary's with Victor Costello as captain before I returned to Barnhall. I felt I'd given all I could to Mary's and I'd been gone from Barnhall for ten years. I'd left them at 18 and was 28 when I rejoined. They'd climbed six divisions in the intervening decade and were now in Division Two of the AIL, with the basis of a good team. Ian Morgan, their coach, approached me. I told him that my commitment would depend on my involvement with Leinster; Matt Williams, the Leinster coach, wasn't keen on his players playing for their clubs.

There were Friday nights when I sat on the Leinster bench in European Cup matches in Donnybrook and I would be brought on with 15 or 20 minutes to go. Afterwards, I'd join the lads in Kielys for one before leaving, just as they were getting stuck into the pints – and wherever the night might take them.

Instead, I went across the road to Eddie Rockets and then home early to Leixlip before driving to Limerick, or wherever, the next morning to play for Barnhall. It wasn't always easy, but that was the kind of commitment I wanted to give to my hometown club, the one I cut my teeth with.

On one particular Saturday afternoon, having left my Leinster team mates in Kielys the night before, Barnhall played Wanderers. I was brought on as a replacement and helped us to victory, but one high-ranking Leinster Branch official from Wanderers took exception.

He apparently went mad with Matt Williams, maintaining that I shouldn't have been allowed to play. Matt relayed this to me. I pointed out to him that as I wasn't getting much game time with Leinster I needed to be playing some rugby if, because of injuries, they suddenly needed 80 minutes from me.

Much had changed since I last played for my home town club. A clubhouse has replaced the wooden shack. They've become more professional. Ian Morgan, was in effect, a full-time coach and they've broadened their search for players to the southern hemisphere – paying for their flights and locating them jobs. When I was with Ireland in South Africa, for example, I'd talked to a South West Districts player called Klein Tromphe who'd played with the Cats and wanted to come to Ireland, so I put him in touch with Barnhall.

My first game back with Barnhall, and my first senior match for them, was against UCC at home. Everyone had turned up to see the prodigal son. In the warm-up my back was in agony but I couldn't let the club down. A band had been laid on. Even the GAA boys were there. So Gerry Waters gave me a good rub and cracked my back.

They'd get 3-4,000 for some games and, as a family-orientated, community-based club, are still well supported. They've a big catchment area all to themselves; Leixlip, Celbridge, Lucan, Maynooth. Aside from those towns, having the Intel Ireland plant in Leixlip also brings in players from around the country. Despite the back, I managed to drag a few of the UCC players over the line with me for a try. By the end of the night, it was nine or ten players. It's the stuff of folklore.

A local old fella said to me one night soon after "I was talking to a fella, Joey Mac, down in the church. He said you carried nine players over the line. It was like that Ginger McLoughlin try against England in Twickenham. Amazing. Amazing."

"Nine?" I said.

"It could have been ten," he said.

On the clubhouse wall, there's even a framed picture of me scoring that try. A Kodak moment.

I managed to play eight matches for Barnhall and we remained in contention for promotion. The leaders, Belfast Harlequins, were on a run of 11 unbeaten matches when they come to town. After Moggy had finished speaking at our team meeting in the bar-cum-restaurant of the Springfield Hotel, I was like a man possessed. I asked if I could speak.

Ignoring the old folks having Saturday lunch with their families, and a few communions as well, I let fly; Belfast Harlequins were no better than us, if the players didn't believe we could win this match today, if we didn't wear the Barnhall crest with pride, if any of us thought we were going to be their 12th victims, if anybody wasn't prepared to put their bodies on the line like I was going to do, they might as well stay and drink pints there for the rest of the day. I really wound them up and we were almost crashing into each other in the car park to get to the club house. We beat them well and Brendan Burke scored three tries. The boys said afterwards that my talk fired them up beyond belief.

We missed promotion by a solitary point and in hindsight, I wish I'd played more games for them. However, I was restricted in the number of games I could play for them by Matt, who said that if I togged out for Barnhall, I wouldn't be involved with Leinster at all the following weekend. It wasn't just me, it was everybody in the 22. Although it's supposedly improved since, I believe the attitude of the provinces back then killed club rugby.

A club like Barnhall depends on a core group of players and many of what you might call their golden generation have retired or moved on, such as the Burkes. Barnhall had always done everything in their power to help Conrad, the eldest and most talented of the Burkes, play on Saturdays.

His computer work took him to London, Amsterdam and elsewhere, but the club always flew him back and forth for matches if they could. Conrad read the game so well, he kicked well, he passed well, he sidestepped well he made gaps and created gaps. Eoin, who's a scrum-half, captain and still there, is a qualified carpenter; Brendan, who moved on to Rotherham, is a qualified electrician. I admired them because they worked and got their trades. Declan and Paul were good players too, and their sister Fiona is a fantastic camogie player and very good at Tag Rugby. A talented family.

William Servat, the Toulouse hooker, accompanied me to Barnhall one day last season and I have to confess, it looks a little run down. Club rugby has changed hugely, but Barnhall is regrouping, and have had some fine under-age teams recently. They were the All-Ireland Under-16 champions two seasons ago and they've had good under-18 and under-19 sides in the last few years.

That 2001-02 season was the peak of Barnhall's climb, although after flirting with relegation two seasons ago, they're on the rise again. In my own mind I was going back to finish off my career with Barnhall for the next three, four or five years before retiring. But the man above had other plans for me.

HARRY WILLIAMS
BECTIVE COACH 1996-97 AND ULSTER COACH 1998-2000, INCLUDING ULSTER'S EUROPEAN CUP WIN IN 1999.

"As a person I can only speak in the highest possible terms about him. Off the field he was an absolutely wonderful fella; full of craic and chat. He had a very deep side to him as well as everything else. He was very family orientated. I know he had a young brother who died and that upset him quite a bit, and he was very close to his mother and father. He would have done anything for you, just a wonderful ball carrier with a heart as big as anything. He was always good craic post-match, he always had a bit of a song and a laugh and a joke; a great character, the sort of fella who lit the room up when he came in. Mad as a hatter, mind you.

To use that horrible word, he was very focussed and he wore his heart on his sleeve. He never took a game lightly, no matter who he was playing for. When Trevor went on to the pitch, whether it was for Bective, Leinster or Ireland, you always got the Full Monty. He was a big-hearted guy, and a big-hearted player. He was always motivating guys; he was never short of a word or two.

We went very well in 1997-98 but then lost to Derry with three or four games to go when we were cruising it. Trevor was the big back-row man, and he made the big hits and did the ball-carrying. We had a great guy on the ground called Stephen Montgomery, or Monty, and Trevor used to keep him going.

We had a lot of good players and I suppose we were fairly forward-orientated, but Bective wasn't the same without Trevor. He was very, very fast and we used to use him quite a bit in terms of bringing the ball up. And he would have brought it up when he wasn't supposed to! He was foolhardy at times, we've got to be honest about it, but he was maturing. We used to spend a bit of time with him before games, just making sure he was calm. We called it the Trevor Clever Routine. We'd sit him down for five or ten minutes and just have a wee quiet word with him and go through the game with him.

As well as myself, our hooker John Carvill was also a calming influence on him – John went on to become a referee. In the early days his penalty count was fairly high but we sort of accepted that was going to be the case, because if you tried to tame Trevor you would lose more than half the player. You just had to work with what you had. He had so much to give, it was a case of managing his enthusiasm, shall we say.

I also came across him when I was manager of Ireland A, when Declan Kidney was coach and Niall O'Donovan was assistant coach. His game had matured a lot. His penalty count wasn't nearly as high but he had the same wonderful enthusiasm for the game and a way of making everyone else feel good. When Trevor was about, nobody was downhearted."

BRENT POPE
COACH TO ST MARY'S WHEN BRENNAN CAPTAINED
THE CLUB TO THE AIL TITLE.

"I first came across Trevor when he was playing with Bective in Division Two and I was coaching Clontarf. We met them in a promotion decider in Donnybrook and I told Dave Moore to get at Trevor and then stay at least one yard away from him for the rest of the match. I don't think I've seen Dave play so well or move so quickly.

As a New Zealander coming from the deep south in Canterbury and Otago, he was the kind of player I would have had a lot of regard for; fully committed, hard as nails, always willing to give 110%. I remember one scrummaging session in St Mary's one night he caught the side of his hand in the springs of the machine and it took a bite out of his palm. He put the hand, which was dripping with blood, into the waistband of his shorts and I said "Trevor, I think maybe you should get that seen to."

"Ah no Brent, wait till after training." Nothing was ever a worry for Trevor.

I think he was seriously 'mismarketed'. I've always said that Trevor should have been the poster boy for rugby in Mary's, in Ireland and in non-traditional areas. He would have been brilliant going around the schools talking about his career given he was a guy who came from the other side of the tracks of rugby in this country.

I'm not saying Trevor was ostracised but he would have been seen as not of the right pedigree. I've seen a lot of that in Irish rugby; what school you went to, what university – and from there you went on to Leinster.

He wasn't the most skilful player in the world, we all know that, but he worked on it and gave you the best of what he had. And he was a fantastic captain. He was great for Mary's. It wasn't a D4 club as such, but it had a very proud tradition and Trevor was a very popular captain. He always came down to the club on Sunday mornings to watch the kids.

We're still the only Leinster team to have won the AIL, and Trevor is the only Leinster captain. He was a captain that led by example. I've played with a lot of good captains; some are talkers and some just get on with it. Strangely enough, his team talks were quite controlled and methodical. Trevor hit the right nerves and hit the right buttons. It's an old cliché, but he was the type of guy that you'd have followed out over the trenches in World War I. There were a few key games, like the semi-final against Ballymena, when Trevor led the team in tackles.

I remember one quite funny story. We were playing Cork Con, it was mucky and wet, and the internationals were just back. Trevor had dunted Ronan O'Gara about three times. I was on the sidelines and after the last tackle Ronan was lying face down in the mud and I heard him say "Is that my old mate Trevor Brennan?"

"Yeah, it's me again Ronan."

I think he was a sad loss to Irish rugby and particularly to Leinster. They have struggled to make a real impact in Europe while Trevor has been instrumental in helping Toulouse to win two European Cups. He certainly should have played for Ireland after he had gone to Toulouse. If you're picking on form, which they always say is the case, then he deserved a run as much as anybody. He certainly deserved to be in touring parties. But he probably ended up having a more distinguished career than if he did stay here.

In fact, I'd go so far to say that Trevor should have been on the Lions' tour. He was the one guy I kept saying would go on the Lions' tour. They were rudderless in midweek and I thought that with Trevor's team spirit and his willingness to keep playing hard the whole game, he would have galvanised a midweek side.

Given some of the clowns they did eventually take he would have been an ideal mid-week captain. Trevor has what in New Zealand we call 'Mana', which could be applied to a hard nut who commands respect. He would pull the others together and he would get more out of the team than the individuals themselves. There's very few players who can do that.

A lot of people would remember Trevor from his younger days as nothing more than a fireball of punches and a hard man. But Trevor worked on his game over the years and his skill level improved big time when he went to France. He practically re-invented himself, which was admirable, but he was the kind of guy who could turn a match around in 60 seconds – whether it was chasing a kick-off or putting in a big hit. Every team needs one. Leinster have lacked one ever since the day he left.

Trevor never accepted second best, and half the time he was bandaged up. How Trevor has played so long I don't know, but he's going to be a sore boy in a few years. It's a sad way for him to go, but it was probably the right time to go out anyway. Typically he went out with a bang, not with a whimper. But you'd always have expected that of Trevor."

CHAPTER 6

THE LEINSTER YEARS: I

ON ZINZAN BROOKE

I remember in the dressing-room beforehand guys talking of him in awe. "Jaysus, he'll kill us," I heard Jonny Kenny say. He was a confident, fiery little scrum-half normally, but I sat there thinking "I'm going to get stuck into him." From the kick-off, whenever he went near the ball, I just went for Zinzan's head. And off we went, the two of us tearing into each other in Donnybrook. Thank God it was only a friendly. No-one was sent off but it gave the boys in Bective something to talk about for a month.

ON BEING NICKNAMED BY NEIL FRANCIS

It was on that pre-season tour to Italy, that Franno nicknamed me Begbie - after the mad character in *Trainspotting*. I was a bit wild, I'd have to admit.

IF YOU'RE A YOUNG PLAYER COMING INTO A SQUAD, THEY'RE NOT GOING TO PICK you ahead of a 30-year-old with years of experience. You have to prove yourself first, be it with your rugby skills or your physicality. I probably didn't have the rugby ability if the truth be told. The physicality came naturally to me, whereas the rugby didn't. My strengths were my tackling, my ball-carrying, my hunger and perhaps my mental toughness. I wanted it all, I wanted to play for Ireland, and I wanted to make sure that I had no regrets. I did not want to look back and say "I didn't give it my best go." I also think every team needs a bit of lunacy, every player brings something different. That's what makes a good team, 15 players who aren't all the same.

In 1995-96 Leinster reached the semi-finals of the first Heineken Cup, but I was mostly on the outside looking in. Apart from a few squad sessions and a couple of games on the bench, my only game time was on a pre-season tour to Treviso when we were well beaten in the first but won our second game. Neil Francis, Brian Rigney, Victor Costello and Steve Jameson were the big names and the big men in the squad. They were an impressive bunch of characters.

In the gym one day I looked at Francis, who had been capped 30-odd times. Almost in awe, I asked him what weights he did. "Weights? Never lifted a weight in my life and I don't intend to start now." I don't think he would necessarily have excelled in the professional era because weights and fitness didn't really figure in his training schedule. He was just one of those naturally gifted players and one that I would have looked up to over the years. It was on that pre-season tour to Italy, that Franno nicknamed me Begbie after the mad character in *Trainspotting*. I was a bit wild, I'd have to admit.

'Jemo' was Steve Jameson; a big country lad, with an impressive chest. I've never seen a man with a bigger chest, with the possible exception of Reggie Corrigan. Loved his rugby, and liked a pint to go with it. Steve was a big man, very tough on the pitch, good line-out jumper at the front and a very solid scrummager. A real throwback to the old era.

The Italian tour, which was also a developmental trip, included Colin McEntee, David Coleman, Ciaran Clarke and Derek Hegarty. As we weren't playing in the second game our manager, Jim Glennon, told us "Right dirt-trackers, those not playing in tomorrow's game are all coming out with us." We were brought out for a meal and a few drinks, the sort of thing management encouraged in those days.

I was starting to fit in, but I knew it would be difficult to break into the set-up. It seemed to be a very settled team. The back-row consisted of Dean Oswald, Chris Pim and Stephen Rooney and there wasn't any space in the second-row with Franno, Brian Rigney and Jemo around. So I just kept the head down and trained hard.

That said, I had a few dust-ups on the training pitch with Pim and Rooney, but that was all part of it. I remember one run-in with Rooney a few years later on a pre-season tour to Loughborough with Mike Ruddock as coach. It was a contact session and we were on opposite teams. I probably started it, but I remember him running around the pitch chasing me like a madman for the rest of the afternoon. I was trying to get into the team and figured the best way of doing that was by a process of elimination. I suppose it came naturally to me at the time. I've definitely mellowed since then; no doubt about it.

I was mad – mad to succeed. I felt no-one was going to give me a chance, so I was going to make a name for myself somehow. Politics, I felt, was still rife in those days, even at provincial level. The team was a closed shop, or at least that was my impression. I sat on the bench so many times and hardly ever got a run, even though the established players – who had been there for years – were being hammered by 20 and 30 points.

Even so, some people believed in me. One was Jim Glennon. He had taken the dirt-trackers out one night, and the next day, I was wearing an Irish jersey I'd bought in Arnotts a few years' previously, when I was about 18. It looked a bit worse for wear as I'd cut the sleeves off it and it had seen many a training session. Before our fitness session, which started with a 3,000 metre followed by 150 shuttles, Glennon came up to me. "I know you had a good night last night with a few of the others. You might be feeling a bit sick today, but I don't want to see you pulling out of any of the runs, or be at the back of the group. I want to see you up at the front all day."

He grabbed the shirt, and said "Listen kid, do you see that jersey you're wearing? One day you're going to have a lot of them and they're going to be your own. The real thing."

"Jesus," I said, "I hope you're right Jim." And that fired me up to run all day.

Coming from a former Irish international who quickly became one of the biggest influences on me and my career, that meant a hell of a lot. Jim gave me some very good advice in my early days. He was a good manager of men, good at keeping the spirits high, especially the dirt-trackers.

I often found myself beside him on plane or coach journeys. He told me stories from his playing days with Leinster and Ireland, and the different training methods back then. I always listened very intently to anyone who had already been there.

Jim was a very hands-on manager and helped out with the scrums and the line-outs. He could be a hard man too. The morning after the defeat to Stade Francais in '99, when a few of us had slept it out for an early departure to the airport, Jim left us there. We came to breakfast and discovered the coach had gone. We hired a taxi and asked the driver to take us to the airport. "Which one?"

"You mean there's two?" We didn't know that as well as Charles de Gaulle, there was Orly. We were frantically trying to contact some of the lads because we didn't have our passports either. They'd all been collected together on arrival. We contacted Jim and he said the passports would be left at the check-in desk, but luckily the plane was delayed long enough for us to catch it. A bit like Roy Keane setting an example at Sunderland. It taught you to be punctual.

I knew if I could break into the Leinster team, the Irish team would be a relatively shorter step away. My reasoning was once I played number six for Leinster I only had three or four players as rivals; Eddie Halvey, Anthony Foley and David Corkery in Munster along with a few others.

That said, when Brian Ashton took over as Irish coach from Murray Kidd, my international career hardly took off. As it transpired, Ashton appeared to have a clear preference for players based in England, like Dylan O'Grady and David Erskine.

When Mike Ruddock, who had coached Swansea and the Welsh A team, arrived as Leinster coach in 1997, everyone began again from a clean slate. He didn't know Trevor Brennan from Adam – or Chris Pim or Stephen Rooney for that matter – and he gave me, Shane Horgan, Kevin Nowlan and John McWeeney our opportunity.

Ruddock's arrival brought a new edge to training and we were always the ones leading the 3,000 metre runs. I remember one on Bective's back pitch when Shaggy and Kevin outran everyone. This was normal as they were like two long-distance runners, always out in front.

Ruddock's approach to a game was physical, physical, physical. Match them up front and take it from there. Mike wasn't a backs' coach. He took Paul Dean on to help him out, but by and large he was on his own. He didn't have the retinue of specialist assistants like today's head coaches. Nor did he have the facilities which are now common place. Although Irish rugby was slower to grasp professionalism than most of their main rivals, he was expected to produce results straight away.

And he did get results, because he had us super fit. I thought I was fit, but I recall coming home from training sessions being unable to climb the stairs, saying I'd sleep down on the couch. He used to have drills which he called 200s. I'll never forget them.

You'd drag a tackle bag up and down the back pitch, with one fella hitting it, and then Mike would call "200". You had to drop the bag, sprint to one touchline, run all the way back to the other touchline, and then back to pick up your bag, before starting the whole process again. We seemed to do that for hours. As well as the 3,000 metre runs, there were his bloody one-two-threes: first you'd hit a tackle bag, then drop to the ground to do ten press-ups, then get to your feet to do a hit-and-spin, i.e. hit the tackle bag and spin off it.

Coming into that first full season with Leinster under Ruddock, 1997-98, I'd never been fitter. I was picked for the seasonal opener, against Ulster. It was a lovely, sunny, end-of-August day with a packed Donnybrook. It was a bad game, a huge anti-climax, even though we won it 26-25. I had a dust-up with Paddy Johns, the two of us going hell for leather in their 22. Paddy Johns is a hard man and I always respected him. A pure gentleman. But these big name players do challenge you on a pitch sometimes, and some players – especially if they're young and relatively new on the block – might back down. But Trevor Brennan would get stuck into him and give him as good as he got. And I think that's what got people talking about me.

The bigger the name, the bigger the challenge. Even more so if he was an international. It was often pre-meditated, ever since I broke into the Bective team. When Northampton played a friendly in Donnybrook, Zinzan Brooke was with them at the time. An All Black legend, and probably still the world's best player at the time, in my opinion. In fact, I would consider him the best back-rower of all time. Hard, ruthless and gifted, he had everything. It's no wonder he wasn't a huge success as a coach, because no player could do what he did on a pitch.

I remember in the dressing-room beforehand guys talking of him in awe. "Jaysus, he'll kill us," I heard Jonny Kenny say. He was a confident, fiery little scrum-half normally, but I sat there thinking "I'm going to get stuck into him." From the kick-off, whenever he went near the ball, I just went for Zinzan's head. And off we went, the two of us tearing into each other in Donnybrook. Thank God it was only a friendly. No-one was sent off but it gave the boys in Bective something to talk about for a month.

Sometimes I thought about this a week before. I could imagine myself playing against the Irish number six. I'd want to tear his head off. I didn't want to just tackle him; on the way up I wanted to push his head into the mud as well. I don't think I was unique, especially in those days. It was the way of the game then. Trevor Brennan from Barnhall and Bective? No-one knew me. And Bective v Old Wesley wasn't normally a headline maker.

On the Monday after the Ulster game I went to Mike Ruddock's office. "Listen, I didn't feel I had a good game, and I know I got into a fight and everything. Just give me another chance against Munster." We lost 15-12 in Musgrave Park. They had a back-row of Halvey, Wallace and Anthony Foley. No quarter given. No tries scored. Another typically full-blooded physical interprovincial.

Mike got us all into the big dressing-room in Belvo on the Monday morning, and being the sort of coach he was, went around the team one by one.

He went to Bob Casey "You're 6' 8", you're marking Mick Galwey and is he a better player than you? Are you afraid of him?"

And to Reggie Corrigan, I can't remember if it was John Hayes he was pushing against "Is he a better f****** prop than you?"

"What is it," he asked, "between Leinster and Munster. Is it a mental thing?

These guys bully you and push you around whenever it comes to a fight."

I remember him saying that he had two pairs of gloves in the boot of his car and he'd challenge anyone to a fight in the car park. "Is this guy for real?"

I remember saying to Reggie Corrigan "If he comes to me I'll go out and take one of the pairs of gloves off him and I'll give him a go in the car park."

"And you Trevor," he starts..."you're all right," before he moved on to tear into somebody else.

I don't remember much else about that Munster match, but so began a long love-hate relationship. You can't take it away from them, Munster were the benchmark, the best rugby team in Ireland. They were, and remain, the ultimate test. It was my start. I played in all the interpro games, as Chris Pim had decided to retire, and we beat Connacht 23-6.

In 1997, I made my Heineken Cup debut, against Toulouse in Donnybrook. They had a great team. Franck Belot and Hugo Miorin were in the second-row, with a back-row of Sylvain Dispagne, Christian Labit and Didier Lacroix – who is still in the club as coach of the Espoirs and who also looks after all the sponsors.

They beat us 34-25, but it was a good, tough game. I just ran around like a lunatic, carrying ball, chasing kick-offs, tackling everything that moved. It was one of those games that I didn't want to end. I was yellow carded and I also put poor Christophe Deylaud – their famous out-half who was known as The Magician in Toulouse, but who left to coach Agen the year I joined – out of the game with a tackle which damaged his cruciate ligament. I was also awarded man-of-the-match; a lovely bronze statue from the Burlington Hotel which now stands in the da's house. "*Man-of-the-match: Leinster versus Toulouse, the Heineken Cup, 1997.*"

Even today, I am still slagged in Toulouse about my performance that day. "Brennan, you used to be mad. Do you remember what you did to Deylaud? And your fight with Dispagne in the same match? You and Dispagne."

I carried ball well, tackled well and was good in the line-outs. I was starting to enjoy playing for Leinster. That was probably the day I really arrived, and the following week we beat Leicester at home 16-9. They had a very strong team, full of English internationals, and were camped on our line for about the last ten minutes. It was Leinster's first significant scalp in the Heineken Cup, and should have been a huge boost to all of us. But because I was slightly concussed, I had to go home while the boys went out celebrating.

I joined them after our next match, even though – being Leinster – it was an embarrassing 33-32 defeat away to Milan. I'll never forget it, the match or what happened afterwards. Mike had told us after the defeat that we'd have training the next morning at 8.30am before breakfast. But lads paid no heed to it, and off we went for a great night. I recall putting Kevin Nowlan in a taxi and sending him home. We went to a night club, and most of us drifted back to the hotel at four, five or six in the morning.

True to his word, Mike and the bag man knocked on everyone's door before 8.30am. We met in the lobby and it was one of the funniest sights I've ever seen. Victor Costello and a few others were still in their Number Ones – shoes, trousers and shirt – from the night before. They hadn't been back long, and had stayed up in the lobby having a few more drinks in the residents' bar.

Mike meant business, and led us out of the hotel. As there was no pitch nearby, he took us to a cornfield for a few laps. The corn was taller than us in some parts. It was crazy, but a laugh. I managed to nab a pair or runners and shorts, and we ran around that field for half an hour. Every now and again he shouted "Hundred", the signal for the last few men at the back to run to the front.

"Victor, move your arse; get up to the front," he kept shouting at Victor.

"Victor, if you don't move your arse, I'll take £250 out of your wages."

And I remember Victor turning towards him and saying, in between gasps "No problem. Who do I write the cheque to?" He didn't budge and stayed at the back of the group.

In our next match we were thrashed 47-22 by Leicester in Welford Road but I do remember one journalist writing "The tackle made by Trevor Brennan on Eric Miller from a kick-off was worth the entry fee alone." Just as he caught the ball I tackled him and banged him into touch. And so began another long-running feud.

Leicester were then at their best. A load of players in their prime and a savage pack with a punishing rolling maul.

We beat Milan 23-6 at home and were beaten 38-19 away to Toulouse. In the Toulouse line-up was Patrick Soula, the restaurateur from whom I later bought my bar, De Danu. It used to be Tommy's Café, which he'd named after his son. During the game, Patrick ran to retrieve a ball that had been kicked through and went down on it. I attempted to jump over him but I clipped the top of his head with my boot. I can honestly say it was an accident.

But it opened up and required 32 stitches inside and outside, leaving him with a scar for life not unlike Victor's on the side of his head. We've had many laughs about it since. He often talks about that match and that incident, and the scar!

That was a particularly eventful night in Toulouse. On the way back from a bar, through one narrow street after another, myself and Declan O'Brien – a number six from DLSP – were struggling to locate our hotel, the Crowne Plaza. Suddenly, we were nearly run over by a car, and received some abuse from the lunatics inside it to boot.

They braked and I said "Think we could be in a bit of trouble here Declan." But if you were ever going to be in a bit of trouble, there was no better man than Declan to have alongside you. Hard as nails. A really good player, and as two aggressive number sixes from rival clubs fighting for the same slot, we fought it out for a few years too. As the five occupants emerged from the car, he just said "Right, back to back here. You take the two on the left, and I'll take the three on the right."

I said "Are you sure?"

"Yeah, no problem Horse."

The police arrived, broke up the fight, discovered we were rugby players who'd played against Toulouse earlier that day and brought the two of us back to our hotel. We came out of it well. No-one was really hurt.

However, the police would be back at the Crowne Plaza before long, for something quite different. Denis Hickie had also arrived back in the hotel with blood gushing from his nose. When we asked what had happened, he said he had run into trouble with some doormen at a night club.

At that stage there were about ten or twelve of us gathered in the lobby, including myself, Declan, Paul Flavin, Shane Byrne, Denis, Reggie Corrigan and others. Someone suggested that he show us where this night club was and we'd sort out the doormen.

Luckily for us and for them, when we did get there, the club was closed. What separated us was a 20 foot high door, probably about a foot thick, which even the Leinster pack couldn't budge.

The police were obviously called, and three or four police cars pulled up outside the club. Some of the lads made off on foot, but five of us were arrested. It was Alain Rolland who came to our rescue. Shane Byrne got him out of bed and Alain and Jim Glennon came to the police station the next morning.

Alain spoke the language and applied the diplomacy, while Jim wrote the cheque. We had never actually assaulted anyone. The problem was the damage we had done to the door trying to get inside. In hindsight, I thank God for the old-fashioned doors. So there was no fight. Just as well.

By the end of that season I'd never felt better, and had even been involved in a few Irish sessions under Brian Ashton. I was hoping to pick up where I left off. For the 1998-99 pre-season training Leinster were brought over to Alton Towers in England. Ehh, that trip went very well...

An unofficial warm-up game was arranged against an English side and Alain

Rolland, who was just starting out on his new career as a referee, was in charge. There were no dressing-rooms or clubhouse, just a field as such. But it was a lovely sunny day as we all changed on the side of the pitch. I wore mouldy boots, because the ground was hard. One of their players went to ground about 15 or 20 minutes into the game and a ruck formed. In the process of clearing the ruck, I made contact with his head. A bit of a scuffle broke out, prompting Alain to intervene and halt the match for a minute.

I think we scored a penalty off it, but as I remember it, the game effectively resumed with a kick-off to them. They'd obviously said amongst themselves that from the next kick-off everybody was to pick one player each, no matter where the ball was, and just hit them. So we were all looking at the ball in the sky and then it was bang, bang, bang. Another almighty fight broke out.

Once order had been restored, there were Leinster players being stitched everywhere. Poor old Dr Arthur Tanner was running all over the place.

Emmet Byrne had about ten stitches while Pat Holden suffered a broken nose. Rollers abandoned the game. Jim Glennon called me aside and told me I was a feckin' eejit, because it was my stamping that had caused the fight and led to the match being abandoned.

Jim made me go to the front of the bus to apologise to the management and the team. That wasn't easy. Pat Holden and Emmet Byrne were still nursing facial wounds that had required stitches. But while Jim could be hard, he was fair and loyal, and stuck by me. He knew how players could go beyond the line, probably because he had done so himself.

You can't say I was sent off, as everyone was sent off. Even so, the Leinster management had to be seen to do something, as these trips are costly. I was suspended for the first match of the season away to Ulster. The reason given to the media by Mike Ruddock was that I needed to become "more focussed".

But the papers soon found out what really happened, with Trevor Brennan the bad guy, as usual.

It wasn't a good week. My good friends, Chris Gallagher and Alan Graham, did their best to cheer me up. We met for a few pints in the Celbridge House, had one or two more in other pubs in Celbridge before moving on to Brady's in Maynooth later that night.

I was drowning my sorrows. I wasn't involved with Leinster that week. I was on the outside looking in again. I seriously wondered whether I'd blown my Leinster career, and with it my dream of playing for Ireland. Luckily for me they got the shite kicked out of them by Ulster and I was brought back in the following week. Even so, at times in my rugby career it felt as if I was fighting against everything and everyone.

JIM GLENNON
FORMER IRISH INTERNATIONAL, EX-COACH AND MANAGER OF LEINSTER, AND RETIRED FIANNA FAIL SENATOR AND TD.

"Having heard of Trevor through his under-age exploits with Barnhall and Ireland Youths, he first came to my attention in my capacity as Leinster coach on St Patrick's Day, 1993. In an under-21s triple crown decider against Wales, in the Glamorgan Wanderers ground, he almost beat his way out of the subs area in his enthusiasm to replace an injured colleague.

His raw-boned passion and courage revitalised an ailing Irish effort and turned the flow of possession in Ireland's favour. Unfortunately his introduction to the fray came too late to rescue the game.

I was totally taken by his 'no frills' attitude, which was badly needed that day. It was not a particular characteristic of the Leinster team of that time. I can clearly recall receiving strong advice from a senior IRFU official against including him in any plans I may have had. Trev, I was told, had no basic skills, and was unmanageable.

His athleticism, commitment, dedication and manifest honesty seemed to be worthless in the eyes of the 'establishment'. To me, and in a 21 year old particularly, these attributes were invaluable, especially so in the context of their marked absence from the vast majority of those coming through the traditional Leinster 'nurseries'. For what other reason were coaches and managers created?

He became part of the squad for the following season, 1997-98 and immediately made what we came to know as the customary Trevor 'double-whammy' impact – a huge physical presence on the field, and an outstanding squad member off it.

That season started with a pre-season training camp in Northern Italy and, from the moment of our arrival at Marco Polo Airport in Venice, he was at the heart of a very happy squad.

He played his first game for us, in appalling conditions, a couple of nights later against Benetton Treviso and had to be substituted midway through the second half. Dr Niall Hogan, our scrum-half, who hadn't trained with us prior to our departure – and hadn't shared a pitch with Trev previously, panicked when he saw the physical mayhem being caused. He then let his medical instincts get the better of him, insisting that Trevor be substituted before Niall's professional skills were required!

The spectacular, sometimes reckless, but always good-humoured, exterior belied a very serious and dedicated rugby player. And he was blessed with a tremendous physique which he was prepared to test to the very limit, whether playing, training, or in the gym.

Unfortunately his ball skills were not of the same quality, nor were his powers of mental application. His critics, and I was among them myself at times, will say that these deficiencies were the defining factors of his career, and I agree with them. But I do so only in the sense that these acknowledged imperfections provided him with the colossal challenge which was ultimately, in my view, to define Trevor Brennan the rugby player, and more importantly, the man.

He ultimately failed to bring his ballskill levels to what Eddie O'Sullivan required of him.

That said, the qualities he displayed, and continually refined, on a daily basis during his career-long struggle to overcome these self-acknowledged shortcomings are, for me, the real definition of not only Trevor Brennan the rugby player, but also, and of much greater relevance, Trevor Brennan, the human being. Someone I am honoured to have as a friend."

MIKE RUDDOCK

FORMER BECTIVE, LEINSTER AND WALES COACH, NOW COACHING WORCESTER.
"Because I had previously coached Bective I kept in touch with a lot of the Rangers – people like Dr Tim O'Flanagan, the club doctor, and Johnny O'Hagen, the kitman with Leinster. And whenever I spoke to them they told me about this lad Trevor Brennan. He was playing with Bective and they felt he could go on to do really well. I think I'd done the interview for Leinster and there was a Leinster Cup semi-final on in St Mary's.

Bective lost, but Trevor was as abrasive and aggressive as I'd heard, and physically he looked a big, strong guy. I just felt that it was a matter of adding to some of his skills to see him move up the ladder and get representative honours.

I had to tame him a little but I didn't want to take that tough edge away. Obviously the laws of the game have changed quite a bit, but there weren't so many yellow cards flying around in those days. He probably got away with a bit more, so playing to the edge and to the referee was an important part of his game.

That said, overall he was a great competitor and one of the first guys you'd want on the team sheet at that time, because he would lead by example. He really was just a fantastic character to have and a bloody great player.

By the time I left Leinster, there was a lot more awareness and skill in Trevor's game. When I first met him, he trained so hard to improve his game but often on the field it was still a personal thing between him and the guy opposite. Over time he still hit guys hard, knocked them backwards and did all the physical stuff. But over the years he matured into a really great player who was prepared to contribute to the game plan and to the style of play. This made him a very effective weapon carrying the ball. With the Toulouse style of play his ball-handling came on and I think ultimately he finished as a really good all-round player.

The first time he was asked to go to an Irish training session, I was involved on the periphery. A number of defensive drills were taking place and Trevor was really trying to make an impression.

A couple of the senior guys had a word with Brian Ashton, coach at the time, to ask that Trevor be held back and temper it a bit. Every now and again he came over to me and out of the corner of his mouth would ask "How am I doing Mick?"

I said "Great Trev, keep on banging them."

I thought it was a real compliment to him and a great example of making a first impression when senior players were asking the coach to keep an eye on him so that he wasn't hitting so hard in the practice. I think he made a mark straight away.

On the lighter side, I can remember him and Victor Costello putting a series of alarm clocks in the room of the physio – the great AK (Alan Kelly), the talking beard.

They placed them at different points in the room so that the alarm clocks went off every half-hour in the wardrobe or under the bed or in a cupboard somewhere, thereby keeping him awake all night. As you can imagine, AK made a meal of it the next day.

I remember playing Glasgow in the European Cup and Trevor was actually on the bench. We were leading quite handsomely but then we let our concentration slip and Glasgow got back in for a couple of tries. We put Trevor on, and he nailed a guy from the kick-off, turned the ball over, and suddenly we went upfield to score a couple of tries and nail the game down. He could make that kind of impact, whether starting or off the bench.

In an interprovincial game down in Munster – I think the game after he had been suspended – he was Man of the Match. I remember him singing *Dublin In the Rare 'Oul Times* in the changing room and the happiness on his face and the pleasure he took from inspiring the team to a fantastic win.

One incident that typified Trevor for me was when we were at Liam Toland's wedding on the Shannon in the summer of 2006. A big gang ended up in the bar in the early hours of the morning. Some local lad came in with a guitar, played a few songs and Trev grabbed the guitar from him with one hand and said "Give it to Mick."

Trevor meant it nicely, but I'll never forget the poor guy's face. It was probably a very expensive guitar, being snatched from his nose and being randomly given to a Welshman singing Welsh songs in an Irish bar.

With the physical size and presence of him, people who don't know him wouldn't realise the good nature of him. He's been through so much off the field but just a great guy with a fantastic family and a guy that you enjoy spending so much time with."

CHAPTER 7

TO CAP IT ALL

ON GETTING HIS FIRST CAP FOR IRELAND

When the moment came, the packs were lining up for an Irish line-out and the fourth official held up the number 22 for number eight. I shouted at Victor to get off the pitch. "Victor, get the f*** off." I went past him, completely forgetting our pact about the high fives.

I hadn't a clue what I was doing. I couldn't even remember the line-out call. For the 13 minutes I was on the pitch I ran around like a headless chicken. We were well beaten, 37-13. Afterwards, at the post-match reception, Victor came up to me.

"So much for the high fives. 'Get off the pitch."

"I'm so sorry Vic. In the heat and hype of the moment, I just wanted to get on."

I'M A PRODUCT OF THE 80'S. ROCKY I, II AND III WERE, FOR ME, CLASSICS. LAUGH IF you will, but I was an impressionable young lad, and easily influenced by Sylvester Stallone's character. Just as I had been by *Rambo* when playing in the woods. VHS videos were relatively new, and watching *Rocky* I truly believed he did train that hard and did become world champion. Just an ordinary guy who beat the best to reach the top.

So my regime had to mirror his. I began mixing six raw eggs and swallowing them for breakfast at about 6.30am, then went for a run on the back roads, before coming home for a shower and heading to school. My brother Ronnie was serving his time as a butcher in Noel Carroll's and I'd call in and ask Noel if I could punch a few carcasses hanging in his freezer. I was 13 or 14 years old, Noel would laugh at me and say "Go ahead kid, I'll put the kettle on for a cup of tea," and he'd send Ronnie next door to the bakers for a couple of cream buns.

The rugby bug was catching, but no matter what sport I was going to take up, I wanted to be the best I could possibly be. I was working in Sammy's chip shop that summer, which used to close between 2.30 and 5.00pm, so I started visiting Motions Gym in the village to train for an hour and a half.

Weights were only catching on in rugby, but working out in Motions three or four times a week was a great relief from Sammy's – especially during the summer months. That was hard work in itself, and before taking up weights, in between peeling and slicing spuds, I'd do press-ups, chin-ups, lift bags of spuds over my head – anything to help make myself stronger.

One day, when I was 15 or so, I jumped on to a 66 bus into Abbey Street and walked to Arnotts to buy a 60 kilo kit of weights – almost £200 at the time. I'd always bought my football boots and other bits of gear in Arnotts. I carried that 60 kilo box and the bench onto the '66' back to Leixlip, then slowly dragged them up the hill and back to the house, where I assembled them. From then on I could lift my weights – bench presses, leg curls, arm curls – as well as do my morning runs. They were the plastic weights, filled with concrete. 'York' were the makers.

Through these developmental years, I played with lads a year or two older than me in Barnhall. I wasn't head and shoulders above my team-mates, but I stood out. People said that if anybody was going to make it from Barnhall, it was me.

Like me with regard to rugby, Rocky wasn't the most naturally gifted boxer, but he realised his dream to become world champion. Mine was to play for Ireland. Even so, back then I thought my dream was just that, a dream. I didn't think it could happen, coming from a small club like Barnhall.

It had no history as such, having been founded as recently as 1969. My rugby education had led me to believe that it had always been a middle-class game. Apart from Munster and particularly Limerick, people who played for Ireland didn't come from a working-class background.

The first chance a team from a club like Barnhall had of playing against say, a St Mary's or Blackrock, was in the McCorry Cup (the Leinster Under-19 competition). You'd be so fired up against them. They usually knocked the hell out of us because they were invariably better coached and more skilful. We were mentally motivated and physically committed; we just didn't have the skills.

But, by jaysus, if a fight broke out, they knew all about it. We usually came out on top in that. Not that that's what motivated me. I just believed that coming from a club like Barnhall, I had to make the absolute most of myself if I was ever to reach the top in rugby. And I guess the proof of that was leaving Barnhall at 19.

And with each move in my career, my game improved. Different coaching and training methods were one reason, having to prove myself in a new set-up another. Most of all, perhaps, it was due to playing with better players.

As Phil Lawlor was the resident number eight at Bective, and an Irish international, Noel McQuilkin told me I wouldn't be playing there. He tried me a couple of times in the second row but then decided on number six, because I was 19 and he thought of me as fast and mobile. In those days a back-rower could break off the back of a scrum before the ball came out, and I could pop up outside the scrum–half or out-half. McQuilkin devised moves using me like that.

Between my time in New Zealand and being coached by a Kiwi, my rucking and mauling game improved immeasurably. He was good at pulling a player aside and giving individual coaching. He designed drills for me, such as running off the goalposts from a scrummaging position to different points on the 22, so as to improve my defence off the base of scrums.

I learned from playing with Phil. Technically he was very good. Phil taught me about lines of running, in both defence and attack. He kept telling me I wasn't that far off the mark. Coming from an Irish international, that was hugely encouraging.

At Bective I was used as a battering man; a big ball carrier. I was young, fit, 19 and quick, and I set it up for the backs. At St Mary's I wasn't just a battering ram anymore. They had Victor Costello, Malcolm O'Kelly, Emmet Byrne and others. I was running onto ball that they had set up. Victor might make a 30 yard break off a scrum and I'd often be the first player in support. If he offloaded the ball in the tackle, he'd help make you look good.

At Toulouse, that was taken to another level altogether, because every one of them could keep the ball alive. There, a player might throw a 50-50 pass over his head or from under his legs, and most of the time it went to hand because the Toulouse players expected it. And if it didn't go to hand, nobody said a word. So that brought my game on to another level again.

There was a fantastic sense of history in Mary's too which helped you believe you could make it all the way. You only had to look at the wall above the bar and see the plaques. I remember when the All Blacks came in the autumn of 1997, John McWeeney, Conor McGuinness and Kevin Nowlan earned their first caps. The club held a celebratory night and in congratulating them all, the club president John Hussey said "There's another player here tonight who'll be getting capped soon. He's not knocking on the door, he's breaking the door down. That's Trevor Brennan."

I had initially been called into the Irish squad training sessions in 1997 under Brian Ashton in the ALSAA complex near Dublin Airport. Warren Gatland was usually in charge of the 'B', or shadow team. He'd take us to one end of the pitch and say "Right lads, you're supposed to be cannon fodder here. Hold nothing back and get stuck in."

I was thinking "Yippee. Here's this Kiwi giving me licence to go mad." So every time I got a chance I'd throw myself around, hitting Keith Wood, the Claw, David Wallace, Anthony Foley and so on.

The story goes that at one of my first Irish training sessions I was putting in a few big hits, including one on Keith Wood. While the two of us were on the ground he told me to take it easy, and I said "That's okay for you to say. I'm just a milkman from Barnhall."

A total myth, I'm afraid.

There might have been one or two little altercations between us but my response would have been more along the lines of "that's okay for you to say, you have all your caps, I don't have any." Or "you're established in the Irish team, I'm not." I might have said something along those lines once.

It was hard at the time too because I remember looking in and wondering "who the f*** is this David Erskine or that other English fella Ashton has brought in, Dylan O'Grady?"

Ashton had, admittedly, given debuts to three of my new St Mary's team mates. But when he resigned after the opening Five Nations' defeat at home to Scotland and Warren Gatland took over, I'm sure I wasn't the only home-based player who felt we stood a better chance of selection.

Playing for Ireland became the pinnacle; the be-all and end-all. I'm sure it was the same for all – well, virtually all – players who have ever played for Ireland. And on the Irish tour of South Africa at the end of the 1997-98 season, I reached the mountain top.

I'd had a good year with St Mary's in 1997-98, I'd broken into the Leinster team and I'd had a big European Cup campaign. Gatty called me in to a few Irish sessions in Greystones before the tour to South Africa. On April 28th I was named in the 34-man Irish squad for an old-style, seven-match tour, including two tests. Gatty took me aside and told me why I'd been included, and outlined what he thought were my strengths; my physicality, my hardness, my tackling, my ball-carrying, my lifting. The weakness, he said from the start, was my ill-discipline.

Gatty tried to bring more fun into the Irish scene. We trained hard during the day, we did our rucking and mauling drills and our scrummaging in Dr Hickey Park.

The day after the squad assembled in the Glenview Hotel, he organised a trip up to Johnny Fox's, where every player was given a duty, or put on one of the ten committees, while on tour. This was a very All Blacks' way of doing things, making everyone feel involved.

Mick Galwey and Peter Clohessy, along with Gabriel Fulcher and Derek Hegarty, were the judges and handed out the duties for each player, as well as the fines. Thankfully I avoided laundry duty. Mike Mullins was in charge of music, social events were under the charge of Denis Hickie – no better man. I was appointed to the Spielberg Committee, i.e. a video cameraman along with Killian Keane and Malcolm O'Kelly and I hit Donal Lenihan, the team manager, for a few video tapes in Heathrow on the journey over.

This meant I had to video bus trips, sing-songs, day trips, dressing-rooms, court sessions, team meetings. I suppose it was like a fly-on-the-wall documentary, and at the end of the tour we were supposed to make a video for everyone involved. It never happened, most probably because some of the video was a little OTT, but I still have the cassettes in a shoebox at home.

We arrived in Cape Town at our hotel overlooked by Table Mountain. After matches or training sessions we had sing-songs on our bus journeys back to the hotel – or Gaillimh and Claw handed out the fines which went into a kitty for a night out at the end of the tour. The squad was full of new caps and new faces. I played some part in six of the seven games, including both test matches. The trip was pure joy from the first day to the last.

Even in South Africa I quickly earned a name for being a hard man. "The milkman from Dublin," was how one South African commentator described me. I hadn't been a milkman for three years at that stage, but that was how they perceived me.

I was brought on 11 minutes from the end of our tour opener, a 48-35 win against Boland. One of their players wanted to swap jerseys with me but Donal Lenihan, aka Mannix, had advised me not to swap my first Irish shirt. The first one, he said, was always special.

I wonder why I keep them. I have Irish blazers from that South African tour, the World Cup in '99, from the Six Nations, as well as tracksuits from the World Cup and other stuff. Paula keeps telling me to throw them away and I don't know why I hoard them; perhaps I might want to show them to my kids or grandchildren one day. Who knows?

I also incurred a fine for using my mobile in the dressing room to phone home. They don't do easy tours in South Africa, and that Boland match set the tone.

Reggie Corrigan took a cheap shot – a kick in his lower back. Myself, Reggie, Victor Costello and Denis Hickie were good mates and I remember him being really downcast on the coach home and all that night.

"I really think the tour is over for me, lads," he kept saying.

"Don't worry, get another drink into you; you'll be alright in the morning when you get a bit of physio," we told him.

"No lads, I really think I'm gone." We kept ordering the beers but the next morning we heard his tour was over. He'd sustained a cracked vertebra, and was in no condition even to fly home.

The second game was a 27-20 defeat to South West Districts. It was my first start for Ireland and I really wanted to prove I was worth my place in this company. Myself and Claw were having cracking games but Gatty replaced us with John Hayes and David Corkery 13 minutes from the end. We were leading 20-14 at the time, but lost 27-20. I thought I had a cracking game anyway. We really matched them up front, and I recall Gatty admitting it had probably been a mistake to substitute myself and Claw. I also won the watch, as it was, for Man of the Match.

Heads were down in the dressing-room, but I had a smile from ear to ear. I'd played well and would draw more good press back home. Journalists now wanted to interview me – I was beginning to make a bit of a name for myself. By and large, I've had good press in my career and I would recommend all young players to grant interviews to journalists. It's no harm being on their good side.

Their influence may be overstated, or not as important as it used to be, but positive press is a boost to players. Maybe there were things I shouldn't have said and I still reckon that they cost me caps. So by the time I went to Toulouse I was a bit warier, and would give interviews only if I had a club translator alongside me. I don't regret having good relationships with most journalists I've known.

Back in Cape Town, we played Western Province in the third match of the tour – the unofficial third test. One night, we were allowed have a drink or two in the hotel bar, but myself, Victor and Reggie decided that we'd head out for a discreet drink or two by the harbour before Reggie went home.

As the night wore on, we lost count of our 'few quiet ones'. Victor was the established number eight, and throughout the night we agreed that if I were to make the bench against the Springboks the following Saturday, I would more than likely replace Victor. I told him that even if that wasn't happening, he was to go down injured. I wanted that first cap. So that was the pact, and when I came on for him we were to exchange high fives.

At about 1.00am we decided to stop off at a bar near the hotel. On the way up the stairs, Victor put his head between my legs, picked me up on his shoulders, managed a few steps and then fell forward. I literally fell head first into the bar. There looking down at me were Warren Gatland, Donal Lenihan and a few others from the management.

I'd caught both shins on the final step and was in agony, but couldn't stop laughing. "Looks like you're not going to play at the weekend," Gatty said dryly. To their credit, they asked us what we wanted to drink. We worried that we might be in trouble but in fact we finished the night with them.

The 12-6 defeat to Western Province was the only tour match I went to wearing a suit. I was like a man possessed in the stands. Eric Elwood, who had pulled out sick that morning, kept telling me "Calm down there China." Everybody was 'China'. I'd stand up and shout at Jonathan Kaplan, the referee who gave us nothing that day. "Sit down there China. Relax. Relax. It's only a match."

The next game in Kimberley in the high veldt the following Tuesday, was like something from an old western, with tumbleweed rolling up the street. The hotel didn't merit one star. We had the whole day to kill because it was a midweek, evening match. Oranges were thrown at the coach on the way into the ground. I remember going around the back of the stand and discovering an assault course, complete with ropes and climbing nets. The groundsman told us that the Kimberley players did this course three times a week. "What are we up against here?" we asked ourselves. The foreign legion popped into my head. They duly thrashed us.

The first test was the following Saturday. The team and replacements were announced to the squad by Donal Lenihan on the Wednesday morning after a one-and-a-half hour coach drive to Bloemfontein. I thought I'd done well on the tour and had a good chance of making the bench. I was sitting at the back of the room; my head and feet sweating. He read out the team from one to 15, then the subs from 16 to 22. My name was last, number 22. When I heard my name everything he said afterwards about the game faded into a distant murmur. I whispered to players around me.

"Did he say my name?"

"Am I in the 22?"

When we stood up most players shook my hand and congratulated me, including David Corkery; my main rival, I suppose, for the blind side/impact replacement slot. From the outside, people would probably have presumed we were mortal enemies, but although we were both similarly aggressive players, the closest we ever came to a scrap was in a Cork Con-St Mary's match. Some players mightn't talk to rivals for their position but it never came to that with us. He was a good, down-to-earth lad off the pitch and we were always mates. When I was picked ahead of him for the 1999 World Cup there was never a problem.

Donal Lenihan and Gatty congratulated me too and we went straight to training before returning to the hotel. I was still wearing my dirty gear – boots, shoulder pads, the lot. All I wanted was a shower. "Horse," came a shout in the lobby. I turned. "Trev." I looked around wondering who it was. Some people were sitting down, holding newspapers in front of them, so I crossed over to peer behind the papers.

There was my father, with two friends of his: Jack Looby and his son Joe, and another friend Paddy Ennis. They had arrived unannounced, in the hope that I would be capped.

Jack was five years older than me, but I had played with him. Like his father before him, he has since become president of the club. Paddy, another ex-Barnhall team-mate, was a friend of mine from our school days. For my second cap, John Caldwell and another former Barnhall team-mate, Sean Kirby, also made the journey.

I asked the Irish team's liaison officer from the South African Union to recommend a nearby restaurant and that night I brought the four lads out to dinner along with the liaison officer and the squad's bus driver. We had the best of steaks and fish, and must have spent a good four hours there.

I had an alcohol free night, but the boys were going heavy on the wine and the shots, and I'd only the equivalent of £200 on me. So when I spotted the da going to the jacks, I asked him for a loan of another £100. The bill, in rand, came to about £178. After I paid up, the chef came out and kissed me, the barman kissed me, the restaurant owner kissed me. I must have tipped big.

Match day. I'll never forget that day in Bloemfontein as long as I live. The gates into the ground were closed and Donal Lenihan had to climb off the bus to persuade them to let us in. The dressing-room was small so the first XV were placed in one room and the replacements were sent to another room full of weights and tackle bags.

Claw, aka Peter Clohessy, and Hendo, aka Rob Henderson, were also on the replacements' bench and they duly lit up a couple of fags. I couldn't believe it. "How could they be doing this? We're playing the Springboks today. Mad."

This was a good hour before the game. I put my socks on, my deep heat, had a quick rub down with the physio Willie Bennett and came back to the room.

"C'mon lads, will we do a warm up?"

"Relax kid. Give it another 20 minutes. It's too early to start the warm-up."

So I started warming up in the room. I overheard them whispering to each other. "He's mad."

We went through the warm-up with the rest of the squad, came back into our little subs' room, and then the whistle blew for us to go out. I couldn't sit still, so five minutes into the game I decided to do another warm-up. I made sure that Gatty, Donal Lenihan and the rest of the management saw me before returning to join Hendo, Claw and the rest of the subs. "You're mad kid, relax."

When they went for a run and a stretch later in the half, I joined them. At half-time we played a little touch rugby amongst ourselves. I had ants in my pants. In the second-half I went to one of the in-goal areas for another stretch. Past the hour mark, I gave up and returned for the last time to the stands. "That's it," I thought to myself and put on my tracksuit. Victor was flying. No sign of him going down. "I'm not going to get my first cap now."

Donal Lenihan signalled to us on the bench. "I think it's you Trevor," somebody said. I ran to the side of the pitch. "Warm-up Trev," said Donal.

"Warm-up?" I said. "I'm f****** roasting."

He laughed at that. "All right Trev, get your tracksuit off. You're going on."

When the moment came, the packs were lining up for an Irish line-out and the fourth official held up the number 22 for number eight. I shouted at Victor to get off the pitch. "Victor, get the f*** off." I went past him, completely forgetting our pact about the high fives.

I hadn't a clue what I was doing. I couldn't even remember the line-out call. For the 13 minutes I was on the pitch I ran around like a headless chicken. We were well beaten, 37-13. Afterwards, at the post-match reception, Victor came up to me.

"So much for the high fives. 'Get off the pitch'."

"I'm so sorry Vic. In the heat and hype of the moment, I just wanted to get on."

A few of us formally received our first 'cap' – myself, Justin Bishop, Dion O'Cuinneagain and Justin Fitzpatrick along with a few new Springboks. I imagined it would have been different had it been at Lansdowne Road. There would have been more friends and family there. We took it in turn to be presented with our caps by Donal Lenihan. I wore mine proudly all night.

That was the pinnacle of my career. I don't think winning Heineken Cups, or the Celtic League, can compare to being capped for your country. That's all I ever wanted. I didn't dream of winning Heineken Cups or Celtic Leagues. My dream was to play for Ireland, and on June 13th, 1998, I did. No-one could ever take that away from me. I'd done it. That night, a second one would have been a bonus, although by the next morning I didn't want to be a one cap wonder.

I can only imagine what it was like in Barnhall. I'm told the club was black with people, and that there were over 30 in the ma's house for tea, beer and trays of sandwiches. The score wouldn't have mattered. As the camera focussed on me at the side of the pitch, it was "shush, shush," before a huge cheer when I came on.

We hit a few bars in town that night, and my father, Jack and Joe, and Paddy came along. My dad sang a song, which went down well. We had difficulty getting a taxi into town so we headed off on foot, eventually hailing a truck with a couple of hunters in the front.

We hopped into the back. There were about seven of us, including Bishy and Mannix. When they dropped us off we gave them a few rand and linked up with the rest of the squad. It was tradition then for all the players to buy new caps a 'shot' so the night gradually became a blur.

The squad flew to Johannesburg the next day, transferring to the Crowne Plaza in Pretoria less than an hour away by bus. I started in the 26-18 win over North West Districts in Potchestroom on the Tuesday, but suffered a dead leg and had to go off at half-time. Another four days on, I won my second cap, replacing Victor after 55 minutes. We were well beaten by then, and lost 33-0 in what became known as the Battle of Pretoria.

Trouble started early in the game when Malcolm O'Kelly was kicked in the head while on the ground and Keith Wood was heavily targeted.

I was barely on the pitch when Paddy Johns and Gary Teichmann resumed their running battle. One of the Springboks came in and hit Paddy from the side. Paddy couldn't have seen it coming and I went bald-headed for the Springbok.

One on one is fair enough, but I wasn't having that. When I turned around there seemed to be dust-ups all over the pitch.

It was like a battlefield from an old war movie. "What is going on here?"

I thought to myself "This is right up my alley."

Twenty minutes of fighting followed until the final whistle. Hardly any rugby was played. The television coverage failed to convey what really happened. Scraps 50 yards off the ball were being broken up by the touch judges, Ed Morrison and Didier Mene.

Peter Clohessy, my fellow pacifist, came on shortly after me. Afterwards journalists asked whether Gatty had told us to run amok, but he had said nothing of the sort.

Woody led the whole squad up to a podium at the post-match reception and in front of the entire South African squad defiantly kicked off our tour anthem, *From Clare to Here*. I liked the song then and thanks to Woody have liked it even more ever since.

The session that night was unbelievable. Our travels took us to a bar with live music, where there must have been a thousand people. When the band took a break, hearing Hot Chocolate's *You Sexy Thing* prompted myself, Malcolm and Justin Bishop to the stage. I'd grabbed a guitar, Malcolm had acquired a bodhrán and Bishy was banging on the drums. We took off all our clothes, bit by bit; blazers, shirts, ties, pants, the lot. All I was left with were my socks, and we strategically used our instruments to give the occasional glimpse! After our audition for *The Full Monty,* we managed to reclaim most of our clothes. The memory of it didn't help my hangover.

After lunch the next day we had a court session, and continued to celebrate the end of the tour and the season, in the airport and on the plane, all the way home. I thought this was what international tours were all about. I knew all the Mary's and Leinster lads, Victor, Malcolm, Denis, Conor McGuinness, but I made some good mates on that tour like Gaillimh, Claw and Hendo. I hadn't known them much before that tour, but they were just down-to-earth, ordinary, honest blokes.

For me, Leinster v Munster had always been battles, likewise the games against Ulster, but you couldn't get a nicer fella than Paddy Johns, our captain. Though on the pitch he was a hard grafter and a bit like myself, he'd turn into Robocop.

We went toe-to-toe in the Leinster-Ulster match in 1997 and Dave McHugh gave us both a yellow card. One morning before training in King's Hospital in the build-up to the 1999 World Cup I was having coffee and croissants with him in Finnstown House, and thought we were the best of mates.

Gatty liked to divide us into two sides but the game wasn't five minutes old when I found myself at the bottom of a ruck and Paddy came in and did a 'windmill' on me. He tore the shorts off me and left his tread marks. I'm sure there were plenty of fellas who would have liked to do the same. But of course, I came up swinging and we had to be separated.

Now Paddy and the boys were my mates and team-mates. I felt on top of the world coming back from that tour. Everywhere I went in Leixlip or Lucan, and back at Mary's, I was told how good a tour I had.

"This is the start of things for you kid."

ALAN QUINLAN

MUNSTER AND IRISH FLANKER.

"I first met Trevor in 1997 when Mick Galwey asked me to come with him to Barnhall to play a charity match. A lot of former internationals played, like Brendan Mullin, Mickey Quinn, Brian Rigney, Gaillimh; a mix of current and former internationals against a Barnhall selection. I'd never met or seen Trevor before and I remember thinking half-way through the first-half "Who *is* this lunatic?"

A few pints had been had the night before, everybody was chilling out and throwing the ball around; it was going to be a game of touch-rugby really. And then here was this young fella clattering into everyone. That was the first time I saw him and I ended up running after him in the charity match. The two of us started tripping each other a bit and I suppose everyone was laughing at us.

I got to know Trevor gradually through playing against him a number of times in Munster-Leinster matches and in Irish squad sessions. So my first impression may have been that he was a bit of a lunatic. But deep down, when I got to know him, I realised he was a decent lad and an honest, hard-working guy who just wanted to try and make a name for himself. To play for Ireland and do well in professional rugby.

He came from the club scene like myself – I came from Clanwilliam –we had a lot of similarities and I kinda respected him for that. It was difficult to break through back then if you hadn't played schools rugby and Irish under-21s, and I hadn't played any of that. I played Irish Youths and so did Trevor, but there wasn't too much attention paid to the Irish Youths.

I suppose he wouldn't endear himself to you on the field; certainly a bundle of energy, an all-action type player and quite aggressive and abrasive. Similar to myself, but Trevor was a much bigger, more imposing player than me, and knew how to throw his weight around. Despite this, I think he's a very likeable fella. Everyone had great time for him and he was a great character off the field. Over the years we developed a good friendship.

We only ran into each other once in his five years with Toulouse, when they beat us in the semi-final. Munster went to Castres a few times and there were nothing but good reports from people as to how he looked after them – especially my mum. Mary, and Donnacha's mum, Marie, very well. He always looked after the parents of the Munster players.

He always wore his heart on his sleeve when Leinster played Munster, and played as hard as he could. That said, there was never any animosity or bitterness off the field. You couldn't but respect him. That's probably one of the reasons why

I liked him. He was a natural guy, what you saw with Trevor is what you got. He was straight-up, he wasn't nice to your face and cut you up behind your back; and I think they're great characteristics in a person.

I followed his career closely. When he first moved from Leinster to Toulouse a few eyebrows were raised, but he certainly had a fantastic time in Toulouse. It's been a disappointing end to what should have been a fairytale story. No-one condones what happened, we were all disappointed for him. I personally felt a lot of sorrow for him.

But for an Irish guy to go to Toulouse and make such an impression in the south of France is a measure of the guy and his character."

CHAPTER 8

THAT SINKING FEELING

ON THE KEFU INCIDENT AGAINST AUSTRALIA

I didn't realise until I saw the video that no Irish lads had come to help me. I was a bit shocked to see the incident unfold. The bandages over my eight stitches had come down over my eyes and my arms were held by two Australian players. I couldn't see and I couldn't move my arms as Kefu went hell for leather on my face. I couldn't see the punches coming, I could only feel them. My head was going forward and back. Thud, thud, thud.

AND ON HIS TWO-WEEK SUSPENSION

There's no way I should have received a two-week suspension in the middle of a World Cup. The only people who backed me, apart from family and friends, were Gatty, Donal Lenihan and a few players. Though maybe some of them felt I deserved it.

IT WAS THE SATURDAY BEFORE IRELAND PLAYED FRANCE IN THE LAST FIVE Nations Championship, and I was sanding floors. I'd missed out on the World Cup qualifiers against Georgia and Romania, as well as the rematch with South Africa in November 1998, to a fit-again Eric Miller. I had just bought a house in Glen Easton Square in Leixlip, and my brother Errol was helping with the painting and decorating.

In my pocket were five tickets for that afternoon's European Cup final in Lansdowne Road. The foreman on the site had been looking for tickets and seeing him go by that morning I'd given them to him.

With two of the four floors completed, we took a lunch break to watch the second half of the final in one of the locals. In the course of Ulster's famous 21-6 win over Colomiers, Andy Ward went down injured.

"Ah you'll probably get the call, horse," said Errol.

"I will in my bollox. Finish up that pint and we'll go back and get these floors done."

We sanded the other two floors, intending to varnish them the next day. The radio sports bulletin speculated that Ward was likely to be ruled out of the French game, and that I might be called in. "Huh?" The phone hadn't rung at that stage.

But the next morning, Donal Lenihan rang to say I had been called into the squad for the forthcoming match against France at Lansdowne Road.

My first outing for Ireland at Lansdowne turned out to be a nightmare.

I came onto the pitch as a replacement for Victor Costello with nearly half an hour remaining. It was a dirty old wet and windy day. We hadn't beaten them for 14 years and they were going for a third Grand Slam in a row. Ireland had been wooden spoonists for three years in a row, and been whitewashed the previous season.

Nevertheless, there was a sense of optimism in the air. Ulster had won the European Cup the week before. It was a bruising, hard match with little rugby, but we had more than enough of the game to win it. We led 9-0 with nearly an hour gone, when they scored a converted try. We went on to lose it 10-9.

Paul Wallace and David Humphreys copped most of the flak, although some of it was directed at me as well. I did blame myself for conceding the territory from which they won the match. From a French line-out on halfway, the touch judge put up his flag and penalised me for a late tackle on their scrum-half Philippe Carbonneau. I thought it was a harsh call.

Thomas Castaignède missed from long range, and I remember telling Conor O'Shea to kick the 22 drop out long, but he hung it short. They recycled it a few times and Wally was penalised for offside. Castaignède kicked that one. I chased the restart and got my hand to the ball. Although we earned a penalty to win the match, Humph's kick from 30 metres out drifted wide in the wind.

I remember leaving the pitch, and from the front rows some alickadoo shouted at me "You lost the game for us today." I was too gutted to respond, and thought to myself 'this guy knows nothing about rugby'. I wasn't the player to give away the penalty that lost the game.

As is custom, we went back to the Berkeley Court Hotel for the post-match banquet, and it's hard walking into that foyer, full of people. You say a quick hello to family and friends, sign some autographs, pose for photographs and then go to your room to change into your monkey suit. Win, draw or in this case lose, you have to sit through that meal for two or three hours. It's an alickadoos' dinner, and most of the players hated it that night. Knowing that your friends and family were out in the bar, you'd sneak out for a pint and check back in to see if the speeches were over.

Before the next match against Wales at Wembley, St Mary's had an AIL game against Shannon in front of a big crowd at Templeville Road. "From hero to zero," as RTE news said of me that night. I scored a try early in the game, and we went on to win.

But I received two yellow cards, which meant a sending-off and an automatic two-match suspension. After the first yellow, a niggling duel developed between me and Anthony Foley, and at the insistence of a touch judge, the referee produced a second yellow.

I still had to join the rest of the Irish squad the next day, and who did Gatty have me rooming with? 'Axel' Foley.

"You're joking?" I said to the receptionist. But there he was in the room, lying on the bed and reading a paper.

"How are you Trev?"

Gatty called me to his room. "How many rugby players get a chance of playing at Wembley?" he said to me, adding "We're going to win it too. You're going to miss out on a win bonus." While admitting the red card had been harsh, he said I had to learn from this. He told me to keep working and I'd be back in the squad.

Ireland won 29-23 but I didn't watch it. I couldn't bear to. Luckily, throughout my career I've always had a good bunch of friends who could help me escape from rugby if I needed to. I watched the highlights on the news, but that didn't make me feel any better. So I missed Wembley, as well as the 27-15 defeat at home to England.

I was recalled to the squad, winning my fourth cap as a replacement in the 30-13 defeat away to Scotland. It was the least memorable and most forgettable of my 13 Irish caps, except for a good night out in the Caledonian and elsewhere. It was the same old story. The Scots were our bogey team back then. We could have sent over the Harlem Globetrotters and we'd still have lost.

Italy had also become a bit of a bogey side. We played them three weeks later as part of their dry run for the 2000 Six Nations, and they had beaten Ireland three times in a row. This was my first start for Ireland. As a sub, I felt I had an awful lot to prove, and always too little time to do so.

"This is your first full one," Gatty said to me. "I can't do any more. The ball is in your court now. You've got to show people why I'm picking you."

And I wanted to reward him for showing faith in me. I must have bought 50 or 60 tickets for that game, from other players and any source I could find. For family and friends, for aunties and uncles, the butcher, bread man, the solicitor....I think the whole of Barnhall was there, as well as both GAA clubs. It felt as if anybody who knew me was at that match, apart from my mother.

Most of them faced us for the national anthems. They were in the lower west stand, where the players are given their allocation. As you line up with the other 14 starters you know you can give it socks from the start, and build your way into the game. Standing at the end of the line amongst the seven subs, the anthems psyche you up. But whereas the 15 starters go out for the kick-off, you have to head back to the stand and wait your turn.

Even then, you might only have ten or 15 minutes to make an impact or do something special. You're trying to get your hands on the ball. You're chasing the game. If you start, you might not touch the ball for the first ten or 15 minutes, but you can still build a rhythm and a feeling for the game.

Or you can be welcomed in by an opponent.

In the first five minutes I was buried at the bottom of a ruck when someone clobbered me, completely opening me up and breaking my nose in the process.

The referee saw blood and called on Dr Donal O'Shaughnessy, who suggested I come off for treatment. No way, I told him, so he shoved cotton wool and Vaseline up my nose.

No broken nose would make me come off that pitch. I tackled well in that game, and carried well too. Team confidence was low. We made mistakes, trailed 23-11 at half-time but pulled through 39-30 with some good tries.

Although the media's reaction was muted, everyone in the dressing-room – coaches and players – was delighted. This wasn't no little rugby nation we'd beaten. This was a strong Italian side who'd had the Indian sign on us.

I played the whole 80 and threw myself into everything. Here I was on a pitch with 29 top internationals, and Trevor Brennan, Horsebox from Leixlip, was announced as the Man of the Match. I was formally presented with a bronze trophy at the post-match reception in the Berkeley Court. Gatty was genuinely chuffed, perhaps because his loyalty had been rewarded and it had taken a bit of pressure off him. Proud as punch, I had a great night with friends and family in the hotel which finished in the early hours of the morning. I felt that I'd made a statement.

The 1999 tour to Australia was a pre-World Cup tour and I was included in the 28-man squad. So too, for the first time, was Brian O'Driscoll. He was only 18 but like everybody who had seen him play for the Leinster As, I'd thought 'this kid will play for Ireland'.

Arriving in Sydney at nearly midnight, after being diverted to Melbourne, we were instructed to assemble in the hotel lobby in 15 minutes in our shorts and t-shirts. For a run – to stretch the legs. We took a left, went down a dark hill and took another left. We'd run about two miles when we saw a big Coca Cola sign and suddenly it clicked. Someone said "This is King's Cross." For a mile the Irish squad ran by transvestites and prostitutes, to a chorus of whistles! Our hotel was practically in the famous red light district.

Tours were fantastic opportunities to see parts of the world you'd never usually see. Staying in the best of hotels, they were free holidays in my mind. You were a tourist as well as a rugby player. If I had any free time to myself I would go down to Sydney Harbour and take a boat trip.

A replacement in the opening win over New South Wales Country Cockatoos, I played the full 80 in a 39-24 defeat to New South Wales. The game went well enough for me, but at the reception my shoulder was killing me. All I could think about was missing the first test in Brisbane.

I trained every day; bike, run, bike, run and lots of speed work with the squad's fitness coach, Craig White. While the rest of the team was training, I was catching high kicks from Donal Lenihan. I duly missed the first test, which was probably no harm, because we got the shite kicked out of us, 46-10.

We flew to Perth on Sunday, and rather than flog us, Gatty gave us the Monday off before organising a boat trip to a steak house in Fremantle on the Tuesday. Mannix (Donal Lenihan) presented a jersey to the restaurant owner and we had a massive singsong on the way back to the hotel. Virtually the entire squad went out that night. Off the pitch, it was another good tour; a good mix of experience, youth ... and singers! Tom Tierney would sing *The Gambler*. My tune was *Dublin In the Rare 'Oul Times*.

Gatty was always very good at sensing when lads were mentally tired, and arranging distractions – clay pigeon shooting, fishing, whatever. On that tour we went to the State of Origin match, had a barbecue and walked Sydney Harbour Bridge. It didn't matter if it was test week. That really surprised me.

Gatty said that the Wallabies had played their best hand, that we knew what their strengths were – we could only play better. There was a big emphasis on defence for the rest of the week and we had nothing to lose. Again, we trained well. The night before the match in our floodlit run in the Subiaco Oval, we hardly put a ball down. We were overdue a big performance.

Victor Costello was dropped, Dion O'Cuinneagain moved to number eight and I was picked to start. In fact, Victor wouldn't be selected for the World Cup and wouldn't play again for Ireland under Gatty. Victor was one of the most utterly, naturally talented forwards I ever played with. I didn't have half his talent. He could have been the best number eight in the world if he had applied himself.

I felt good and fit all week. But on the Friday before the game I woke up in the middle of the night puking my guts up. Food poisoning. What timing. Just as I'd got myself right and had been picked to start for only the second time! I was rooming with Victor. "Victor, get the doc." The doc gave me loads of medication and told me to take plenty of liquids.

Luckily the match was scheduled for an 8.00pm kick off. I didn't eat anything that whole day until 5.00pm. The hotel had a swimming pool on the roof. My legs were heavy. I was aching all over. The pool was ice cold, but that was good. Myself and Dion did lengths up and down that pool.

When we reached the ground, I was struck by the professionalism of the Australians. They had oxygen masks and bikes at the side of the pitch for their replacements to work on. They appeared to be way ahead of us. But it was a totally different game from the first test.

Claw scored an early try, which gave us a huge lift, and we outscored them three tries to two. I was very aggressive throughout that match and rucked really hard. I remembered our video session the previous Monday, when Gatty told me not to hold back at certain points – that it was better to give away three points rather than seven. George Gregan had a big overlap from the bottom of a ruck so I climbed over it and took him and ball. It was one of the better penalties I conceded in my career.

In the end, though, we lost 32-26 due to a number of stupid errors. It was a game for the taking and we didn't take it. I played virtually the whole game but typical of my luck, I was called in for a drugs test. Perhaps because of the food poisoning, I couldn't piss to save my life.

To say I was dehydrated would be an understatement. It's one of the worst feelings in the world. The doctor stayed with me – literally – accompanying me to the shower, watching me dress and then escorting me to a room where I had to provide a urine sample. You're asked if you've taken any drugs. Your team doctor normally accompanies you and signs off on the form.

Then you start the process of drinking and waiting to piss. I drank about ten Powerade energy drinks, before I managed a dribble. I was there for almost three hours. The other player had been and gone within an hour, so now I was alone.

Sample provided, I went looking for the rest of the squad at the post-match reception at the Subiaco Oval. No sign of them. The reception had finished. Just a few stragglers. Balls! The team coach had left without me. I couldn't believe it.

I left the ground wearing my Irish team blazer and tie. As the taxi pulled up, I began to puke. Nothing but pure blue liquid. He asked me if I was drunk. I told him I had just played for Ireland against Australia but had been delayed because of a drugs test. I didn't have any beer, just too much energy drink. 'Yeah, a likely story' was written all over his face. Eventually he believed me. "Aw yeah mate, close game. You guys cudda won." And, long story short, he gave me a ride back to the hotel.

Immediately after the long haul home, I flew out to New York with Paula and Danny for a family holiday. From one mad flight to another. Talk about jet lag! Jeremy Davidson and Malcolm O'Kelly had dyed my hair in Australia, which came out more ginger than blonde. In America I tried to rectify that, but it turned out white. We were in Providence, one of the gay capitals of America.

One waiter threw the menu to Paula, turned to me and said "Hi, your hair is gorgeous." I went home that evening and shaved my head.

In early August there were two rounds of interpros. Leinster played Connacht in Donnybrook, and poor Girvan Dempsey had his knee smashed, ruling him out of the World Cup. Then my shoulder went again in the same game. It was hanging off me and I needed an operation.

Mick Molloy, the IRFU team doctor, ruled me out of the World Cup. He said I had a dislocated shoulder; an A/C joint, grade three. But Gatty and Donal Lenihan said they'd give me every chance. I went to a doctor I knew and had cortisone injected in my shoulder to get me through the World Cup. No regrets. Some players may get one chance to play in a World Cup and, as it happened, that was my only chance.

However, I still had to prove my fitness against Connacht a week before Ireland played Argentina. Then there was the final announcement of the 30-man World Cup squad. Alan Quinlan, uncapped at that stage, guested for Connacht and left his mark on that match – as well as on a few boys – by two tries. He was later called into the team when I was suspended for the fight with Toutai Kefu. Strapped up like an Egyptian mummy, with some bubble wrap under my shoulder padding, and with a bottle of pain-killers, I came through the match. That gave me the time to receive daily treatment.

The following week we beat Argentina 32-24 in a World Cup warm-up match. I was taken off nearing the hour when we were leading 32-3 before they scored three tries. As I said in an interview afterwards, the wheels came off the bus when I was replaced. My dad agreed. "We nearly lost the game after you were taken off," he said.

Coincidentally, Alex Wyllie had left most of his big guns on the bench – Agustín Pichot, Felipe Contepomi and Ignacio Corletto – before bringing them on for the last half-hour. An hour or so after the game, Donal announced the squad a day ahead of schedule. I'd made the 30-man cut.

Ireland prepared for the World Cup by beating Ulster, but were turned over by Munster in Musgrave Park. We were based in the Finnstown House in Lucan, which was a bit weird for me as I only lived down the road in Leixlip. My mother would ring me and say "Son, there's a stew on, can you make it down?" So I used to pop home in my new car and occasionally some of the lads in the squad came with me. Art McCoy, a car dealer in Lucan, had given me a sponsored car for a year. "Trevor Brennan, sponsored by McCoy Motors". In fact, I seemed to spend more time in my ma's house than in Finnstown. I got to see Paula and Danny, who'd just been born, nearly every day.

It also meant that friends and family could call in for a cup of coffee and a chat. This was a double-edged sword, because there were too many distractions, and too many people calling to the hotel looking for tickets. Somehow, I'd always imagined that if I played in a World Cup, it would have been a more exotic location, such as France or the southern hemisphere.

When the team for our opening match of the 1999 World Cup against the USA was named on the preceding Tuesday, I was last to leave the team room. My selection was still sinking in. We had training straight away in the grounds of King's Hospital school. No time to ring anybody, and I wanted to tell everybody.

A large crowd had gathered there, but I managed to pick out my uncle Colm as I climbed off the bus. I whispered to him "I'm starting. Ring the family. Ring everybody." I spent that evening on the phone.

I remember Gatty's speech in the team talk. "This little p****! Who does he think he is? He's not going to come here and beat us," he said, or words to that effect, referring to their coach at the time, Eddie O'Sullivan. He called him and his team quite a few things. Little did he know that after the World Cup, Eddie would become his right-hand man and later take over from him.

The game went well. We beat the States, and I survived the first 49 minutes before Eric Miller replaced me. The shoulder felt good and I was just thrilled to survive the game intact. Woody scored four tries, a record for a hooker in a test match.

He was a terrific player, genuinely world-class, at a time when we didn't have so many of them. At the time, he was probably the best hooker, and one of the best players, in the world. I found Fester a funny character. His greeting was usually along the lines of "You mad Irish bastard, how are you?"

"Yeah, how are you Fester?"

"You're crazy. You're a looper, aren't you?"

"Yeah how are you going Fester, alright?"

No matter whether it was breakfast, lunch or tea, that was how he greeted me. I was always a bit wary of him. I'd had a couple of run-ins with him at training sessions. I never felt comfortable around him. It wasn't that I took personal offence to the way he greeted me. That was good-natured, and he characterised nearly everybody in the way he said hello to them.

That said, I thought there was something funny about the banter. I also felt that as captain he had too much influence on selection, so I didn't know whether to snuggle up to him or avoid him.

There were also the cliques; our own Leinster clique, the Ulster clique, the English-based clique and the Munster clique, of which Fester was one. Yet outside the Leinster clique, I felt most comfortable with the Munster clique. I was accepted quite readily in the back seats along with Claw, Hendo and Foley. Gaillimh wasn't selected for that World Cup, although he should have been.

Before the game against Australia, Donal Lenihan arranged a four-day break in the Inchydoney Island Lodge & Spa in West Cork, a beautiful spa hotel on the beach. The sessions in Clonakilty were open to the public, which created a real sense of hype about the World Cup that hadn't existed in Dublin at that stage. After training there for a few days, we left with a best of luck message inscribed on the beach in massive letters.

By now, the World Cup had hit me. The media coverage had taken off, and the walls of the team room were plastered with goodwill texts and faxes – while personal ones were left folded or in envelopes on a table – another of Gatty's ideas borrowed from his All Blacks' days.

For the next game against Australia, tickets were like gold-dust. My mother had never been to an international but I insisted she come to this one. She had never seen me play for Ireland in the flesh. She never liked to watch me play, as she worried about me, or my brothers, being injured.

I was 25, but still a bit raw and inexperienced. Gatty took me aside to discuss their back-row. They had a big number six, Mark Connors, and I was there to do a job – to stop him and Toutai Kefu rumbling forward. On the day of the game,

Sunday October 10th, I read some of the personal goodwill messages to me in Finnstown. There was one from Blackrock College which paid tribute to my aggression and wished me well. As the day wore on I became more hyped up.

That particular game was a fateful one for me. We had high hopes of giving them a match but were well beaten by a team that just strangled us by keeping the ball – as they did to everybody they played in that World Cup. And my performance was remembered for all the wrong reasons.

Early on, I had to leave the pitch for stitches after catching a knee to my head when making a tackle. The medical room in the middle of a match is one of the weirdest places you could ever find yourself in. There's a TV in the medical room, and a nurse in attendance, as the doctor makes his running repairs with a needle and thread. You're asking the nurse what the score is. You're telling the doctor to hurry up; you want to get back on the pitch. Bizarre. An out of body experience. He tells me to relax, and eight stitches later I'm running down the corridor and back onto the pitch.

While chasing one of our restarts, I accidentally clipped Jeremy Paul with my elbow – though few people believe me. I never meant to clip Jeremy Paul. I don't know how it happened. I watched it on the video, and whatever way I ran past him, my elbow clipped his head. I was looking at the ball and all of a sudden, wham. It was genuinely an accident, and he was alright. If I was going to do it deliberately, I'd have done it right.

All I remember, and all anyone remembers of my performance after that, is the fight with Kefu. Some maintain that the incident with Paul was the catalyst. There were even suggestions that I racially abused Kefu. Rubbish. I've never racially abused him or any other player in my life.

I tackled him in their 22 and a few bodies piled in. The ball popped out and they cleared to touch. Then whatever way myself and Kefu stood up, we threw a dig at each other and began to exchange a few punches. Or should I say, he exchanged ten for my one. My head was used as a punch bag for 20 or 30 seconds as my arms were held down. The Aussies were awarded a penalty after the mêlée, and I played for a few more minutes before being replaced.

Some people asked me afterwards how I felt that none of my team-mates jumped to my defence. Did I feel that they'd let me down? I didn't realise until I saw the video that no Irish lads had come to help me. I was a bit shocked to see the incident unfold.

The bandages over my eight stitches had come down over my eyes and my arms were held by two Australian players.

I couldn't see and I couldn't move my arms as Kefu went hell for leather on my face. I couldn't see the punches coming, I could only feel them. My head was going forward and back. Thud, thud, thud.

But I don't blame anyone for not coming to my aid, for the simple reason that it had occurred in their 22. Their fullback Matt Burke had found touch around half-way and most players had turned to follow the ball.

All I felt after that game was embarrassment. I felt sick. I wanted to approach Kefu during the reception in Lansdowne Road and kick it all off again, but I couldn't find him. I asked several Australian players "Where's yer man Kefu?"

"He hasn't come down yet."

Word must have spread that I was a man on a mission. Team-mates sat me down. "Let it go." I didn't eat my food but I didn't see Kefu either. Later we went back to Finnstown House.

Bob Casey had won his first cap and was full of beans, so a few of us went off to the Salmon Leap pub in Leixlip, which was having a busy Sunday night. I was delighted for Bob, and it never dawned on me that my World Cup might be over.

The next morning Donal Lenihan told me that Kefu and I had been cited, and we'd have to travel to Twickenham the following day. It would become even more surreal. Paula rang to ask me to come shopping with her that Monday. Why, in the name of Jaysus, I ask myself, did I go shopping the next day? I've never felt so uncomfortable. People were looking at me or coming up to me to discuss the incident.

It was a bizarre situation, as myself, Donal, Kefu, their manager, John McKay, and Daniel Herbert – who had been cited himself for a high tackle on Kevin Maggs – checked in together and sat beside each other en route to Twickenham.

Again, it was like sitting outside the headmaster's office as we were called inside in turn to face a disciplinary committee.

We were summoned first. Donal spoke for me, and their manager for Kefu, as we each gave our side of the story. The Disciplinary Committee was chaired by Sir Alan Holland, and included Peter Trunkfield and Terry Wright – a former All Blacks' winger. They acknowledged that the video was not entirely conclusive but reckoned that a slight element of blame be attached to me for raising my hand first.

They did concede that I was held back whilst Kefu went on swinging punches. Even so, they suspended him for 14 days, and me for ten – which amounted to the same thing – as Ireland had a quarter-final play-off against Argentina the following Wednesday. Therefore, both suspensions amounted to two-game bans. I never quite understood that.

No-one was badly hurt, not even me. My pride hurt far more than my head. I was like a wounded animal. Worse acts have been committed on a rugby pitch. He came back for the semi-finals and played in the final, earning his winners' medal, but my World Cup was over. Gatty did tell me to keep the head up, stay focussed. After we beat Romania 44-14, he told me to come to France, and that if we beat Argentina, I'd be back in the frame for the semi-final. But that Lens qualifier was a disaster for everybody, even for me.

It was a Wednesday night match, and earlier that day after two hard training sessions with the Irish fitness trainer, Craig White, I went to the ground to take my seat in the stands. There was a buzz in the build-up to kick-off. The organisers must have given thousands of free tickets to school kids to help fill the ground. But it was a dreadful, nervy match. The referee, Stuart Dickinson, blew his whistle non-stop. We were ahead most of the way, but they turned it around with a try and we camped on their line for nine minutes of injury time. Pick and go. Pick and go. When the final whistle blew we all just looked at each other in total shock. Gatty and Mannix did the same. We'd just gone out of the World Cup to Argentina. I was afraid to leave my seat. Irish fans booed the team off the pitch. Donal Lenihan called us in to the dressing-room.

I stood in the corner of the room near the showers with my arms folded along with the other lads who hadn't played. The boys gradually came in, some of them crying. For minutes, you could have heard a pin drop. Nobody could talk, not even the management. They were in shock too. There was no "right lads, lift the heads". There was nothing to say. The silence seemed to last ten minutes before Donal said something about wrapping up the World Cup, have a shower, pack up and we'll go.

We had a wake in our little hotel outside Lens, and flew home the next day. Some went to Finnstown, where we were based for the quarter-final against France the following Sunday. We'd left our bags there, but Argentina had arrived before us and set up shop. They were using our team room and had checked into our rooms. They were literally having a party as we quietly went amongst them gathering our stuff.

Rala, our kit man, had a load of jerseys and told us to take what we wanted. I took an Irish number six jersey. Other lads had to drive or fly to various corners of Ireland or England. I rang the da and had him pick me up. It was like going home from a Barnhall match. I'd safely say I was first home.

My da buys every paper and I went through them over a pot of tea. They all slated us. I was living in no-man's land. Like others in the squad, I'd no idea of when, where – or if – I'd be meeting up with them again. Unless you were Brian O'Driscoll or one of the main men, you didn't know how long that Irish experience would last. I felt the cloud over me was the darkest.

That was probably the lowest point of my career. "This fella is a loose cannon: good luck," seemed to be the popular feeling.

That Australian defeat, my citing, my suspension, having to sit out both the win over Romania and worse, the loss to Argentina, and then watching the rest of the World Cup on television, were among the worst days of my career.

That was not a nice time.

Horrible, horrible, horrible.

I had travelled and trained with Ireland after the Australian match every day in the desperate hope that they would qualify for the semi-finals. My suspension provoked plenty of media coverage, none of it complimentary, and there weren't too many people backing me. Certainly not in the IRFU.

I don't think one of them said a word on my behalf.

The IRFU should have piled in behind me and made a much bigger deal of it. There's no way I should have received a two-week suspension in the middle of a World Cup.

I felt that the only people who backed me, apart from family and friends, were Gatty, Donal Lenihan and a few players. Though there might have been a few who felt I deserved what I got.

Gatty said at the time that there was no reason why, at 26, I couldn't play in the next one or two World Cups. "Are you off your head Gats?" As it happened, my playing career might just about have taken in another two World Cups but I didn't make either of them.

That was my only World Cup, and that was how it ended.

DENIS HICKIE
ST MARY'S, LEINSTER AND IRELAND TEAM-MATE OF TREVOR BRENNAN.

"One thing that a lot of people mightn't know about Trev is that he is one of the worst liars I have ever met. He'd be there trying to tell you a story and it would quickly become apparent that most of it – or at least some of it – would be made up. Not that he lies a lot or anything like that. But what would happen would be that he'd finish a story and, even if it sounded far fetched, he might get away with it – because he always seems to be involved in genuinely bizarre situations.

But then he'd just burst out laughing and say something like "ah Dinny, sure I'm only pulling your leg, what actually happened was ..." He's just one of those guys who's better off being straight up all the time, even if he gets himself into more trouble by telling the truth.

A good example of him being straight up came during a bruising encounter in the AIL out at Clontarf's ground on Castle Avenue. I can't remember the exact year, but it was during those halcyon days of the AIL when there was more then a couple of thousand at every game and most sides would have been composed of a few internationals, a few interprovincial players and a few die-hard club servants/hard men.

Clontarf especially had plenty in the latter category and, like a lot of games that St. Mary's played at that time, Trev had been singled out by the opposition as a guy who could be targeted and provoked into giving away penalties, yellow cards etc... Sometimes he deserved them, sometimes he didn't. Either way, about 20 minutes into the first half, there had already been plenty of niggles, rows and off the ball stuff involving players from both sides.

Trev was having a good 'ol ding dong with his opposite number – a tough customer who would have been well able to look after himself. The ref had spoken to them both already but – not surprisingly – given that neither was the type to take a backward step, the lads started at it again.

I happened to be in the vicinity when the ref started trying to separate them. By this stage they were both so fired up (and the fact that he was at least a foot smaller than either of them!) that they continued to have each other by the throat and completely ignored him. What I do remember is how it ended – and I remember it as clear as if it was yesterday.

In the middle of all the pulling and dragging, Trev just took a step back and said (right in front of the poor ref) "Listen Bud, I'll just tell you now: if you want a fight, I'll give you the fight of your life."

This time, Trev wasn't lying and that was the end of it.

CHAPTER 9

THE LEINSTER YEARS: II

ON MALCOLM O'KELLY

In all the years I've known him, he is the most laid back player I've ever met. You'd wonder how such a character could have won so many caps. But then again, he is one of the most naturally talented forwards Ireland has ever had. No-one can ever take away what Malcolm O'Kelly has given and done for Irish rugby.

He dyed my hair when we were in Australia. I shaved his head when we were in South Africa. You could always be sure that Mal would walk in to team meetings 15 minutes late or arrive to a match with no boots. "Oh my boots, I forgot to pack the boots." That would be Mal and it wouldn't bother him; he would never get upset about it ... as Phil Danaher once said "Mal lives in his own world, but it seems like a nice world."

I WAS ALWAYS A CONFRONTATIONAL PLAYER, AND OVER THE YEARS I CAME UP against a variety of opposition hard men. It got me into a lot of bother. But the one forward I probably failed to confront was myself, robbing me of many career highlights and caps.

After my in-house suspension for the events in Loughborough (when the match was abandoned due to fights breaking out in the wake of an incident I was involved in), I was on my best behaviour. I felt I'd let down both my team and the coaches. I was brought back for Leinster for the game against Munster in Dooradoyle. We won that 24-18 and I was given an extended run of starts throughout September and October. My Leinster career was back on track.

Leinster were, however, still having their usual hiccups – like losing to

Connacht 24-23 in the Sportsground due to a last minute try. It was games like that which earned us our reputation for lacking 'bottle', but Connacht were a good side. Mike Ruddock stormed into the dressing-room and overturned a table of soft drinks and hot tea. He went bananas. The walls are thin in the Sportsground, and we could hear Connacht belting out their anthem *Red Is The Rose*. Warren Gatland was making his name with them at that stage. None of us rushed to the showers or the post-match reception that day.

We were also still a little out of our depth in Europe. A case in point was the trip to Stade Francais in the 1998-99 season. I knew that was going to be a disaster from the moment we ran onto the pitch in Stade Jean-Bouin.

We ran through some papier mâché, and then saw something that I had never seen before. In fact, no-one in Leinster had ever seen this. We were met by two lines of cheerleaders lifting their legs six feet into the air. About 40 blondes and brunettes. All of them models, wearing mini skirts and belly tops. They gyrated in two chore-ographed lines. As we were waiting for Stade Francais to join us on the pitch, myself and Victor looked back toward the tunnel.

"Holy Jay-sus!" were my exact words.

He goes "Horse, what is the story?"

The models were still dancing as the Stade players ran onto the pitch to loud, pumping techno music. We were playing at the Super Bowl! This was typical of how their owner Max Guazzini has always presented rugby in Paris; a show he has since taken to capacity crowds of 80,000 in Stade de France. But it was our first taste of it. The nearest we'd had was the Ringsend Irish Dance School, or something, in Donnybrook.

We chased shadows for 80 minutes, and I played the full game. They beat us 56-31, after easing off in the second half. It was Super Bowl rugby too, and we were terrible. Afterwards, we were asking 'how could you play with all that stuff going on?'

The week before, we had beaten Bègles/Bordeaux 9-3 in a real battle up front. But they were old-school French. I loved that match. Richie Murphy, in a rare outing at out-half, kicked three penalties. He could kick them from anywhere – either touchline and up to 50 or 60 metres out. He had a hell of a boot.

There were no prisoners taken on either side, and at times it spilled over. We had some real warhorses up front; Pat Holden, Gabriel Fulcher and Craig Brownlie, and a front-row of Emmet Byrne, Shane Byrne and Angus McKeen, along with myself and Victor. We didn't back down. The rucking was vicious. The pack's aggression was non-stop.

Nearing the end, Bègles pummelled our line looking for a converted try to win. They tapped countless penalties, went through about ten "pick and goes" close in, and when that didn't work they went wide. I ran across the pitch behind my goal-line at the Wesley end, just watching the ball flash across their backline. Their French international centre, Julien Berthe, broke through and was literally over the line when my tackle on him in mid-air forced him to knock the ball on.

Because of the World Cup and my shoulder injury, I missed most of Leinster's 1999-2000 season. After the World Cup, Dr James Colville in the Blackrock Clinic operated on my shoulder. He told me my shoulder was infected and needed to be cleaned out. The cortisone shots probably hadn't helped.

I shared a room with a horse trainer, who was having a hernia removed from his back, and a Kilkenny hurler, who was having a disc removed from his. We were there for a few days and I was last to have an operation. The trainer said he'd arrange tickets for the RDS Horse Show, the hurler for GAA matches in Croker, and me for Leinster matches. We were all going to watch each other when we had recovered.

The day after my operation was a huge day of Six Nations rugby on television, and we were exchanging banter when in walks this young fella.

"How's it going lads?"

Grand, we said.

"Are you watching the rugby today?"

He joined us and we got talking. We asked what had brought him here. He'd had a shoulder operation too.

"It was smashed up playing a rugby match," he said.

"Where do you play?" I asked him.

"I play out in Leixlip."

"What club?" I asked him.

"Barnhall."

"Ah, ye play for Barnhall." I decided not to let on who I was.

"Where do you live?"

"Lucan," he said.

"Ah right. Do you know many of the lads out there?"

He started naming a few of the lads he knew in Barnhall. "I know Kenny Charles, I know the Burkes, and I'm good mates with yer man Trevor Brennan."

The ears on the two boys across the room picked up. I was clean shaven, I had no goatee, my hair was a little longer, as I wanted a nice hospital look for the Black-rock Clinic.

"Do you know him well, do ye?" I asked.

"Ah yea, we'd have the odd drink at weekends in Courtneys or Kennys in Lucan. I see him around alright."

I told him we would definitely have the rugby on later. Then I hit him with it.

"By the way, I'm Trevor Brennan."

"No you're f****** not," he says.

I said "I f****** am Trevor Brennan."

"You're not," he maintains. "I drink with Trevor Brennan." But he's glancing across at the two lads and starting to look a little embarrassed.

"I tell you what," I said. "Look at the name on the chart at the end of the bed there."

He picks up the chart, peers down at it, lets it drop and legs it from the room without a word.

Needless to say we didn't see him until the next day when he came back, apologised and gave us a few cans of something as a present.

Matt Williams had come in as assistant coach to Mike Ruddock in the 1999-2000 season before taking over in 2000-01. We lost away to Edinburgh Reivers before beating Biarritz 35-9. I was sin-binned for offside when I stepped over a ruck to get the ball, but the referee saw it differently. I was yellow carded again in the win away to Northampton, then the European champions, and after beating them at home we had a chance of qualifying. But we let a big lead slip at home to Edinburgh and then needed to win in Biarritz to make the last eight.

The Italian referee gave a penalty count of what seemed like 20-2. He penalised me for not being bound at a scrum or breaking early. We lost 30-10 and we gave it socks that night; the squad and the management. We met up with a few of the Biarritz lads, Serge Betsen, Olivier Roumat and others. I'd swapped shirts with Betsen at the end of that game though he'd nearly cut my nose clear off when he stood on my face.

They took us to a beachfront bar owned by Pascal Ondarts, the legendary French prop. He was delighted to host us, and after a few Basque songs I was asked to sing. I think I sang *Willie McBride* and that started a French-Irish sing-off. We left Pascal's place at about 2.00am and he showed us around the night spots of Biarritz.

Back in the hotel, we were hungry and myself and another player raided the kitchen for some cooked chicken and baguettes.

Well fed, we had a baguette fight in the lobby when Matt walked in and tried to stop it. We turned on him instead. Some of the bedrooms over-looked the lobby and I vaguely remember one or two of the blazers looking down on this. There were some messy, messy heads getting onto the bus to the airport the next morning – some of us nearly missed it. A few Leinster Branch officials weren't too happy.

That's what Matt was up against. There were great characters in the Leinster dressing-room, and not just the players; our bagman Johnny O'Hagen, and our two doctors, Arthur Tanner and Harry Beacham, our fitness trainers Jason Cowan and Dave Fagan. I took as many knocks as anyone, and few men did more to help me onto a rugby pitch than the physio; Alan Kelly, the great AK, hands like magic, always had the Calvin Kleins, the slick car, the sun beds, the well-trimmed goatee, the eternally youthful looks, the story teller and, as he'd say himself, "physio to the stars. There's only one AK"!

I got on very well with Emmet Byrne, Liam Toland, Reggie Corrigan, Denis Hickie, Shane Horgan, Bob Casey and Victor Costello. Denis is just a lovely fella, and always the same. He doesn't have a low or a high, he never changes; and is so down to earth. If you rang Denis and said "listen there's a benefit night out in Barnhall, any chance of you coming out?" or "listen I need a jersey or a pair of boots for a raffle" he'd give you whatever you wanted at the drop of a hat, if he felt it was for a good cause.

The same with Malcolm O'Kelly. Mal's given me jerseys for the bar and for a Toulouse charity raffle, 'Maillot de Vie' for childrens' hospitals. And it's true what they say about him. In all the years I've known him he is the most laid back player I've ever met. You'd wonder how such a character could have won so many caps, but then again he is one of the most naturally talented forwards Ireland has ever had. No-one can ever take away what Malcolm O' Kelly has given and done for Irish rugby.

He dyed my hair when we were in Australia. I shaved his head when we were in South Africa. You could always be sure that Mal would walk in to team meetings 15 minutes late or arrive to a match with no boots. "Oh my boots, I forgot to pack the boots." That would be Mal and it wouldn't bother him; he would never get upset about it.

"Ah number ones, do we need number ones for this match?"

"Yes it's a European Cup match, it's away, in Stade Francais Mal."

"Oh right, I just brought the civvies."

As Phil Danaher once said "Mal lives in his own world, but it seems like a nice world."

Reggie Corrigan is the Michelin Man. Or the Honey Monster. I used to love having a drink with Reggie because the more Reggie drank the funnier and more loving he got; the big hugs, he loved you, he loved everybody. He even loved complete strangers. He has some great stories because he came up through the old school from Greystones.

Emmet Byrne, the Warrior, is a good lad as well. Very genuine, very intense. "Can I borrow your phone for a minute?" An hour later he'd still be on it. He can talk – as viewers can see when he's doing the commentary or analysis for Setanta. Very intense. Intense about everything; scrums, technical aspects of the game. He's also big into his health and his body.

During those seasons, if we were to play Bègles, Stade Francais or other teams in a boat race, we'd beat them. We had some good drinkers, and there was a drinking culture in Leinster. I suppose it didn't help that as well as Bective and Wesley, we had Kielys and Longs just up the road. And if you were still standing after making your way through a Donnybrook pub or two, there was Annabels or Leeson Street.

That same night in Biarritz, though, Matt told us we had to vow to change our ways. To become much more professional. Sessions became longer, our preparation more detailed. Matt himself was perfecting our defence and bringing in Willie Anderson as forwards' coach as well as Alan Gaffney as backs' coach. He restored Roly Meates as scrum coach. The floodlights had to be used in Anglesea Road because the sessions went on so long. Roly Meates had his time with the forwards on scrummaging, then Willie took line-outs and maybe some mauling and rucking.

It helped too that the Celtic League was introduced in the 2001-02 season, which I started in cracking form. Leinster had begun playing me in the second-row. I partnered Bob Casey, Leo Cullen and then Mal O'Kelly when we beat Bridgend 51-32 away. Afterwards Liam Toland, who had been a replacement that night, told me even he was shocked by how well I'd done. For a lock, he said, I was mobile and that could be my future position.

Three days after the September 11th, 2001 attack in New York, we played Pontypridd on what was an eerie night. I had another good game and scored a try; little knowing that Jean-Michel Rancoule, the Toulouse scout, was in Donnybrook. Actually, I believe he was there to watch Victor Costello.

I went head to head with their hard nut Dale McIntosh. The reaction to that try in the corner at the Bective end did me no harm either. My best mate, Alan Graham, had asked me "What's the story with you when you score? You have that big serious head on you. Why don't you give the crowd a wave or something?"

Right enough, I didn't score that much, but when I did I didn't like to show any emotion. But that night I knew that my family and friends were sitting in the main

Heart and Soul: **A life in pictures**

"hat I loved about Trevor was his passion. Everything about Trevor was heart-on-the-sleeve, both on and off the field. You
ew when he was playing he'd give you 100%. And you knew if he came off the bench he'd give you 100%. And if he wasn't
he 22, he was the one guy cheering and shouting the loudest for the team. Those are the sort of qualities that you want
m a guy in your squad. And I think he had the ability to galvanise a team with his sense of humour and his ability to have
g-songs and bring the guys in the squad together. That was one of his strengths as well."

rren Gatland, former Irish, Connacht and Wasps coach.

raining in Brisbane, Australia during Ireland's tour in 1999. I missed the first
est through injury but started the second in Perth — which we lost 32-26.

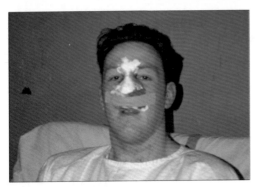

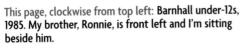

This page, clockwise from top left: Barnhall under-12s, 1985. My brother, Ronnie, is front left and I'm sitting beside him.

■ My confirmation photograph with Damien on my lap, and brothers Ronnie and Errol.

■ In full voice while on tour with Ireland in Australia, 1999.

■ My grandmother, Mary, with my brother, Damien, who died aged 13 in 1995.

■ In a New Zealand hospital in 1993. I had to have my nose reconstructed following another full-on game with Taumarunui. It was a small club on the north island where I worked hard and played hard during the four months I was there. I loved every minute of it.

This page, clockwise from top: **The Brennan family: Ronnie, Errol, myself, Rory the da, Iris the ma, and baby Damien.**

■ The lads enjoying summer in France, 2007. From left: Joshua, myself, Bobby and Daniel.

■ Myself and Paula on the day of our wedding, June 20th, 2003. We returned from the wedding in Mauritius to our newly bought house in Castelginest.

This page clockwise: **Playing for Barnhall and wearing the jersey with pride in 2002, shortly before I left to start my new life in Toulouse.**

■ **Fending off Wanderers' Jonathan Garth while on the charge for Bective.**

■ **Slowing down Aidan McCullen of Lansdowne during the AIL club final at Lansdowne Road which we (St Mary's) won in 2000. That's Victor Costello coming in from the right.**

■ **Celebrating our victory in that final with Daniel in my arms.**

■ **Far page: Going high against Lansdowne's Stephen O'Connor in an AIL match during the 1998 season**

Clockwise from top of far page:
Referee David McHugh lectures
myself and Ulster's Paddy Johns.
■ Holding the line for Leinster in
the Celtic League.
■ Victor Costello and I pack down
for Leinster. He's one of the most
talented athletes I have ever met.
■ Victor, Brian O'Driscoll, myself
and Leo Cullen leave the field after
a disappointing evening's work in
the European Cup, 2001.
■ Happier days in Donnybrook as
we celebrate a win.

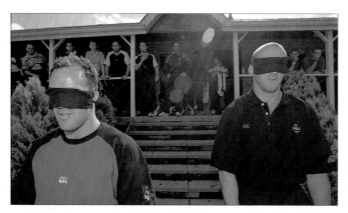

Clockwise from top, this page: **Taking down Italy's Alessandro Troncon at Lansdowne Road in 1999 when I received the Man of the Match award.**
■ Getting on the case of Samoa's Siaosi Vaili in 2001.
■ Emmet Byrne, Frankie Sheahan, myself and Ronan O'Gara share a joke in the Irish dressing room
■ Mike Mullins (left) and myself take part in a team building session with the Irish squad near Killaloe

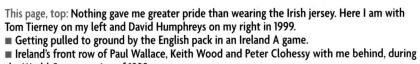

This page, top: **Nothing gave me greater pride than wearing the Irish jersey. Here I am with Tom Tierney on my left and David Humphreys on my right in 1999.**
■ Getting pulled to ground by the English pack in an Ireland A game.
■ Ireland's front row of Paul Wallace, Keith Wood and Peter Clohessy with me behind, during the World Cup campaign of 1999.

Above: The infamous 'Kefu' incident during the 1999 World Cup against Australia at Lansdowne Road. My pride hurt far more than my head. I was like a wounded animal. I thought it pretty rich that I was the one to receive a suspension. This ruled me out of Ireland's fateful match against Argentina in Lens.

■ On the move in a friendly against Samoa at Lansdowne Road in 2001.

Doing the grunt work with the wonderful Malcolm O'Kelly against South Africa, in 1998, when I won my first cap.

Toulouse days, from top of far page and clockwise
The giant of French rugby, Fabien Pelous, in action for Toulouse in the 2003 Heineken Cup final.
■ A word of comfort for Ronan O'Gara following our epic 2003 Heineken Cup semi-final victory over Munster.
■ Toulouse coach, Guy Novès, who saved my life in more ways than one.
■ The boys celebrate our Heineken Cup victory in 2005 when we beat Stade Francais in Murrayfield.
■ With my great friend William Servat.
■ With former President Jacques Chirac following our Heineken Cup win.
■ With my 2005 Texaco Rugby Sportstar of the year award.
■ The legendary Freddy Michalak, star of Toulouse and French rugby — and practical joker extraordinaire!

Days like this: **The first of two Heineken Cup final victories – this one against Perpignan at Lansdowne Road, 2003**

stand toward the Bective end. I'd spotted them at a line-out when one or two of them shouted at me, and I had tried not to react.

When Girvan Dempsey made a break, I ran inside him and chased him all the way. He drew two players – it must have been 60 metres out – and passed the ball inside to me. Okay, maybe it was ten or 15 metres. I went over the line, and gave the Bective end a biggie, then a bit of an Irish jig for the family and friends. All that was missing were cartwheels and back flips, but I couldn't manage them. I got such a reaction from the crowd in that area, that I'd say if Jean-Michel was anywhere near them he couldn't but have been impressed.

That 52-14 win was our fifth in a row, and meant we'd qualified for the knock-out stages of the Celtic League. Our next game, away to Swansea, was our last before our Heineken Cup campaign kicked off at home to Toulouse. However, while Matt's methods were definitely making Leinster more successful, this season saw a split develop in the camp. And it was a very real split.

Toland, or 'Toley', had been captain a couple of seasons before and, as he was also a captain in the army, had organised the odd dinner in the barracks for the lads on the fringes of the first team. Hence, they became known as the balloon corps.

This included Benny Willis, Peter Coyle, John McWeeney, Niall Treston and, I suppose, myself, amongst others. Although I'd had a run of starts, we'd had a few injuries in the second and back rows, and I could see what was in store for me a mile off. The front-line players would leave for international duty, then come back and slot straight into the team. It was a difficult one for coaches to manage, but that's why it became an us-and-them scenario.

On the week of the Swansea game, Matt called the whole squad into Belvo, where we were squashed into a room before training. He explained that he really wanted to look at everybody, and that's why he was resting all the automatic starters. For the rest of us, it was supposedly our big opportunity to play for a spot in the Heineken Cup.

And, "in reward for his hard work and being a true Leinster man, we are going to make captain for this match"...I'd no idea this was coming..."Trevor Brennan". I can only imagine what the rest of the players thought of Horsebox being made captain. The front row was Peter Coyle, Gavin Hickie and Niall Treston. We had a good second row, Bob Casey and Leo Cullen, with myself, Toley and Aidan McCullen in the back-row.

Benny Willis and Nathan Spooner were the half-backs, David Quinlan and Adam Magro in midfield, John McWeeney and Simon Keogh on the wings, and Peter McKenna at full-back. Most of them weren't getting any game time, and most wouldn't start again for months. Only Leo and Nathan were regular starters that season. This was the balloon corps XV.

We knew the score. Calling the lads into a huddle in training, I said that even if we all scored three tries apiece not too many of us would be starting against Toulouse, no matter what Matt had said. Lambs to the slaughter.

We travelled to Swansea to play a strong Swansea side, full of internationals. I really wound up the lads in the dressing-room beforehand.

"We've been written off here. The coaches don't even care how we do or what the result is because we've already qualified. But I'm not here to get 60 points put on us. If not for the coaches or the other players back in Dublin, let's do it for ourselves."

It was a sunny day in St Helen's, beside the Sophia Gardens cricket ground, and it was a sensational performance. John McWeeney, who scored two tries, and Benny, who also scored a try, had stormers; myself, Toley and Aidan double and triple tackled, and Bob and Leo carried ball all day. The referee gave us nothing, Leo and Adam were both binned, but we beat them 34-18 and by four tries to nil.

There was no way we were conceding a try. Leinster had already qualified. This was our second-rate side, which had nothing to play for. Swansea missed out on the quarter-finals and were destroyed by the Welsh papers the next day. We wanted to prove a point to Swansea, to our coaches, and to the other Leinster players.

A few of us, including myself, made the bench against Toulouse, but only Leo and Nathan started.

That early run of games had helped push me back into the Irish set-up, but when I came back to Leinster after the November internationals I was used purely as a replacement. This continued until the Celtic League semi-final, when I came on for Eric Miller. Matt had told me he was considering me for that game, as Victor had had a tackle count of one in the previous game. But it was a way of geeing Victor up as well, and he had a stormer against Glasgow.

When we beat Munster in the first Celtic League final in Lansdowne Road, I was left on the bench for the full 80, because Eric had been sent off in the first half. At first I never gave it a second thought. I sang the first or the second verse of *Dublin In The Rare Oul Times* before we lifted the cup in Lansdowne Road.

It was a great day. There was a huge crowd, chants of "Lein-ster!" echoed around the ground, and despite having 14 men for most of the match, Leinster scored a couple of brilliant tries to win 24-20. I felt sorry for Eric when he was sent off.

I'd been down that road, and I hoped, for his sake, we wouldn't lose. If we had lost that game, at Monday's video session… God love him. That's all I'll say.

Because we won, it was largely ignored, and because of his two-game suspension I started away to Newcastle. About six of my family and friends, including my father and my uncle George travelled over. It was very funny on the morning of the match. The ground was covered by snow and ice, and I remember George pushing his keys into the ground and telling the referee that the pitch was playable, but the game was cancelled.

We went, instead, to see Newcastle United play – my first ever soccer match. I've seen only one since, Toulouse at home to Lyon in my fourth year in France. I've never been to a Republic of Ireland or a National League match. I can't recall Newcastle's opponents, or the result, but I do remember it was a cracking atmosphere in amongst all those football lunatics shouting abuse at each other. We left before the end.

The rugby match was cancelled again the next day, our flight home was fog bound, and we had to charter a flight to Dublin on the Sunday night. It was the worst case of planes, trains and automobiles I've ever experienced. On Monday I went to the pictures with Paula in Blanchardstown, where I had a phone call from Ken Ging. We were to meet in Belvo the next day to travel to Leeds, the game's new venue, and bring enough gear for a week, as we were going straight on to Toulouse for our final group game the following Sunday. Against Newcastle, I did my usual double act – sin-binned and Man of the Match in a 17-15 win.

We flew to Toulouse and were given the green light to go out that Wednesday night. We had four nights to kill before the game, and some lads did the Thursday and Friday as well. It was January, we were unbeaten all season until that point, 15 wins in a row, but the preparation for that game was awful.

We somehow held Toulouse to 3-0 at half-time, but we'd given everything; then the travelling and the preparation caught up with us. Fatigue set in, and in the second half they cut us to shreds to beat us 43-7. I was carrying a bad rib cartilage injury from the Newcastle match. Funnily enough, it would be my last ever start for Leinster, and the defeat cost us a home quarter-final. We were away to Leicester.

Eric Miller completed his suspension and was immediately recalled for the quarter-final. I didn't bear him any grudges. It wasn't a personal battle between Eric and me. He's an individual, who kept to himself more than most. But at the same time, he was very much part of the team.

I broke into the Leinster squad in 1996, and my first sighting of Eric Miller was when he played for the Lions in South Africa in the summer of 1997. Sitting in a bar on my holidays, I watched him, Keith Wood, Paul Wallace and Jeremy Davidson and from my viewpoint, Eric was the most amazing. He had phenomenal ball skills and when he did join Leinster, I knew he would be a massive threat to me. I did feel threatened, but at the same time, I felt challenged.

He pushed me to train that bit harder. Training generally started at 10.30am in Old Belvedere and when I'd arrive at 10.00am, Eric would already be on the pitch hitting tackle bags with Jason Cowan, Leinster's fitness coach. No-one trained harder. He was driven. In drills, Eric hit every bag as if it were the last he'd ever hit.

Later on one morning, I called Jason aside and asked him "How long has Eric been out there?"

"Oh, he's been here since 9.30am."

So I asked Jason "What days are you not doing extra bag work with Eric? Is there any chance you'd do extra bag work with me?"

And in the end, it wasn't because of Eric Miller that I left Leinster. It wasn't because of Eric that I put my tail between my legs and skulked off. No less than Denis Hickie more recently, I thought Eric retired prematurely at 30. In my opinion he possibly had another three good years left in him.

Eric was a world-class player but I had become very frustrated with this state of affairs. Whether he was coming back from injury or suspension, he slotted straight into the team.

When Matt picked him in the starting line-up against Leicester, I told him "If that was me who was sent off in the Celtic League final and suspended for two games, you wouldn't have picked me again for the rest of the season."

And Matt had no answer to that, because it was true.

By the time I came on in the last half-hour, Leicester's maul had already done the damage, Nathan Spooner was playing on one leg and we were beaten 29-18.

Most of the lads had their heads down in the Welford Road dressing-room, but I showered and dressed pretty quickly to head into the bar. Players, family, friends and supporters were down, but I've rarely felt so unaffected by a defeat.

I think that day triggered the idea of moving on.

Deep down, I knew I wouldn't be with Leinster the following season.

It made for a bad end to a good season. The backline, effectively the same as today's, had scored tries for fun. If these lads retire from the game without having won the Heineken Cup it will be a shame. I think it's one of the most talented backlines in Europe, and I wouldn't be alone in Toulouse in thinking that.

It also made for a sour end to what had been a brilliant five years with Leinster. But I was out of the loop. Nothing was happening for Trevor Brennan in Leinster or Ireland.

MATT WILLIAMS

FORMER COACH OF NEW SOUTH WALES WARATAHS, LEINSTER AND SCOTLAND.

"I always valued his absolutely incredible physicality on the field. I've never coached or seen anyone with more physical commitment than Trevor. There wasn't an ounce of his body that he didn't put into it, and that made up for a deficit in some skills.

I think that was exemplified by a physical performance away to Toulouse when we had a lot of injuries and were well beaten. Toulouse were quite magnificent, even though Leinster had qualified and they had been eliminated. But Trevor's performance that day was quite extraordinary and I believe that was what caught Guy Novès' eye, and eventually got him a contract there.

During that period I was very keen to keep Trevor at Leinster. We'd moved him into the second row and he had become a very valuable bench player to us. Trevor didn't like that role – like all players he wanted to start – but Trevor performed a very good role for us in that he could play back row and second row. I had Eric Miller in front of him and Trevor didn't agree with me. He has never really forgiven me for it, yet during that time I fought very hard to keep Trevor at Leinster.

Unfortunately, the money was set by the IRFU and Trevor had dropped off the national radar. We had approached sponsors, we had tried to organise Trevor to be partners in a business; we had done a lot of work to keep him. Yet the money from Ireland was small by comparison.

When Trevor rang me and told me what he was offered by Toulouse, I told him it was a great opportunity, with one of the best clubs in Europe, and he'd have been mad not to take it. I thought Trevor had appreciated the work we had done to try and keep him, and even if he wasn't happy with the selection, he understood that we did want him to stay at Leinster.

No-one thought less of him for leaving because of the financial situation, and the need to look after his family. I was extremely disappointed in subsequent years that at every public opportunity Trevor had, he criticised me for letting him go and not selecting him. Given the efforts we put in to keep him and to convert him into a second-row, I felt very, very hurt. It came to a head when I went down to Toulouse at the time I was coaching Scotland and he introduced me to Gareth Thomas by saying "This is the bloke who wouldn't pick me at Leinster."

I stopped him short, explained what had happened and asked him not to say it any more because it wasn't true. He apologised, bought me a beer and I've never heard him say it again.

I picked Eric Miller ahead of Trevor because he had more skills and linked better with the backline we had. The game we were playing was a high tempo, high skilled game and Miller wasn't physically poor. Still, there were four or five games in his last year at Leinster when Trevor played really good rugby. I think if he'd stayed, he would have forced his way back into the Irish set-up, just like Reggie and Victor. But taking the offer from Toulouse was absolutely the right thing to do.

He played on the edge of the laws and sometimes there were extraordinary feats of athleticism. One that comes to mind was of Isitolo Maka charging toward the line for Toulouse against Leinster in Donnybrook. I thought no-one could possibly stop him but Trevor leapt off the ground and caught him in a bear hug and the result of the collision was that Isitolo Maka got over the line but couldn't ground the ball. Maka was a passenger for the rest of the game until he was replaced.

In the same game, Trevor single-handedly collapsed a maul when they were going to score a try and he hurled his body at Yannick Bru. These things sort of go unnoticed in a game.

He was extraordinary, fearless and totally committed, and it's understandable with that attitude that he would step over the line. He was exactly the same in training. There was one beautiful moment when we were getting ready for Newcastle, with Trevor defending off a short line-out. I asked Shane Horgan to take it up the middle like Jonny Wilkinson and Trevor just completely pole-axed him. Shaggy was knocked senseless. I said "Don't be angry with Trevor."

"He said "I'm not angry with Trevor, I'm angry with you. As soon as you picked him I knew that would happen. Why didn't you pick one of the other blokes?"

Trevor brought a lot off the field as well. He has a brilliant sense of humour, he's a team man and the brutality of his physical game is equal to the brutality of his honesty.

He puts his own hand up and he doesn't let other people off as easy. People won't admit this, but if you ran onto the pitch with Trevor Brennan a lot of people were scared of him. And they had every right to be.

He was the hardest guy I ever coached. I've coached more skilful but I've never coached anyone harder."

CHAPTER 10

THE COLD SHOULDER

ON BEING DROPPED FROM THE IRISH TEAM

My name vanished off the radar. I can't help but think this was at least partly because of what I had said to the press. In fact, you can be damned sure of it. Ireland beat Scotland 44-22 and the rest, as they say, is history. Including my test career, more or less. I wasn't picked for a year and eight months.

... My head was in the shed again. As much as I wanted to play for my country, this whole episode left me disillusioned. As well as vanishing from the radar for the rest of that season (even for the A's), I wasn't included in the 28-man squad to tour the Americas, was overlooked the following autumn against Japan, the 2001 Six Nations, and even the Romanian match in June when Ireland were short six Lions.

I'M NOT USUALLY ONE OF THE FIRST OUT OF THE SHOWERS, AND I WISH I HADN'T been at Twickenham in February 2000. Eddie O'Sullivan had arrived as assistant coach after the 1999 World Cup, and the bulk of the side was retained for that Six Nations opener. We were beaten 50-18. Although I'd only been a second-half replacement along with Mick Galwey and Girvan Dempsey, John Redmond asked me and a few other players to do the post-match press conferences. I should have said no, in hindsight, but John insisted that I do it as no-one else was volunteering.

How do you answer a barrage of questions from journalists when you've shipped 50 points? "We were unlucky?" We had talked all week about being men, about standing up to be counted, about wrapping up ball and man in the tackle. But on the day, we had done none of it. I spoke honestly and from the heart.

"They (England) just offloaded in the tackle with ease. I think we should have tried to wrap man and ball up. We weren't 100% committed in the tackle, and when you're not 100% committed in the tackle it just makes it easier for the man to offload. What fellas said, the commitment they'd give, during the week and in the dressing-room before, it just didn't seem to be carried out onto the pitch, which was disappointing really."

I also said that the decision to kick for the posts or the corner when we were already well beaten was disheartening. "If we'd just tapped and put it through hands and put them under the same pressure that they put us under in the first-half. I think that's the way forward really. Not to slow things down. I can't see any point in going for three points when you're 30-40 down with 20 minutes to go."

If I was a coach, or a captain, of any team that would be the last thing I'd be telling my players to do. Something I've learned even more since coming to Toulouse.

Kieron Dawson was just as candid. "We were awful. Our defence was all over the shop. We were at sixes and sevens half the time. Our tackling was sub-standard. Very poor in fact. Obviously you're not going to do much with these flaws."

All of that was true too, and the pundits rubbished our performance.

I was widely quoted in the next day's papers.

One player took me aside and suggested that speaking in such a manner might jeopardise my selection prospects, and that I really shouldn't be so candid.

Kieron remained in the team, but, whether it was coincidental or not, I wasn't picked for the next game at home to Scotland. Ireland made five changes to the starting line-up. Even though I'd been on the bench in Twickenham, I was dropped from the 22.

Why drop someone from the bench? I could never quite figure that one out. It doesn't make sense. Anyone will tell you that if a player is dropped, it should be the one who started, not the one who came off the bench.

What happened was, in my view, totally wrong. They dropped a player who came on for the last 32 minutes when the score was already 32-3, made a massive hit on Lawrence Dallaglio, gave away no penalties, and could hardly be blamed for Ireland losing by 50-18.

Changes had to be made after Twickenham. But if anything, myself, Gaillimh and Girvan had made a positive impact from the bench.

To be honest, I thought I had a good chance of being promoted. But they brought in five new caps; Peter Stringer, Ronan O'Gara, Shane Horgan, John Hayes and Simon Easterby. And they recalled Gaillimh, Girvan Dempsey and Denis Hickie.

I rang Donal Lenihan. He told me to train with the A squad, who were preparing to play Scotland in Donnybrook.

"How are you Trev? Good to see you," said A coach Declan Kidney, greeting me warmly. Before adding "I'm afraid you're not playing."

I thought to myself "This is going from bad to worse."

In fact, I wasn't included in any of the four remaining A games. Even on the bench. It looked like they were making a point. My name vanished off the radar. I can't help but think this was at least partly because of what I had said to the press.

My test career was more or less over.

I wasn't picked for Ireland for a year and eight months.

My head was in the shed again. As much as I wanted to play for my country, this whole episode left me disillusioned. As well as vanishing from the radar for the rest of that season (even for the A's), I wasn't included in the 28-man squad to tour the Americas, I was overlooked the following autumn against Japan, the 2001 Six Nations and even the Romanian match in June, when Ireland were short six Lions.

I owe my last recall to the foot-and-mouth epidemic, (which meant re-arranged matches the following September and October), a lousy Irish performance in a 32-10 defeat to Scotland and Gary Longwell breaking his finger.

Desperate times call for desperate measures!

I was playing out of my skin for Mary's and Leinster, and I suppose that might have had something to do with my brief recall.

Matt Williams had been using me as a second-row as well as a back-row. After one game in Donnybrook, Gatty came up to me and said "Well played Trev. Keep it up and I might have a place in the World Cup squad for you."

"Is that all you've got for me?" I said, being a bit of a smart ass.

By then I didn't give a toss about them. I reckoned I had nothing to lose. I was enjoying my rugby, but no more was I going to be the little doggy. Gatty's congratulations meant little to me at the time. I couldn't care if he thought I was Zinzan Brooke re-incarnated.

But one day soon after, in my parents' house, I got a call out of the blue from

Irish manager Brian O'Brien.

"How are ye going kid?"

"Alright thanks. Who's this?" I asked, not recognising the accent.

"Brian O'Brien."

"Yeah?"

"Yeah, Brian O'Brien – Ireland."

'Brian O'Brien – Ireland. Who the hell is Brian O'Brien?' I thought to myself. Donal Lenihan had departed to manage the Lions the previous summer. As for Ireland, it had been nearly two years since I'd played for them. I knew Brian to see, obviously, but it just hadn't registered.

"Kid, listen. The big man from Ulster had an accident today."

"Who? What big man?" I asked.

"Gary Longwell."

The penny dropped. "What do you want me to do?" I said, now realising who it was.

"Ah, we need you to come out here."

"For what? Do you want me to hold bags?" I said. I'd been asked along to the odd session here and there, when that's what I'd mostly done.

"Nah kid, this looks like the big one. Gatty wants you on board and on the bench."

This was the Tuesday or Wednesday before Ireland played Wales in the Millennium Stadium, in the second of the re-arranged matches. It was horrible arriving in the Glenview Hotel, Wicklow that evening. I drove up the M50 through rush hour traffic and arrived as the squad were having dinner. I checked in, put my stuff in the room and went down to join them. I shook hands with some of the lads I hadn't spoken to in over a year and said hello to the management, letting on I was delighted to be there.

"Get yourself a bit of grub and settle in there, kid."

They carried on eating, so I grabbed a plate of food and looked around for an empty seat, before going back to my room and unpacking. I went to training the next morning. Throughout the week there was no one-on-one communication with any of the management to explain why I'd been recalled. I didn't feel a part of it at all. Then one day I asked Brian if I was entitled to tickets for the game.

"Oh yes you are, kid. How many do you want?"

I asked for two. But it was all last minute stuff, the hotels were booked up and nobody from my family could make it over. The night before the game, I recall walking around Cardiff on my own. No-one really recognised me apart from two young Irish lads standing outside a pub asking if anybody had tickets. I went back to them.

"Have you no tickets for the game lads?"

"No." they said.

"Here you go, lads. Here's two stand tickets for you."

"My da is inside, will you wait here while I tell him?" said one of them.

His father came out and asked me to come in and say hello. He was delighted that I'd given the tickets to the lads and insisted on buying me a drink. I had a coke with them and made my way back to the hotel.

The pressure on both teams to win was huge. And it showed. I came on in the 58th minute for Mick Galwey, alongside Malcolm O'Kelly in the second row. I was comfortable playing with Mal. We'd played together at Mary's and Leinster. Ireland were leading 15-6 at that point. We went on to win 36-6 with three tries in the last six minutes.

Mal called for the first of the Welsh restarts after I came on, but I shouted "Mal, leave it." I did the same with the next one. It felt good to be back in the zone.

For the next game against England I was retained on the bench. They were going for the Grand Slam. On the morning of the match we walked to Lansdowne Road from the Berkeley Court and practised our line-outs on the back pitch behind the East Stand. They went really crisply. There was no confusion over the calls. Hardly a ball was put down. On our way back to the hotel I remember Gatty saying to me "It feels good, doesn't it?"

"I don't know what it is Gatty. But there's something in the air. I have a good feeling about today."

"So do I." he agreed. "I have that feeling too."

England used the same calls as the Lions, and as Mal knew them all, we cleaned out their line-outs. Myself and the Warrior, Emmet Byrne, came on in the 67th minute, with me replacing Gaillimh again to play alongside Mal.

I thought I'd made a good impression. I put in a big hit on Jonny Wilkinson, and made a tap tackle on Austin Healey. I was happy, not least because we beat them.

We didn't beat England too often in those days, and had lost to them six times in a row before that game. Although much was made of Martin Johnson and Lawrence Dallaglio being injured, that was still a very good English team; Greenwood, Catt, Wilkinson, Dawson, Leonard, White, Shaw, Grewcock,

Corry, Back, Hill... all of whom would go on to win the World Cup. The Lansdowne Road crowd were incredible that day and it was marvellous to be a part of it.

The day after the English game we went clay pigeon shooting, had a couple of pints in Aughrim, and returned to the Glenview. I was wrecked after the night before, but Gatty said that it was obligatory for everyone to come for a meal in a restaurant in Bray. "You'll enjoy it. It'll be a good night."

I sat at the dinner table with Gatty to my right and Rala (Paddy O'Reilly, the Irish bagman) to my left.

"Is he here yet?" Gatty asked Rala across me.

"Not yet," said Rala.

I interrupted them. "Is who here yet?"

"Ah there's a bit of music organised for the boys," Gatty said. "Say nothing to the lads."

"Is it a band?"

"Kind of," he said.

"What kind of music is it?" I asked him.

"A bit of traditional music."

"Oh I love the old bit of traditional Gatty," I said.

"I know you do, Trevor."

After a lovely meal, we went downstairs to the bar below the restaurant and in walked Christy Moore. Gatty knew I loved Christy. I was like a kid in a sweet shop. At first there were only another 20 people in the bar, but after a flurry of texts, by the time Christy was into his third song, it was more like 200. We were right at the front. As I'd been singing along, he asked me to join him.

So I belted out *An Ordinary Man* with him and then we presented him with a signed, framed Irish jersey. I was delighted to sing with him and I took off my Irish polo top to give to him. One of the nights of my life. I have an autographed, framed picture of the two of us on my wall, back home in Castelginest.

Two weeks later, I was on the bench again for the match against Samoa. Myself and Simon Easterby came on for Eric Miller and Anthony Foley at half-time, and we won 35-8.

To be honest, the night was more memorable than the match. I'd been in the bar having a few drinks with my family, and was a little late for the dinner. There were no seats left except at a table with six or seven Samoans.

I was lucky to have a long chat with their coach Michael Jones, one of the legends of the game dating back to my New Zealand trip in '93. I told him of my time there, and we exchanged a few stories. Normally the post-match dinner is a staid affair but the Samoans walked to the front of the room, took off their jackets and shirts, and put on a show of songs and war dances.

I played drinking games with the seven Samoans, and traded songs. It was a really relaxed night. Little did I know that I'd never play for Ireland again. Or that I'd never be in that Berkeley Court function room again.

Maybe I was naïve, but I truly expected things were going to kick off for me from there. When we played New Zealand the following week, I wasn't even given a ticket. I fulfilled a speaking engagement on the day for some sponsor and asked him "Would there be any chance of a ticket?"

"You need a ticket?" yer man said, shocked.

I'm sure I could have acquired one from the Union, but I didn't want to ask. Ireland played superbly. Miller scored a brilliant try and at half-time I said "Jaysus, Ireland are going to beat the All Blacks today." The All Blacks, though, were awesome in the last half-hour and won 40-29.

If Ireland had won that day, Gatty wouldn't have got the heave and I'd probably have earned a few more caps. But the defeat to the All Blacks gave them their excuse. Gatty's cards were probably marked after the Murrayfield defeat. Perhaps my cards were always marked.

Fellas can get 13 or more caps in a season, but I earned my 13 over a three year period. When I think of all the different teams I've played with, in many ways the least enjoyable were with Ireland. With Ireland, players come together from different provinces and clubs, and I never felt entirely comfortable in that set-up. I never felt it was long-term. It always felt short-term.

The last three caps were especially bad. I was delighted to get them, but I hated them in some ways. When I was recalled for that Welsh game, after 20 months out of the loop, I'd been told to get some grub... and that was it.

I played some good rugby for Ireland. My best and only decent run of starts were the four games against Australia in Perth, the World Cup warm-up match against Australia and the two World Cup games against the USA and Australia.

The fight with Kefu – and the citing that followed – was one of only two bad experiences I had with Ireland; the other was the 10-9 defeat to France in '99. But it's worth stressing that I never picked up either a red, or even a yellow card, playing with Ireland.

My best games were probably against Italy, in my first start and against Argentina and the USA, when Woody scored his four tries. I think it was an achievement merely to play for Ireland, given where I came from. It always will be.

But I also believe I should have won at least 20 caps more. At the absolute minimum. If you go through the list of 20 or so players who've since played for Ireland in the second row - or at number six, or combining the two - ahead of me, some are undoubtedly class acts. But you can't convince me that all of them were head and shoulders above me. And that's not including all those who've played for Ireland 'A'. Many of them were playing on losing Celtic League and Heineken Cup teams.

At the same time, I was playing for one of the top clubs in Europe, and indeed the world, keeping French internationals off the Toulouse team. At the end of my first season, I was voted one of the best back-rowers in France on *L'Equipe's* team of the season 2002-03. With players like Serge Betsen and Olivier Magne behind me.

Maybe I wasn't forgiven for being unavailable to tour New Zealand in 2002 when I needed a shoulder operation before joining Toulouse. I wasn't included as one of the 37 players used on the summer tour to Australia, Tonga and Samoa in the summer of 2003. I believe I was better than some of them, and that I should have been in the World Cup squad in 2003.

In my second year with Toulouse, we reached another European Cup final. But I was completely overlooked by the Irish management all season – even for A squads.

And so on it went.

I wasn't even picked for a tour to Japan in 2005, when Ireland had ten or more players with the Lions. I didn't even make the Churchill Cup.

Surely there was an argument, on a horses for courses basis, for picking a player in form playing on a successful team?

In three years we reached three European Cup finals. I was on the bench for the first game, against London Irish, and then started every other European game in those three years. We were twice champions of Europe, and made the semi-finals or final of the French Championship every year.

Can anyone tell me I wasn't good enough to go to Tonga and Samoa, or Japan. Or even the Churchill Cup? I believe it was decided that my face didn't fit. Who knows. I don't. No-one has ever told me. It still rankles after all these years.

I arrived in Toulouse, and in France, with no baggage. They knew little or nothing about me. Of all the teams I've ever played with, I feel that Toulouse was the only one where politics played no part in the selection process.

If you performed, you were picked. That's what I love about Toulouse. And if I was dropped, I was told why. "You gave away three penalties in the last game," Guy Novès would tell me.

In all that time, I was called into the Irish squad just once for training – the week when Ireland played England in 2004. Victor was carrying a knock, but he came through. I remember becoming a little excited about that. "Maybe there's hope here."

The club were delighted for me. Guy Novès told me that I deserved it and had worked hard for it. Though I'm sure he would have had mixed feelings about me returning to Irish duty.

But nothing came of it and Ireland went on to win the first of their recent Triple Crowns.

I do feel lucky to have played for Ireland. There are many good players in Ireland who have never won a single cap. I made many good mates, and always socialised easily with players and alickadoos.

But I never got Ireland's call again.

Behind it all, I don't feel my face fitted with Ireland.

PETER STRINGER

MUNSTER AND IRELAND SCRUM-HALF.

"I first watched Trevor on the tour to South Africa in 1998 and he looked like a complete headcase. But he was so clearly proud to be Irish. Watching the way he performed and got stuck in, it was like he took on the whole South African pack himself. He showed such complete courage in doing so.

When I finally got to meet him and play with him, I saw how emotional he got before a game. How much it meant to him to be playing for Ireland and to be wearing the green jersey.

On a cold, wet Monday of an international week, it might take you a bit of time to get warmed up and to get into the physical side of things. But I remember, with Trevor, there was no easing into a session. It was just hell for leather right from the start. It was fascinating to see. I genuinely believe he enjoyed that sort of thing and enjoyed wanting to make an impression.

I never had any run-ins with him, but I might have had a bit of banter with him on the pitch. It was the same with Victor. I got on really well with the two of them because I respected them.

I suppose he didn't come across as a typical Leinster player, in that he wasn't

D4 and came from Barnhall. I got on really well with him, and I found him to be a great person. A real genuine person. There was no shit about him.

What you saw was what you got, and that was it. There was no hiding behind an exterior. That was the one thing about him; a fantastic guy and a very approachable and friendly fellow. It didn't matter who you were or where you came from, he didn't care.

If you played rugby and you were committed to it, then that was good enough for him."

CHAPTER 11

'ALLO, 'ALLO!

THE AGENT'S PITCH

"Pack the swimming trunks and the sun cream. Tell Paula to do the same." I was laughing to myself. He was describing life in this club in the south of France; swimming pools, their facilities, the French championships they'd won, all their famous players. Like Fabien Pelous, Emile Ntamack, Xavier Garbajosa, Hugues Miorin, Franck Belot, Franck Tournaire, Christian Califano, Patrick Soula ... little did I know that the very year I signed, ten of them were sacked, transferred or retired.

THE LANGUAGE DIFFICULTY

The only word on the menu I recognised was steak, so I ordered the steak tartare and thought I asked the waiter for well done. When I saw a lump of raw meat with a few onions through it I nearly died ... it was like a scene from a Mr Bean film.

WHEN MY CONTRACT WITH LEINSTER FINISHED, I COULD HAVE RENEWED IT without any problems. I simply didn't want to. I was still only 28, but no matter how well I played, I had been pigeon-holed as either an impact player or to provide cover for other players. Even if I made an impact as a replacement, it was only going to underline my name as an impact replacement. I couldn't win. And this in turn meant I couldn't further my chances of playing for Ireland.

I let it be known that I wanted to change clubs. I'd never had an agent, so I asked a few people to recommend one. One guy got me in touch with Dick Best. He phoned to tell me that he could quite easily get me a club in England. He sent over one of his agents to Dublin, and I signed a contract to have his company represent me.

Some months later, Sevi Saverimutto, whose brother Chris had played for Ireland, telephoned me to say that a club in England called Orrell – then a first division team – wanted to talk me. I was flown over and shown around the JJB Stadium. The chairman explained that if they were promoted to the English Premiership, this was where they would play. And that they had expectations of playing in Europe. Not a bad selling point. It was a very impressive stadium.

I was shown the weights room, the chairman's and the president's office. The possibility of playing 'League' for Wigan was also mentioned. At the time Gary Connolly was playing League for Wigan and was being talked of as a convert to Union with Ireland. I did a medical, and after lunch we spoke about figures. They offered me £100,000 plus bonuses. I came home and thought about it long and hard.

At the time, I was on an Irish contract worth €50,000 plus match fees and a car – which wasn't bad. But Orrell were effectively offering me three times my wages with Leinster; or, as I looked at it, three years' salary in one year. They may have been first division, but at 28, I was never going to earn that kind of money in Ireland.

I wasn't going to play for Ireland if I couldn't nail down a spot in the starting line-up in Leinster anyway, so the thought of earning a few extra quid was very tempting. I had an offer from Pontypridd too: £60k, Mercedes, accommodation etc. Thankfully, I turned that down too because the club subsequently ran into serious financial difficulties.

Then a call came from Warren Gatland to come to Wasps – £40k and another £20k at the end of the season. The end-of-season 'reward' kind of threw me. Sometimes these things, if they're not cast in stone, might or might not materialise.

Even though Gatty was the coach who gave me all my 13 caps from 1998 to 2001, I also felt he'd let me down a little – notably by parking me on the bench against France in 2001, when Brian O'Driscoll scored three tries.

I have to say that Gatty had been very good to me by and large, but it just didn't seem like the right move. Especially as property and the cost of living were so much more expensive in London.

Paula would have to give up her job – a very good job at the time – as a family therapist. Overall, I reckoned I would probably be no better off than I already was with Leinster.

In any event, money won me over and I decided on Orrell. I signed a letter of intent, indicating that I was very interested.

I was scheduled to travel over the following Saturday for a final medical, to meet the chairman and sign a full contract.

Friday lunchtime. I was at home when the phone rang. It was an agent called John Baker. I'd met John on several occasions after Leinster and Ireland matches, and I knew he represented quite a number of players. He asked me if I had signed for a club. I told him that I was due to go to Orrell to sign a contract the very next day. He begged me not to go and to meet him. He had an offer I couldn't refuse.

When I asked him what it was, he kept repeating "I'll tell you when I meet you. I'll tell you when I meet you."

"It had better be good John," was my reply.

We met in the Spawell Hotel an hour later. He'd heard that my time with Leinster was over. He kept asking me to guess which club it was and kept me on tenterhooks for 20 minutes.

"The best club in Europe. Toulouse." he said. "A great opportunity for your family."

He added "Pack the swimming trunks and the sun cream. Tell Paula to do the same." I was laughing to myself. He was describing life in this club in the south of France; swimming pools, their facilities, the French championships they'd won, all their famous players, like Fabien Pelous, Emile Ntamack, Xavier Garbajosa, Hugues Miorin, Franck Belot, Franck Tournaire, Christian Califano, Patrick Soula…. Little did I know that the very year I signed, ten of them were sacked, transferred or retired.

I didn't know what to do but I felt I couldn't let Orell down. We stayed there all afternoon drinking tea. John spent three of the next four hours on the phone to a company called GSM (Toulouse's representatives) seeking more details about the deal. It transpired that Toulouse had contacted GSM but were unable to acquire my number. The IRFU don't give out personal numbers without players' approval. Toulouse contacted John Baker.

John informed GSM that if Toulouse really wanted me, they needed to have me there the next day (Saturday). After about 20 cups of tea, and about 20 phone calls, John had us on a flight to Toulouse the next day. I rang Saverimutto with some sad story about being sick and unable to fly.

When I left the Spawell, my mind was racing. It was May, near the end of the season, and I was still training with Leinster. I'd played in a President's XV for Eddie O'Sullivan in Ballymena on the last weekend in April, when Munster were playing Leicester in the Heineken Cup final. I played out of my skin that day. In the second-row, number six, number eight – I played everywhere. But now, thoughts of making the New Zealand tour had been overtaken by events.

I didn't know what to do. The first person I rang was Paula, my girlfriend at the time. Then I called Ronnie. I've always turned to the older brother for advice since we were kids. I could feel excitement down the phone. He said "Listen, go for it. That's great. I'm delighted for you. I'll call up and see you later."

My mind was still racing. I met with John the next morning. We flew to Paris and then on to Toulouse, as there was no direct flight at the time. We were met in the airport by Jean-Michel Rancoule, a scout for Toulouse, an ex-player and a very good friend of Toulouse coach Guy Novès. He'd seen me play in the Celtic League at home on September 11, 2001 against Pontyrpidd. That was when I got the Man of the Match award for my performance in the second-row. He'd also watched me in the back-row against Llanelli in August.

The number of journalists and photographers at the airport, and at the club on my arrival took me by surprise. Word had obviously leaked out that Toulouse were holding talks with me. Everything about Stade Toulousain was impressive.

We had lunch in the club's restaurant, complete with a Michelin star. I was amazed at all the trophies in the cabinets, all the rugby photos on the walls, and the six massive plasma screens showing old Toulouse matches.

I felt all eyes were on me. People were whispering, but the only word I could make out was "Brennan". John said wasn't it lovely – the 'it' referring to the champagne. I didn't know what to think. Why stop at the champagne? Neither I nor John had a word of French, so Jean-Michel was translating everything for us in his pidgin English.

We were to hear the president, René Bouscatel, and Fabien Claude-Elliesse, who was the money man with Toulouse, while Guy Novès, the coach, would join us later. Fabien Pelous came in with Emile Ntamack during the meal to welcome me to the club. They both spoke English.

The only word on the menu I recognised was steak, so I ordered the steak tartare and thought I asked the waiter for well done. When I saw a lump of raw meat with a few onions through it I nearly died. Everyone having been served, René Bouscatel said "Bon appetit," and they tucked into their chicken and lamb.

It was like a scene from a *Mr Bean* film. I didn't want to be rude or insulting, so I picked at it and while they weren't looking, tried to hide some of it under my salad. I was starving but I couldn't eat it. I eventually slid the whole thing into my jacket pocket and excused myself to go to the toilet where I flushed it away.

No sooner was I back at the table when someone noticed my clean plate.

"Encore, encore, Trevor?"

"No, non, no... merci, no, please, no... "

Meanwhile all around me, the lads were stuck into the most fabulous dishes while my tummy ached for some cooked food.

By the time the meal was finished, John Baker was tapping Guy Novès on the back and the stomach and telling him that he was in great shape for his age!

Even at that first meeting, Guy Novès conveyed this presence that I'd never experienced before. He hardly said a word to me over lunch, which was scary.

He just looked me up and down, save for tapping me once on the stomach and saying "Not bad."

After the meal we went into René's office to sign papers. A big room with leather couches everywhere and rugby photos and paintings decorating the walls. I didn't know where to look. John kept saying "Jaysus Christ, Trevor, you wouldn't see this in Leinster. The AC Milan of rugby," he kept repeating.

I just wanted to sign and get out of there before they realised they had the wrong man and changed their minds!

After I had signed "Loue approuvé" about 20 times on sheets of paper, I was brought on a tour of the club and introduced to the players who were about to start training. One guy stood out to me, David Gerard. I didn't know he was to become my best friend in my first season in Toulouse.

He said he'd had a good night with me in Kielys after we'd played them in Donnybrook in September. He spoke to me in perfect English and said that if I needed anything, in settling in or finding a place to stay, I wasn't to hesitate in calling him. When I eventually did join Toulouse, I did just that. Virtually every day for about a month.

It was a hectic schedule, in and out in a day. I had no time to look at houses or apartments. It was arrive, have lunch, sign and return home. "Are you interested?" "Yes,". Bang, bang, bang.

It was a two-year deal. I signed for €152,000, including a relocation fee of nearly €20,000 and an accommodation allowance of almost €8,000. So all of a sudden, I went from earning €3,000 a month with Leinster to €10,000 a month with Toulouse. It was ridiculous. The whole contract in that first year earned me nearly €180,000. If I played more than 20 games, which I've done every year since, the bonus was approximately €13,000.

Ultimately, though, I didn't really give a damn about the money. If they'd offered me 20 or 30 grand less, I'd still have accepted it gladly. It was, after all, Toulouse. And when you're asked to play for Toulouse, you can't say no. French players have since explained to me that they might have made more money joining other clubs, but reasoned "There's only one Toulouse."

Jean-Michel Rancoule drove us through the centre of Toulouse, taking in the

Stade shop, Place du Capitole and Toulouse's famous bridge, the Pont-Neuf. As we flew home, I kept thinking about Orrell.

When we arrived in Dublin, John said "Look, you're just going to have to ring this guy Saverimutto, and tell him that you're not interested anymore. That you don't want to go to Orrell."

He told me to do it there and then, before we left the airport, which I did. Saverimutto obviously wasn't happy and the next day my move to Toulouse was on the *Planet Rugby* website. I was supposed to be in Orrell that Saturday, but *Planet Rugby* had revealed that I was in Toulouse signing contracts the same day. They had got hold of the story through the photographers and journalists in Toulouse.

The next few days were madness. I got a call from Orrell claiming that I was legally bound to them, that the letter of intent was enough. I was with my solicitor Con O'Leary every day. I had explained the whole situation to him. He spent hours on the phone to Orrell fighting my case, along with his colleagues Michael and Sheila.

Orrell rang Toulouse to tell them that I had already signed for them. Toulouse rang me, and also rang GSM, wanting to know what was going on. We assured them it would be sorted out. I felt bad. The chairman of Orrell wanted to fly over to meet me and talk about more money, etc.

Money was no longer the key issue. It was simply Toulouse. The south of France, *La Ville en Rose* (The Pink City). I fell in love with it straightaway. Paula fell in love with it. I knew there was a great future there for me, her and the kids. It was about playing for the best club in Europe.

Okay, they hadn't won the European Cup for seven years, but for me they were the best team in Europe. It was the chance of a lifetime. And it kept alive my chances of playing for Ireland again. In theory, at least.

Orrell had spoken about their ambitions of playing in the Premiership and the Heineken Cup. And ground-sharing with Wigan at the JJB Stadium. In the end, they never made the Premiership or Europe. They dropped like a stone and went out of business as a professional club. Wasn't I lucky!

Con asked Orrell for a copy of what I had signed, but they wouldn't fax it.

After a week of sleepless nights I was convinced I was going to lose out on both Toulouse and Orrell. It was a very real fear. I remember walking up and down the town, half thinking of throwing myself from a bridge.

"You've got to make a decision," Con told me, "and it's your decision at the end of the day. We don't know if they really do have you legally bound in Orrell. They're not giving us the information. It's really your call."

So I made the call. I would risk the consequences, whatever they were, of going to Toulouse. I've never looked back. I just had that gut feeling that I could finish my career at the top.

I travelled to Toulouse with Paula and the children for five days, paid for by the club, to search for a house and see a bit of the town. They put me up in the Mercure Hotel, just off the Place Wilson. We were wined and dined at night, and during the days I did medicals and trained. I was still training with Leinster, and even though I hadn't told anyone, word was getting out.

Ireland were due to tour New Zealand at the end of that season. As part of the build-up later that week, the President's XV played in Ballymena, the same day that Munster played Leicester in the European Cup final. The lads were full of questions about my possible move.

As I'd missed out on the initial selection for New Zealand, I thought this match would be a good opportunity to prove my point. Ballymena had a few guest players from the other provinces to beef up their side. I played in the second-row, at number six and number eight. After the game I was given a lift home from Victor Costello and Reggie Corrigan. They reckoned I'd had a brilliant game and was sure to be going on the trip.

I was in excellent shape, as I'd been doing a lot of extra work on my own; running etc… I used to run to Celbridge and back three or four times a week. I was determined to arrive in Toulouse 100% fit.

The phone rang during the journey home. It was Brian O'Brien, who said I was wanted at the Glenview; there was a possibility of my going to New Zealand. A few Munster players had picked up knocks in the Heineken Cup final.

I wouldn't be the first player in such circumstances to automatically think "I'd booked a holiday with Paula". I'd also just bought the Spanish apartment and had to go there to close that deal. Then there was the move to Toulouse. My head was spinning.

Added to all that, my shoulder had been troubling me for a few months. When I arrived at the hotel, I met the physio Ailbhe McCormack – a lovely, lovely fella. He told me on the QT that Eddie O'Sullivan wanted me fit, and that I would travel if fit.

Ailbhe treated my shoulder and advised me not to train after lunch. Since the squad was leaving the following Saturday I had the whole week to get it right.

They made an appointment for me later that day in the Blackrock Clinic to see Dr James Colville, an orthopaedic surgeon whose area of expertise is shoulder reconstruction.

After examining me, Jim said it might get through the trip to New Zealand or it could go in the first match. Alternatively, I could undergo an operation. My head began to melt again. Jim had operated on my left shoulder after the 1999 World Cup, so I trusted him completely. He is one of the best in Europe. Amongst his patients have been Brian O'Driscoll and Rob Henderson.

We spoke about Ireland and the move to Toulouse. We agreed that I didn't have a contract with the IRFU (which I didn't) whereas Toulouse would be paying my wages for the next two years. If my shoulder went in New Zealand, where would I be? Talking about it with Jim helped me come to the decision that I had to make.

I went to the Irish management and told them that my shoulder did not require an operation, but that my advice was not to go on tour. Leo Cullen was called into the squad in my place.

If I am to be honest, it killed me. I'd played through a lot of injuries in my career. All players know how to play through pain.

I didn't know then whether I had made the right decision and it still haunts me. My missus often asks "How can you let that haunt you? You've won European Cups!"

I say to her "Paula, if I'd gone on that trip I'd have added to my caps. But I didn't. The shoulder might have gone, and it might not, but I made that decision with Jim. Maybe I could have got through it."

For those few tortuous days I was on the horns of a dilemma. Toulouse *would* be paying my wages. And after putting them through that drawn out transfer saga, to then turn up with a busted shoulder? They might never forgive me.

All the same, I still wonder if I made the right decision. If I'd gone on that trip, how many more caps would I have won? I'll never know. In any case, Leo made his debut in the second test in Auckland, and then played in 13 of Ireland's next 15 tests.

I never won another cap. But a new life was about to begin for myself, Paula and the kids.

CHAPTER 11: 'ALLO 'ALLO!

ERIC MILLER

FORMER IRISH INTERNATIONAL AND LION.

"He was a hard-nosed player, no doubt about it. We got on fine. I didn't dislike him. We were pretty much the same kind of player. When Matt Williams was there, we were fighting for the same position. We were both very aggressive players, so we had our run-ins from time to time, as others did. We got on okay off the pitch. It wasn't that we didn't get on, but we were so hell-bent on getting one-up on each other on the pitch that nothing ever developed off the pitch. I got to know him, but I never got to be great friends with him.

In saying that, I only came back to Leinster from Ulster for a couple of seasons before he went to Toulouse. We were in competition for that short period, and I can't say I knew him too well before I went to the UK. It was definitely one of the fiercest rivalries I ever had, but it was also a healthy one.

We'd have our dust-ups, but the great thing about Trev was he'd forgive and forget straight after training. There weren't any grudges held. Neither of us would step back an inch. Or give each other any room. It wasn't that we fought all the time – we had a couple of run-ins in training, but there were never any bad feelings on my part. It was part of training and that was it. I hope he felt the same, I don't know if he did.

Maybe he did target me, maybe he didn't. We certainly seemed to run into each other a bit more than he did with the others. There's no doubt about it. I'm sure, deep down, if you were to ask him, he probably would say 'yeah'. It took me a while to get into the Leinster team under Matt Williams. Trevor was there, and then I took his place. So there was always that niggle there, but I would call it a healthy one as opposed to a grudge-bearing one.

I totally respected him as a player. I kind of identified with him in some ways, in that he was absolutely 120% on the pitch, like myself. I always tried to be fearless, with full-on aggression. But I would say he was probably his own worst enemy at times.

Leinster have since missed his leadership. He led on the pitch and we missed him when he left. I don't think Leinster have had a personality since then. Leadership comes in many forms, Drico (Brian O'Driscoll) and Paul O'Connell are different leaders in many ways. Trevor led with his heart on his sleeve and he was a great guy to get the dressing-room going. He had the combination of leading on the pitch and in the dressing-room, and that's hard to find.

Leinster haven't really found any one since then, to be honest, and I'd equate it to the Dublin GAA team. There are remarkable similarities. I don't know whether it's a Leinster psyche or a Dublin thing.

He didn't do himself any favours and it's a pity the way his career ended. That said, it was liable to end with a bang. I'm sure he'll look back on the good as well as the bad things. I wasn't either happy or sad to see him go, to be honest; I didn't really feel anything. I was probably just focussing on getting back into the Irish team.

Fair play to him for what he did in Toulouse. He went from being shunned from the Irish squad – and he wasn't the only one – to going over there and making it. And to make a name in that business, you take your hat off to him. I totally respect that. French league rugby is different, and is totally suited to him. He obviously thrived in it."

CHAPTER 12

BIENVENUE EN FRANCE

WELCOME TO OUR WORLD

I was gently eased in as a second-half replacement. Bodies piled on top of me as my head was left sticking out the side of a ruck. Then I was hit by two haymakers. This was my first match in France. A friendly. 'Bienvenue en France'.

By the time the ruck broke up there was blood gushing everywhere. But my pride had been wounded more. Here I was, just arrived, and people were still talking about my fight with Kefu at the World Cup in 1999. That's all Trevor Brennan was really known for in France. The mad Irishman who got into a fight with Kefu.

I went berserk looking for the guy who clobbered me, even pushing the referee out of the way. I had to have 12 stitches in the dressing-room. Seven in my eye and five in my lip.

Toulouse, 2002

HAVING MISSED OUT ON THE 2001 SUMMER TOUR OF NEW ZEALAND WITH THE Irish squad, I was brought to Poland on a pre-season training camp. A classic case of getting the short straw. On the player grapevine, I'd only heard horror stories about these Polish trips. In between the three daily training sessions, we were directed into the cryotherapy chamber. Also known as 'the cry-out chamber'. It was basically a fridge. All we wore was a pair of shorts, a headband, gloves and wooden clogs. Each stretch lasted about three minutes at around minus 100 degrees. I'm not sure what the exact temperature was, but it was brass monkeys'. The body needed about 15 minutes to feel warm again.

At the end of the Poland trip I spoke to Eddie about keeping in contact. He said I'd gone from fourth choice second-row a few months earlier to sixth or seventh at this stage. He also said he'd look at any videos I sent him of my games in Toulouse.

We stayed in Warsaw on our last night in Poland. We had a sing-song in the residents' bar of the hotel with Rob Henderson leading the way. And in an Irish context, that was that.

The next time I saw or heard from Eddie O'Sullivan was the following season, when we beat Munster by a point in the semi-finals of the European Cup. He and Niall O'Donovan came to the changing-room, and we had a chat about the match and my new life in Toulouse. It was all good-humoured. I felt happy that they took time out to come into the Toulouse dressing-room, and thought maybe this offered a glimmer of hope for the summer tour of the Americas.

Barnhall marked my move to Toulouse by laying on a massive barbecue. On a lovely sunny May day, Ian Morgan, Eoin Burke, Ian Stewart and other lads in the club assembled all the tables from the function room onto the grass area in front of the club house. Hotdogs, burgers, chicken fillets and, of course, plenty of beers were provided. A couple of hundred people enjoyed a sing-song with a live band.

It started in daylight and finished well into the night. Fittingly Paul Deering, the man who had put me on the first rung of the ladder, presented me with a lovely Barnhall plaque. It featured a few words in French wishing myself and my family the best of luck in France. It is framed in the pub in Toulouse. As is a lovely photograph they gave me that night of my first try in my first game back with them.

I spent two weeks in Marbella before beginning my new life and career in Toulouse. I trained every day, went easy on the drink, and spent hours by the pool listening to Linguaphone French CDs, trying to pick up the basics of the language.

I left Ireland at the start of July and moved into a hotel. I trained every day with my agent, Laurent Lafitte, who translated everything the physical fitness trainer said or advised. It was difficult in Toulouse for the first few weeks, as their French international players were not due back till August. I trained with the Espoirs (the youths' squad) and heard that Toulouse had lost about ten players and were rebuilding.

I wasn't aware that Franck Belot, Hugues Miorin, Franck Tournaire, Didier Lacroix, Jerome Cazalbou, Stephane Ougier and Christian Califano were leaving and that the squad was being rebuilt – as was the club itself. Their home ground had suffered structural damage from the AZF explosion on September 21st 2001. The club was, in effect, a building site.

The new signings included Jean-Baptiste Elissalde, Vincent Clerc, Yannick Jauzion, Jean-Baptiste Poux and my good self. To be honest, the first few months were awful. It felt like being stuck in a bubble. I had no-one to talk to and was unaware that all these great players had left. When the French guys eventually came back, we went to Montferrand for a pre-season training camp and to play a friendly. It was my first game in the Toulouse red and black.

I was gently eased in as a second-half replacement. Bodies piled on top of me as my head was left sticking out the side of a ruck. Then I was hit by two haymakers. This was my first match in France. A friendly. Bienvenue en France.

By the time the ruck broke up there was blood gushing everywhere. But my pride had been wounded more. Here I was, just arrived, and people were still talking about my fight with Kefu at the World Cup in 1999. That's all Trevor Brennan was really known for in France. The mad Irishman who got into a fight with Kefu.

I went berserk looking for the guy who clobbered me, even pushing the referee out of the way. I had to have 12 stitches in the dressing-room. Seven in my eye and five in my lip. Instead of travelling home with the team, I was given a lift by William Servat and Benoît Lecouls.

When we arrived back in Toulouse, I asked the two lads if they'd come for a drink. I was a bit thirsty. Paula hadn't come over with the kids yet. It was my first time to socialise with any of the players. They agreed to join me for one in the Bar St Pierre. We didn't finish until the early hours. These were two fantastic guys, as I was to discover. We drank jugs of beer followed by pastis. I crashed out on a sofa-bed in Will's house. Those two did me a real favour. I was down in the dumps and needed a blow-out.

On the Monday morning we watched a video of the Montferrand match. Guy Novès commented "I've only one thing to say, never touch a referee." He left it at that. It looked even worse on video. I had literally picked up the referee and put him to one side. Guy never said anything about the fight; he never said anything about going bald-headed for yer man. He just said "never put your hands on a referee". And he was dead right. You should never touch a referee. "Touche pas l'arbitre. Jamais. Jamais."

I swore then that I would never let anything like that occur again in France, but that I also wouldn't let myself be beaten up like that. Every week, for about two months, I seemed to be involved in a tussle. I refused to back down. I know some of the older players in the club respected that, even though Guy was big into discipline.

All told, I was in France for almost six weeks before Paula and the kids came out. It was a funny six weeks. I used to go into a coffee bar called the Cardinal every day for lunch. I'd have a coffee with the boss, a man called Francis, who didn't speak English but was a mad 'Stade' fan. Like apparently everyone else in Toulouse.

He'd blab away in French and I'd nod the head. Then I'd speak English and he'd nod the head. That's how we communicated for about two weeks.

One day when I came in he had a translator, Denis Carrier, a guy who taught English to French-speaking kids, and French to English-speaking kids. It was brilliant. For the first time in a couple of weeks we could actually understand each other. This translator was also a massive Stade fan, and the brother-in-law of Cristian Gajan, the ex-forwards coach at Toulouse until the season before, and now the head coach at Castres.

I was still living in the hotel and I started paying Denis for French lessons. To be honest, I thought the club could have done more. They have improved over the years. When Aidan McCullen was due to come over three years later, I told him to make sure that he had his house, insurance and all that stuff sorted out before-hand. At least he had the advantage of speaking the language from his season as a young fella with Dax.

I explained to Denis that I'd had problems in securing a house and that my wife and kids were still in Ireland. They'd be over when we had our own home rented out and the wife had finished her job. Paula still had to complete her notice.

The club had set up two or three house viewings, but neither they nor the agent were really much help in finding me somewhere to live. Admittedly, the AZF explosion a year previously had left 10,000 people homeless, so it was hard to acquire a house or an apartment, even to rent. There were people with worse problems than me.

I didn't want to buy something before I had my bearings. When Denis arrived one day for a lesson he mentioned a house for rent across the road from his home, but which wouldn't be ready for a few weeks. I went to see it. It was old and needed work, but it was in town, beside schools, shops and, most important of all, beside Denis. He was my saviour. Later, when I had to pay a gas, electricity or phone bill, if I wanted to buy a bed or a table and chairs, or have the kids enrolled in school, it was he who did it. He translated everything for me. I simply couldn't have done that kind of thing on my own.

I said "I'll take it."

While it was being renovated, Denis insisted on putting me up in his spare room. He said it would save me the cost of a hotel. I moved in with his wife Anouk, a beautiful woman, and his son Romain and daughter Sophie. They were very easy-going.

A week later, all my stuff – furniture etc. – arrived from Ireland on a 40 foot lorry. Denis hadn't much storage space. He persuaded some neighbours to store some of my property for me. When the 40 foot lorry arrived, the neighbours helped us unload it. After another week of being fed like a king every night, he informed me that they were off to Biarritz for their holidays. He handed me – a complete stranger until a couple of weeks before (and a Paddy who had just signed for Toulouse) – the keys to his house.

He told me to make myself at home. His mother-in-law, who lived a few miles away, would bring me dinner in the evening or have me over to her house with her husband Patrick. Patrick was an air pilot who had fought in the Vietnam War and who spoke perfect English. We got on well and he recounted some of his child-hood experiences; bringing supplies on his bike to the French resistance and seeing his father shot by the Germans.

Other friends of Denis, Bertrand and his wife Marina, were also very generous. When I eventually moved into the house, Bertrand helped me put beds together and paint the walls. He was a handyman who could do anything. He fitted all the light bulbs and connected up the washing machine and dishwasher – things that I am useless at. Denis had obviously asked him to give me a dig-out.

No money changed hands, even when I stayed in Denis' house – all this was typical of the goodwill I encountered. I bought flowers or chocolates for his wife and presents for the kids – as I did for his mother-in-law. It was the least I could do. I'd have preferred to have dinner with the lads so as to get to know them better, but you couldn't have asked for a more pleasant way to dine every night.

Paula arrived in Lourdes on a direct flight from Dublin. My abiding memory of that day was Danny coming through arrivals in his Superman t-shirt and little Joshie in a buggy. They had grown so much. We drove back to Toulouse. Paula couldn't believe the generosity we were encountering.

Bertrand had taken a day off work to drive me to Lourdes in my sponsored Peugeot 307, as I hadn't a clue where the airport was. It was 11.00 at night when we arrived at his house, where a barbecue was laid on. It was to be the start of some good friendships.

Denis had helped me enrol Danny in a school. (Joshie was only eight months old.) Denis said the best way for Danny to progress in France was to put him straight into a French school. He was only three and a half, he hadn't been to school in Ireland. Kids that age are like sponges, they soak up everything.

The following Monday I was walking down the road with Dan, who started school in Jules Ferry in the Minimes. I was so proud of this little man, at three-and-a-half years old, going from kindergarten at home straight into the unknown – with complete strangers who spoke only French. I thought he was so brave. Paula cried her eyes out for the whole day. It is a superb school, and it wasn't long before he started to pick up the language. He and his brother Josh now speak French fluently, as well as English.

When we found our feet, we discovered a nearby village, called Castelginest, where we bought a house.

The first year, in rugby terms, was brilliant. We lost a few but won a good few more. We trained harder than I had ever trained in Leinster. Much of the work was based on aerobic fitness: running and circuit training in the gym. On the field, we always trained against opposition. When we scrummed it was against 'live' opposition. The same with line-outs and mauls. Team runs, on Tuesdays or Wednesdays, were usually full-on and just like a match i.e. we attacked for 30 minutes, then defended for 30 minutes.

As the Espoirs were our opponents, many of these sessions became heated and sometimes ended in injuries. The Espoirs were always keen to prove a point, as they were the next generation coming through. It was their chance to impress. It was also good for us and kept everyone on their toes.

The amount of fitness work we did was astonishing. We went for long runs and sprints. We might complete around 24 to 36 one hundred metre runs on a Monday, followed by circuit training in the gym. Two sessions on a Tuesday, two on a Wednesday, Thursday off, Friday team run and a match on a Saturday. This would be followed by pool recovery on Sunday. Six days a week you were doing something. Thursday was the only day off.

I found the first few championship matches particularly tough, especially the sheer pace of them. I used to claim I needed a new set of lungs after a match. They ran it from everywhere, off-loaded in the tackle, and made big hits from one to 15. After a few weeks of the coach screaming his head off at me to stay on my feet and not go to ground unless I absolutely had to, I began to get the hang of their style of play. At first, I was terrible. As soon as I ran into someone, I went to ground and waited for a ruck to form. Guy was going mad. "Trevor! Joue debout!" Play standing up!

I really had to adapt. The same with turnovers. Until then, my gut reaction was to pin the ears back and go straight into contact, but the first option with Toulouse was always to look to pass. Guy stressed that this was an opportunity to work the ball to the backs and counter-attack.

I found a new dimension to my game; my kicking. If a Leinster forward kicked a ball, he got a bollicking on Monday. Irish rugby, by comparison, was more about gameplans and field position dictating what you did. If the ball was caught by the full-back inside the 22, 'clear the lines'. With line-outs there was more of a tendency to take the ball down and drive. In your half, the norm was to give the ball to the number ten to kick to touch off mauls, scrums or slow rucks.

In France, they played more off the cuff from their own 22, or opted more for off the top line-outs to get the backs moving quickly. With Toulouse it was like playing with seven or eight Brian O'Driscolls, who ran from everywhere. And who, like Brian, could do magical things with a ball.

Whilst all our internationals were away on Six Nations duty in February 2003, we played a friendly away to Castres. A nothing match, or so I thought, with a team made up mostly of the Espoirs. As we were doing our warm-up, there was a big hullaballoo near the tunnel from the dressing-rooms. I turned around to see what was going on.

Guy Novès was trying to scale the fence onto the pitch but was being prevented from doing so by a massive Samoan/Tongan-looking guy. Guy's assistant coaches, Philippe Rouge-Thomas and Serge Lairle, were trying to explain who he was. But this guy kept repeating "No pass, no entry."

I went over and began hurling abuse at him in English. Philippe and Serge were telling me to get back to the warm-up but I ended up literally peeling yer man off Guy, pulling the barrier open, letting Guy in, getting into a tussle with the security man and returning to the warm-up.

After the game Guy said "You're mad, you're mad." The following Monday, I was called into the President's office. There waiting for me were René Bouscatel, Jean-Michel Rancoule and Guy Novès. I was sure I was in trouble. Perhaps the security guard had lodged a formal complaint, as I remembered ripping his blazer.

Guy asked me "Are you happy in Toulouse?"

Oui.

"Is your wife happy?"

"Yes, my wife is happy."

"Are your kids happy?"

"Yes they're happy."

Unlike my initial meeting with the same three people, I had no agent or anyone else with me, and eventually I get up to leave.

"What is the problem? What is going on?" I asked.

"We want to talk to you about re-signing," Guy said.

"Is it the third year option?" I asked. At the time, I was six months into the first of my initial two-year contract at Toulouse, with an option on a third.

"Yes, with a fourth as well," he explained, adding "We want to look at a four-year deal with you."

They asked me if I wanted to talk to my wife about it. I have to confess I said "No, just give me the pen and I'll sign now." As in that same room the previous summer, I just wanted to sign before they changed their mind. 'What have these guys been drinking? Maybe they'd drunk too much vin rouge with lunch.' I thought to myself 'you might not get a second chance. This is a one-off.'

On returning home I asked Paula how she was and to put on the kettle for a cup of tea. We were still in our rented house in Minimes. We went out to the garden and watched the boys playing. It was a glorious, day. The sun was splitting the heavens. I pictured the swimming pool and jacuzzi we'd planned on putting into our own garden one day.

The longest contract I'd ever signed, for Leinster and Ireland, was for two years. Until this point, rugby had never given me much financial security.

Yet here I was, just a few months into my contract and suddenly, in my late 20s, I was being offered job security for four years. This meant we could afford to buy a house immediately, and in the long run, the financial security to explore the whole idea of buying a pub as well.

So many doors opened as a result of having that four years, and the option of a fifth. It was one of the best days of my career and my life. It really was a turning point. I'd come over here with about €300 in my pocket. I hardly had a bean. I'd thrown every penny into the apartment in Spain.

I was 29. The end of my career was sooner than the beginning and I could see it coming. In fact, I could see it when I first signed a two-year deal with Toulouse. Two years with one of the greatest clubs in the world. That, I thought, would be the end. Then, I thought, I'd be out to graze in the long grass with The Barn. Player/coach maybe. That was always in the back of my mind. The second homecoming for the prodigal son.

I said to Paula "Isn't this the life?"

Paula agreed.

"I've been asked to stay on for another two years at the end of my current contract," I informed her.

"That's great," she said "When do you have to re-sign?"

I laughed a little guiltily. I said that I'd done it straightaway. She laughed too.

But I know I couldn't have done it without her and the kids, that she gave up a good career as a family therapist, to come out here. I know she misses her work, friends and family at times, but she sacrificed all that to allow me to follow my dream and I'll be forever grateful to her for that.

"Two more years?" she said. "What if I had said no?"

I said "Well I'd be flying back and forth a lot!" A rugby player's career is short, and some are shorter than others. I didn't want to have any regrets. That contract would take me up to the age of 33, and ultimately 34. I can't have any complaints. For the last year or two, I was feeling worse the morning after every match. Giving it up is hard to take, as it's been in the blood for the last 23 years. Yes, incredibly, that's right. I've been playing rugby for 23 years.

I reckon that little incident with Guy didn't do any harm. He loved that bit of fighting spirit in me, even though before every game he emphasised the importance of discipline. And you were hammered on the Monday after a game if you gave away penalties. I didn't always understand exactly what he said, but I knew he was angry and I took it well. He was The Boss and I had no problems with that. Better still, he was going to be The Boss for at least three more years.

GUY NOVÈS
TOULOUSE COACH AND FORMER FRENCH INTERNATIONAL WING.
TWICE WINNER OF THE BOUCLIER DE BRENNUS AS A PLAYER WITH STADE
TOULOUSE, WITH WHOM HE PLAYED FOR OVER A DECADE.

"While on the look-out for the 'rare bird' – a player still going strong physically, with talent for either the second or third row – I was immediately drawn to Trevor Brennan's performance during a Leinster v Stade Toulouse European Cup match.

His exemplary behaviour on the pitch made me want to get in touch with him and offer him an interesting but difficult challenge. One which I know Trevor the player – and especially Trevor the man – was well up to.

Today, I know that I was lucky to have found him.

Coaching Trevor was an honour and a pleasure.

On the pitch, he showed previously unsuspected qualities. He was able to make a fresh start by coming to France and he responded, with all his talents, to Stade Toulouse's demands.

Becoming a European champion with our team, he was able to bring a sense of togetherness well beyond simple loyalty. He achieved this through his generosity, his commitment and his precision to the entire team, its coaches, its president and, not least, the Toulouse and French public.

I myself played rugby from 1976 – 1988 and I rediscovered in Trevor's game the behaviour of those amateur players giving their all for their jersey, their colleagues and their club.

He was ever-present in all those unseen contests on the pitch. He was subject to numerous injuries, sometimes leaving him unable to walk or jump on a Monday. Nevertheless, when I'd ask him how he was, Trevor's answer was always "No problem, Guy." I knew that I could count on him.

He has been an indispensable, unquestioned and deeply loved element of our team. Now that he has retired we are, once again, looking for 'the rare bird'.

As Trevor was not a conventional player in marking his team-mates and his opponents on the pitch, he has marked them in everyday life. His assimilation into our city – thanks to his courage, his sociability and his affection for others – makes this man an exceptional human being. He has become a life member of Stade and a Toulouse man forever.

The public were in no doubt at the time of our last match in 2007, when the applause for him on the day exceeded that given to his team-mates. Even to the star of French rugby, Frédéric Michalak.

I'm proud that I was able to share with him the difficult, painful, joyous, and now and then, intimate moments that rugby gives us.

Trevor will not leave a large void because, as he deserves, the club will now rely on him to pass on all his experience – and especially his human qualities – to all our young players.

I'm sure that he'll bring that something extra of his to future generations of Stade Toulouse.

As for me, Trevor has, without knowing it, taught me a lot.

I know that I can count on him.

He knows that he can count on me.

JEAN-MICHEL RANCOULE
TWO-TIME FRENCH CHAMPIONSHIP WINNER WITH TOULOUSE AND NOW CHIEF SCOUT AT TOULOUSE.

"As we were preparing for the 2002-03 season, one of the first thoughts of the staff was that we needed an aggressive player. Not especially Trevor, but an aggressive lock. My job is to find such players. I was in Donnybrook for a game between Leinster and Pontypridd, shortly after the attack on the World Trade Centre, not to watch any one player in particular. Trevor was playing, and when he first touched the ball, I was very surprised by the reaction of the public. There was also a huge cheer when he scored a try. It was even interesting to watch him when he did not have the ball. Whenever he made a tackle, there would be more huge cheers.

So, in April or May of the next year, when Guy Novès and the president said we needed an aggressive lock, I looked through my notes and I remembered Trevor's match. I suggested Trevor to Guy Novès and he said 'Ah, Trevor Brennan. Good. Good.'

I called his agent, and Trevor came over with Paula and his family. The first quality he brought was his heart. At this time in Toulouse, the team did not have much heart and we needed a hard spine, like Fabien Pelous, Yannick Bru, Trevor and Finau Maka. He is a fine player and he brought many things. But the first thing was the heart.

Within six months of coming here, all the public were singing 'Trevor, Trevor' and waving Irish flags. In the main stand, there could be 20 flags. They were Irish fans but also French fans. Before Trevor, no foreign player had that level of support."

CHAPTER 13

ALLEZ, ALLEZ, ALLEZ

**ON PLAYING MUNSTER IN THAT EPIC
2003 HEINEKEN CUP SEMI-FINAL**

The referee came in three minutes before the kick-off and we had our final few words together. What a roar entering the pitch. "Mun-ster, Mun-ster, Mun-ster." "Tou-lou-sain, Tou-lou-sain, Tou-lou-sain."

The chants reverberated around the ground to the backdrop of drums and bodhráns. In the nine months I'd been playing in France, I'd never experienced an atmosphere like this. Le Stadium was full to its 36,000 capacity, including 12,000 Munster fans. A sea of red and black.

Although it's an all-seater stadium, everyone was on their feet, jumping up and down. "Qui ne saute pas n'est pas Toulousain." He who doesn't jump is not Toulousain.

FIVE MONTHS INTO MY CONTRACT, I HAD A PHONE CALL FROM TOM ENGLISH of *The Sunday Times*. He wanted to interview me and talk to my team-mates about my integration into Stade Toulousain. I was happy to receive Tom but, as always, a bit wary of a journalist; just not knowing what kind of a story he might be looking for.

I gave him a tour of the club before one of our training sessions, introduced him to a few of the lads and then left him to his own devices. The players emerged from a gym session and Tom couldn't believe how approachable they were. But that's another difference between French and Irish or English players.

Later that evening I met Tom in town for dinner and brought along David Gerard for company. David speaks English fluently and could give Tom an insight into what the French championship means to French players, and how the European Cup compares. As I had been only a few months at Toulouse, that would have been very difficult for me.

I have to admit I was both surprised and in awe as David explained the history of the trophy they call Le Bouclier de Brennus; the prize for the winners of the French Championship. David explained its century of tradition and how, since the early 1900s, every single club in France and every single player sweated blood to win Le Bouclier. Many failed, and one name stood out for me in particular, the legendary Serge Blanco. Despite such a wonderful career, he had retired without ever winning Le Bouclier de Brennus.

David cited an example from his own career. In 2001, Toulouse beat Montferrand 34-22 in Paris to win Le Bouclier in front of 80,000 people at the Stade de France. David recalled how, a few days later, he carefully loaded the giant wooden shield into the boot of his Peugeot car and covered it with some rugby jerseys to protect it. He then drove 500 kilometres from Toulouse to his family home in Toulon. During the trip he kept wondering what people would say when they saw his precious cargo.

We were interrupted during this story, and the meal, when the chicken wings came with a complimentary bucket of beers sent from a table of Stade Toulouse fans on the other side of the restaurant. I told Tom that this happened on a regular basis. We waved over to the lads and then signed a few autographs when they came over to us. This being a regular haunt of David's, the service was excellent.

As we ate and sipped our beers, David continued his story. He told us that eight members of his family, including his grandmother, had made the three-day, 1,100 kilometres trip to Paris in a hired mini-bus. All to see their boy David help Toulouse claim the Championship shield against Montferrand in front of 80,000 people at the Stade de France.

David eventually arrived outside the family home in Toulon, and was greeted by his father Thierry. That summer I had been to Toulon with Paula, as Thierry had given us the use of his beach apartment for a week, while he moved in with his girlfriend. He had been a parachute jumper in the army and on his arm had a tattoo that read "GO!" – as in "Jump!". He was a seriously hard man and, having left the army, became a welder on the ships in Toulon, where there is a nuclear base. Because the job entailed working with nuclear products, he had been permitted to retire at 50. Thierry had played in the second-row (like David) with Toulon and to this day still has the granite, square-jawed look from that old, hard school of French rugby.

David gave the jersey to his dad, who was overcome. But when Dave opened the boot of his Peugeot 307, his dad was in shock. Until that day, Dave told us, he'd never seen his dad cry. But that day, he let rip. He said he wouldn't touch it because he had too much respect for it.

"Ce n'est pas possible. Le Bouclier de Brennus ici; chez moi." It's not possible. The Bouclier de Brennus here, in my house.

David said "Dad, I won this for you."

His dad kept saying "It's not real. It couldn't be." He'd watched French teams in finals for years on television, but had never dared to dream of a day like this.

The hairs were standing on the back of my head. Does it really mean that much? I didn't realise there was over 100 years of history behind Le Bouclier.

It really is mystical.

In that first year in Toulouse I soon discovered what drove this club, and every other club in France; to win Le Bouclier de Brennus. With that, came a recognition that I hadn't expected. Having signed for one of the biggest clubs in France, and probably the world, I was saluted no matter where I went. I thought I had been fairly well-known around Leixlip and Dublin, and maybe even Limerick, but in Toulouse the recognition was ten or twentyfold.

I couldn't go anywhere. I couldn't bring the young fella to school, because it would take me an hour to get home. I even had to time my trips to the boulangerie when there weren't queues. Everybody wanted to talk to me about how I was integrating, how I was getting on in Toulouse and whether I thought we'd win the next match. In boulangeries, boucheries, supermarchés etc, they shouted 'Allez le Stade', or 'Allez Brennan'. Drivers would hoot their horn at me and hang out the window shouting 'Allez Brennan'. 'Gagne Samedi'. Win on Saturday. To be honest, I didn't mind. It actually gave me a lift, and usually put a smile on my face.

People wanted to talk for ages. Mostly about the French Championship, what it meant to the club, who would win it this year. While others still wanted to revisit the loss to Agen in the semi-finals the previous year. I was told I'd been brought to Stade, not to improve their performances in Europe, but in the French Championship. I was reminded more than once of that semi-final in Montferrand when Stade Toulouse scored three tries to Agen's none, and still managed to lose the game by giving away the seven penalties which Francois Jelez kicked.

The forwards had been out-muscled by Agen and that hurt, as Toulouse packs were renowned for their physicality and their ability to wear teams down when it got physical. I asked Yannick Bru about this. He said that before the semi-final, Guy Novès had warned them about discipline and not to retaliate if provoked.

'Discipline, discipline.' 'No penalties.' I was to hear those words about discipline and not to retaliate many, many times over the next few years.

During his visit, Tom interviewed a few players but I didn't find out what they had said until I read the article. He had spoken to Yannick Bru, who had won six Boucliers in eight years. Yannick had said that the team had become lazy; that all the trophies and the adulation had made them soft; that for all their talent, there was something missing. Guy Novès had more or less said the same, but added that in Brennan he believed he'd found it. When asked what 'it' was, Novès just said "Tres dur." Very hard.

Fabien Pelous, when asked about me, had simply said "He's a proud man." Emile Ntamack had said I was "a warrior". Emile had won everything and done everything, both on and off the field, and was Stade Toulousain to his core. He said I'd played in 90% of the games, had given everything, and hard though it was to admit, "it took an Irishman to come here and remind us what hunger is."

Yannick also said that they had signed me to replace Hugues Miorin, a club legend of 17 years, who he said was irreplaceable. But that thanks to my big heart, I had managed to fill the hole.

I have to admit to feeling pretty happy reading all this. After all, Emile Ntamack and Fabien Pelous were legends, with Fabien on his way to winning 100 caps for France. From that point on I had even more respect for them, and I was even more determined to win something with them.

I'd go to the club on Monday mornings and look at Fabien, knowing it was extremely unlikely that he or any of them had ever read *The Sunday Times*. But, likewise, I didn't want him to know how much his words meant to me. Instead I simply trained harder than I'd ever done before. And when I was handed that Stade Toulousain jersey on match days, I remembered what they'd said about being physical, about being hard and about being there for one another when the shit hit the fan, as it did so many times on a rugby pitch in France and elsewhere in Europe.

Our first game in that season's European Cup was against London Irish. I was brought on as a replacement in the second-row. I can still recall the feeling of joy both on the field, and afterwards in the dressing-room, when told I had made a real impact.

The club always lays on cocktail receptions in a marquee which holds nearly 3,000. That was where I met some London Irish players and their supporters. They were armed with bodhráns and green wigs. It wasn't long before a sing-song started.

The French looked on in amazement. As well as my dad, brother and friends, Bobby Casey, Justin Bishop and Barry Everitt joined in along with the London Irish supporters in a corner of the marquee. As the sing-song gathered pace, the bottles of whiskey, wine, champagne – you name it – which were normally drunk in moderation, were downed until security threw us out at closing time.

Later that night myself, Paula and a few family and friends met the London Irish players and their supporters in the Floridia Bar. They had taken over the bar. Big Bob C was 'DJ" and insisted that I sing. I sang *Willie McBride* as Bob, Barry, Justin and others joined in. What a night.

We played Edinburgh in another pool match in December. I asked David Gerard for a few specific French phrases. The weather on the day of our arrival was awful and the pitch we played on was waterlogged. But the hotel was excellent. Even with my limited French I knew that, as usual, my team-mates were a little dispirited.

Despite the hotel's facilities, these guys love the comforts of home and always find something to complain about. Come match-day, it didn't help the team's mood that Edinburgh had allocated us two adjoining away dressing-rooms because they were so tiny.

So when we went onto the pitch – with the few phrases I'd learned from David – I gave it to the lads in my best French. "Aujourd'hui, on n'a pas d'excuses." Today there are no excuses. "The flight was great, the hotel was five-star, the food was good."

Well, it was for me anyway. But all these little things can easily disturb the French mentality. If the food's not right, if the bed's not right, if the pitch isn't right, if it's not just like Toulouse, they can be thrown off their game. It's the same even within France. They are just so used to their home comforts, and when taken away from them, heads can drop.

"On doit etre fort mentalement." We must be strong mentally. They looked at me in amazement. The game itself was a good deal tougher than the 30-9 scoreline might suggest, and in our cramped adjoining dressing-rooms afterwards, the lads really slagged me. No more would they speak English. "Tu es vraiment Francais." You're a Frenchman now!

We could afford to lose our final pool game away to London Irish and still secure a home quarter-final against Northampton. Which was unforgettable in its own way. The day before the match, Northampton were left outside the stadium on their bus. They weren't allowed in on time for their captain's run – while we continued training. Before the game, Guy Novès gave an unusual team talk in our hotel to psyche up the lads. He began with the usual stuff. No penalties, no cards, defence.

At this point I usually switch off and go into my own little world, to think about my own personal little match. I've done this whether the coach was speaking

English, French or Russian.

Then suddenly, a few words made my ears prick. "Trevor ... Trevor ... la famille ... Angleterre ... Trevor ... la mere ... la grandmere"

I was thinking "What the f***?" He used my name about ten times! "What's going on here?" I asked myself.

When Guy had finished, everybody looked at me. "What the hell did he say?" Lads were hitting me on the back as we left the room and boarded the bus, saying "Today was for me," and "bastards." "Merde, merde, merde ..."

On the journey to the ground I asked Yannick Bru, who speaks English fluently, to tell me what Guy had said.

He revealed that Guy had criticised the English at length; about the war, the French versus the English and the Irish versus the English; that he then mentioned me, The Famine, my grandmother, the English, the raping and pillaging, people being burnt out of their homes, the suppression of the 1916 Rising and how the English were still in our country.

It mightn't have been a strictly accurate interpretation of history; he may have taken some liberties!

Yannick asked if it was all true. I just nodded and went quiet until we reached the ground. In the dressing room I did my ritual 'shinking' – which to the uninitiated is thinking and shitting at the same time – generally brought on by nerves. I always spend a few moments like that on my own, gathering my thoughts and thinking about the game.

Then I laughed out loud. "Off his trolley" How did he think of all that stuff to wind the boys up?"

We won that match 32-16 to earn a semi-final against the legendary Munster Monsters. However, after a big hit on Andrew Blowers in the Northampton game, my leg was hanging off me and I had an MRI scan on the Monday. A torn thigh muscle. Balls, balls, balls. Guy said he'd give me until match day to prove my fitness, which was two weeks away. There was no match I wanted to play in more than this one.

I wasn't involved in the Championship game against Pau on the intervening weekend. Toulouse hammered them. I concentrated on upper body weights and 20 minute cycles for two weeks. I tried to stay out of town as the quarter-final neared because Toulouse gradually turned red with Munster supporters, and I knew I needed to focus.

As with the Northampton quarter-final, the semi-final was to be played in the Toulouse FC stadium with its 37,000 capacity. With Munster getting half the allocation, the demand for tickets was ferocious. A huge queue formed outside the ticket office on the Monday, as a story in one paper claimed that Munster were handing back 5,000 of their tickets. Some chance of that happening!

Typical of Guy, there was no mention of the Munster match until the video analysis of the Pau game on the Monday. He then said that Ronan O'Gara would make us pay if we did this or that, or gave away penalties. Guy also told me that the press conference was all about TB; would he play or would he not? To make a long story short I did, and it was incredible.

On the Thursday, the first of three scorchers in a row, myself, Emile Ntamack and Yann Delaigue did a 20 minute run. By the end of it, I looked like a tomato. I love the sun, but the sun doesn't love me.

The team was announced and I was picked to start, but I still had to do the team run on the Friday. Some Irish people staying in our hotel told me that the Munster fans had taken over Toulouse. The city had never quite experienced anything like this kind of invasion before – nor this level of alcohol consumption. I'd say the bars and hotels wished Toulouse were playing Munster every week.

The team run went brilliantly for me. I still had the torn 'quad', but I could run on it. On Friday night I roomed with Finau Maka, otherwise known as Jimi Hendrix. Maka wants to be a rock star more than a rugby star. One of these guys still living in the '70s. Around town, a few Munster supporters sported the Maka wig. Finau was surprised about the level of his Irish support, having never set foot in the country.

There were the usual antics at the team meal the night before the game. Being the last to sit down at our table, my chair had been left soaked through by a bottle of water. I found out Yann Delaigue, sitting to my right, was the culprit. Toward the end of the meal, I ordered a cup of tea with a hot pot of water and left my spoon soaking in it for ten minutes. Then I left Yann running around the room with a third degree burn on his left ear. The lads hadn't seen this one before. 'The hot spoon' is an old Peter Clohessy trick.

Newspapers, such as *Midi Olympique*, speculated whether TB would play or not. The boys thought this was amusing, as it seemed that the game was all about me. So I had them translate an old Oscar Wilde saying "There's only one thing worse than being talked about, and that's not being talked about."

After dinner, Guy Novès said that the antics had become a little out of control. Maybe it was the manager being hit with a bread roll while the soup was being served. Maybe it was Freddy Michalak being stabbed with a fork by Fabien Pelous. And Xavier Garbajosa's back was killing him as he'd been attacked by Patrice

Collazo for stealing his phone. I'm not making any of this up. It goes on with most teams, but seemed to happen a bit more with Toulouse.

A sleepless night followed as I played the match in my mind about four times. I had been in bed by 10, but I remember it was about 3.20am when I last looked at my watch. We'd won the match, we'd lost the match, I'd been sent off, Quinny had been sent-off. And meanwhile Jimi Hendrix had been snoring since 11.00pm.

The atmosphere on the way to the stadium was unlike any other game I'd known in Toulouse. A few riot police swelled the customary police escort, kicking cars, vans, bikes or anything else that blocked our passage through the traffic. Most of the players were on their feet observing all this. When we arrived at the ground, the bus came to a halt. Thousands had gathered outside, around the hot dog stands and beer tents. The bus started to rock as the Munster fans began to good-naturedly bang it while *You'll Never Beat The Irish* rang out on my discman. It was time to change the CD.

I'd had another x-ray later in the week and was told to give it a go and see if it held up. While the lads went out for a walk around the pitch as usual, I waited until the warm-up.

Guy grabbed me in the dressing-room "You are friends of the Irish? You are afraid of the Irish, no?"

And he kept pushing me. I'd been doing some more French with Denis during the week as I had a hunch Guy might say something like this.

So I just said "dans une autre vie peut-etre", in another life maybe, "mais pas dans celle-ci", but not in this one.

"Bonne réponse," he said. Good answer. And he walked out onto the pitch for the warm-up with his arm around me. He does that, little niggly things to wind you up before a game.

The referee came in three minutes before the kick-off and we had our final few words together. What a roar entering the pitch. "Mun-ster, Mun-ster, Mun-ster." "Tou-lou-sain, Tou-lou-sain, Tou-lou-sain." The chants reverberated around the ground to the backdrop of drums and bodhráns. In the nine months I'd been playing in France, I'd never experienced an atmosphere like this. Le Stadium was full to its 37,000 capacity, including 12,000 Munster fans. A sea of red and black.

Although it's an all-seater stadium, everyone was on their feet, jumping up and down. "Qui ne saute pas n'est pas Toulousain." He who doesn't jump is not Toulou-sain.

Munster dominated the first 40, line-outs, scrums, mauls. All we could do was defend. Every time there was a turnover Rog put us 60 metres back down the pitch. I busted my eye in the first five minutes tackling Hendo on one of his crash balls. I stood up as one eye closed immediately and said "Thanks for that one, Hendo." I couldn't see out of the eye for the rest of the game, and was a bit dizzy for about ten minutes. He sustained a sore ear. As well as a burst ear drum.

In the second-half, the game began to flow more. Which suited the Toulouse boys. Two good sides, and one had to lose. Guy made some inspired changes. Freddy Michalak was switched to out-half when Jean-Baptiste Élissalde was introduced for Yann Delaigue, and Freddy scored an opportunist try to help us to a one-point win. I don't know if I've ever played in a game that was so intense and nail-biting right to the very end.

After the match I swapped jerseys with Alan Quinlan. I respect him as a player, he plays on the edge and makes life difficult for you all day. Wouldn't have it any other way. Hendo, Quinny, Axel and a few of the lads also came into the dressing-room for a good chat.

When I emerged from my shower who should be standing there but Eddie O'Sullivan and Niall O'Donovan. I hadn't had any contact from them since moving to Toulouse. It was nice of them to take the time out and wish me well for the final. They asked me how life was in France. I gave them a few French phrases and had a little laugh with them. "Not a bother on you, Brennan." said Niallo.

Alan Gaffney is a man for whom I've always had huge respect. And I know, from my time there, that every Leinster player did as well. Munster were very lucky to have a man like him. Typical of the bloke, he made time to find me in the tent after the match.

I remember a Munster player coming to me in the car park and I said bad luck to him. "Never mind that," he said, "just beat those Leinster f****** in the final."

That night remains a blur of drinking and sing-songs with Munster fans around the city. I recovered by watching the Leinster-Perpignan semi-final with more Munster fans in Place de St Pierre. For them, bad and all as it was to lose to us, even worse had been the thought that if they couldn't win it, Leinster might.

My old boys in blue were just 80 minutes away from ensuring I met them in a Heineken Cup final in Lansdowne Road. And that's really what should have happened. Whether Leinster froze on the day, or just thought they had to turn up, I don't know. But they were capable of playing much better than they did. I felt sorry for friends like Denis, Victor and Reggie – guys who had been there for a long time. Drawn at Lansdowne Road in the quarters, semis and final, I thought it was a great opportunity for them, and I had been looking forward to playing against them in the final.

Even so, it seemed as if my professional rugby career had come full circle, back to where it all started. It was also a chance to give the fingers to some people, I suppose. Every Toulouse player gave me tickets for the final – and how I needed them! I allocated about ten to family and friends as well as supporters from Leixlip and Barnhall who hired five buses which departed from various pubs. Even the GAA club provided coaches. I made time to meet my brother in the club, and my old fella in Killiney Castle, for them to divvy out the tickets.

Over dinner the night before the final with Fabien Pelous, Emile Ntamack and David Gerard, they had suggested that I lead the team out onto the Lansdowne Road pitch. "No, no, no. No way," I said. "Fabien, you're the captain. You lead the team out."

"No," Fabien insisted. "This is for you. This is your city. This is your ground."

"Ok so, lads." I agreed.

Disappointingly only 26,000 turned up as it would have been a full house if either Leinster or Munster had been in the final. On the other hand, it didn't matter a damn to me if there was just one man and his dog there. It was a European Cup final. And not only did we go out and win the thing, but I played 70 minutes.

Before the game, I lined up in front of the Toulouse players, and the only thing I remember is Emile Ntamack coming up to me. He put his arm around me, and spoke into my ear. "This is your day. This is your home. All this season has come down to this. We're going to do it for you today."

If I wasn't pumped up enough playing in a European Cup final in my home town already, I was after those words from Emile. I tried to keep my head down. Tunnel vision. I raced onto the pitch, straight past the Cup, and as I turned around started to say "C'mon lads, let's get stuck into... Where is everybody?" No-one had followed me onto the pitch, not even the Perpignan players. I was left there standing on my own for what seemed like 30 seconds. An eternity. I had to give it the old 'Mary McAleese'; a royal wave to all four corners of Lansdowne Road.

Vincent Clerc and Yannick Jauzion were on fire that day. Clerc scored the try that rewarded our good start. We went well up front, although we had some problems against Perpignan's scrum. And Yann Delaigue kicked beautifully to keep us in front.

Finau Maka was brought on for me with about ten minutes to go and I was joined on the sidelines by all the gang, Paula, Danny, Joshie, the da, his mate Corky, Mick Davern (a garda sergeant in Donnybrook), Pat Cremin (the owner of Kielys) and more. Pat was telling me to come up to Kielys and bring the Cup and the Toulouse boys with me.

We looked to be cruising, until Manny Edmonds shaped to kick one way and then kicked, banana-style, to the blindside wing for Pascal Bomati to score. With about a minute to go, it was suddenly a one-score game. But thankfully, there were no more scares and I raced onto the pitch to join the lads. I brought both Danny and Joshie with me, but Joshie was bawling crying. He was a bit scared by it all, and Diarmaid Murphy, then the ERC press officer, who subsequently became its commercial manager, took him back to Paula at the side of the pitch.

I've rarely felt so elated as I did in those few minutes; running to the Toulouse fans at the Lansdowne Road end of the ground or when we all posed with the Cup. I'd played for Leinster since 1996 and we'd had some great wins. I'd also won Celtic Leagues, interpros and AILs. But I don't think we ever really believed we could win a European Cup. Toulouse players did believe, and I truly felt a part of them.

I'd come and earned my place at number six ahead of Finau Maka. I started every Heineken Cup match bar the first against London Irish. Of all the teams I'd played with, I felt that this was the least political when it came to selection. I'd earned my place on merit.

To be honest, I was also already thinking of getting a few pints in. The players were telling me that there would be thousands waiting for us in Toulouse, no matter what time we returned. I couldn't wait. We'd earned this night. I'd earned this night.

The post-match dinner was held in a marquee on the Lansdowne back pitch, but I was still being hounded by people in Kielys to make it to the pub and Pat, the owner, asked me if I could bring the Cup. "I won't be able to bring the Cup but I'll definitely be there," I told him. So I grabbed David Gerard and we skipped the post-match dinner. The only problem was transport.

Fortunately, I bumped into Diarmaid Murphy in the car park and he generously dropped myself and Dave to Kielys, where we had three hours of bliss.

Champagne, trays of 'Die Hards' and pints flowed. There were about 200 there from Barnhall, Bective and St Mary's, and the Barnhall boys sang their club version of *Red is the Rose*, i.e. *Blue is the Rose*. David couldn't believe it. His father, some of his family and his friends were there too. I'd arranged accommodation for them with my family – anybody who could have them, rather than hotels – as a return favour for all the generosity David and his father had shown me.

Time ticked away, as it does when you're enjoying yourself, before Dave pointed out to me that the Toulouse plane was due to leave in about an hour. I went to Pat and said "Listen, taxi, as quick as possible. We need to be in the airport ASAP."

Pat came back to me within minutes and said "I'll do one better for you. I've got you a police escort." Mick Davern, a great organiser who has been deeply involved in rugby through coaching and his own son's playing career, said "There's a car outside with two of the lads who are going that way. They'll drop you over."

About 100 people gathered outside Kielys to cheer us off and we were driven across town from Donnybrook to Dublin Airport in about 15 minutes – with sirens blaring and lights flashing. "This would never happen in France. Never," said David. We arrived the same time as the team bus. They were suitably impressed.

Anyone reading this book will probably think I'm an alcoholic – along with many other rugby players. But it's worth putting this in context. We mightn't have been out on the lash for weeks or even months before this game, and it was a European Cup final. On match nights, players let loose. And although French players are more reserved, when they do celebrate, they go for it.

As the players had forecast, a crowd of about 2,000 were waiting for us in Blagnac Airport. I happened to be holding the Cup in the terminal building beside the carousel when some fella grabbed it from me. I had to climb over the security barriers to reclaim it. Blagnac, as anybody who has been there will know, is a small airport and cars were double-parked everywhere.

Myself and a few of the lads climbed through the coach's air hatch to parade the Cup on the roof, the driver taking off at about five miles an hour while we were still up there. The club laid on a free bar for anyone and everyone who turned up.

At about 4.00am, a few of the lads said some of the night clubs and bars wanted to see us. By the time the night ended for me I think it was around 9.00am the next day. I might as well have been brought home in a wheelbarrow, for all I remember, before William Servat and Benoît Lecouls put me to bed on a pull-out sofa in William's apartment. Paula and the kids were still in Ireland.

The next day, a civic reception was arranged on Place du Capitole. The team manager phoned me inquiring after the whereabouts of the Cup. Through his inquiries, he'd learnt that we'd been seen with the Cup while drinking and eating steaks in the market at seven that morning.

"Have you seen the Cup?"

"Oh, the last time I saw it was this morning in the market and I haven't seen it since."

He explained as there was a reception at 2.00pm and as the Cup was nowhere to be found, they were phoning every player.

"Well, I haven't seen it," and hung up on him.

I turned over and heard a clink. The Cup was under the sheets. I'd gone to bed with it. I immediately tried to ring him, but his phone was engaged for half an hour. I eventually got through to him.

"Listen, I have the Cup. Myself and the Cup slept together last night."

After that European Cup final we had two very heavy weeks of travelling, partying and playing. It was physically and mentally draining, and it caught up with us. To begin with, we had two massive days' celebrations, and paraded the Heineken Cup trophy in the Place du Capitole the day after the final. Then a trip to Paris to meet President Jacques Chirac. I felt none of this should have been done until the French Championship was completed.

We went back into training on the Tuesday, and travelled to Montpellier on the Wednesday before our semi-final against Agen three days later. This was our revenge match for the semi-final 12 months before – they'd beaten us 21-15 even though Toulouse had scored the only two tries of the game. It was that defeat which had prompted Guy's summer cull.

Stade Francais would have the advantage of playing, and winning, their semi-final in the cool of a Friday night in Bordeaux, whereas our semi-final was played under a burning Saturday afternoon sun. The temperature reached 45 degrees that day. Our warm-up felt like the longest warm-up ever. I tried to slink away and do my warm-up in the shade of the stand, but Guy spotted me.

"There's nowhere to hide, get out here!" he said. "In a few minutes you're going to be doing this for real." Ah, bottles of water over my head. I wanted the warm up to be over and the match hadn't even started.

There was a fight from the first kick-off. This was why myself – and others – had been brought to Toulouse, to put it up to Agen, and we did. The first few minutes of that game were hell for leather, punches everywhere. But every Toulouse player stood up that day.

Although Guy had given his usual spiel about the need for discipline, the forwards had agreed that we weren't going to take any shite from Agen. So when I saw David Gerard and Christian Labit getting in a scrap with two of their boys, I must have run about 20 yards to help him out. Then someone else came in. Discipline? What discipline?!

Agen didn't know what hit them. They had lost the final the year before to Biarritz, after extra time,. They were the form team coming into the semi-finals, and were favourites to beat us again. But we were not taking a backward step that day. Serge Lairle had told us where François Gelez would kick his restarts and, right enough, he put them in the same spot, i.e. on me, all afternoon. I caught some lovely balls that day and it felt good. Though I've never been so happy to be substituted, as happened after an hour.

I didn't watch the last 20 minutes. I just lay down on the bench and had some of the lads pour bottles of water over me. I was so dehydrated that when we won, and everyone was jumping about, I had to find a cool corner in the dressing-room and stick my head in an ice bag. I kept opening and closing the door of a big Coca-Cola fridge in the dressing-room and put my head inside. Not that it made any difference. The lads just laughed at the Paddy trying to climb into the fridge with all the ice bags.

That was a big win, and was celebrated accordingly. We had another civic reception for the Heineken Cup win, this time in Toulouse. I thought that was madness. We went to Paris on the Wednesday prior to the final.

Again, madness in my view. Too much time to kill. We stayed in a big, old chateau about an hour's drive from Paris – or an hour and a half in traffic. It was hot. Oppressive. Almost suffocating. I felt tired and yet restless.

It took more than an hour on the Friday to drive to the Stade de France for our team run. The same for the journey back – even with a police escort! We should have stayed in Paris that night. Instead, we had to pack our bags on Saturday morning as we were moving to a hotel in Paris after the final.

The night before the final, I walked around the grounds with Guy and he informed me that in his previous 12 finals with Toulouse they'd never lost.

He told me "Tomorrow you'll be a French champion!"

"That's great," I replied.

"I have never lost a final, do you know that?"

"Ah Jaysus no, I didn't know that, no."

"You will be a champion tomorrow," he vowed.

There must have been 40 people from Leixlip and I felt so disappointed for them, because I'd got them tickets amongst the hardcore Toulouse fans behind one of the goalposts. We gave it everything for 40 minutes and led 15-6 after 33 minutes – all penalties. Yann Delaigue was sharing the kicking duties with Freddy Michalak.

But this was to be Fabien Galthie's day of destiny. He had been the main talking point in the build-up, being one of those legends of French rugby never to have won Le Bouclier in his time with Colomiers. He had joined Stade Francais for a year at the end of his career to reach his Holy Grail.

Just before half-time he sneaked in off a maul for a try and then Brian Lieben-berg kicked a long-range penalty to put them in front. You could see heads dropping in the dressing room at half-time. I'd also sustained a dead leg just before the end of the first-half.

Early in the second-half I was left one on one against their full-back, Ignacio

Corletto. Rather than attack him, I just froze. I stood still, thinking he'd try to run through me, but he sidestepped me and all I managed was an ankle tap. No use five metres from my own line. Just to remind me, one newspaper the next day carried a picture of him scoring with me ankle tapping him. Diego Dominguez added another penalty. Suddenly it was 29-15 and game over. They went on to win 32-18. I was taken off for the last 20 minutes or so and found it impossible to watch.

Our dressing-room was full of champagne bottles. Nobody opened one. Lads cried for ages, and I became a little pissed off with them because they wouldn't stop. I was thinking "We lost it, get in the shower. Get on with it, get on the bus, let's go to the reception."

Individual players stayed quiet at first, analysing their own performances. At the reception, the coaching staff were in a corner talking amongst themselves. They had recalled Patrice Collazo from injury to the front row and had dropped Jean-Baptiste Poux, who'd had a good European Cup final.

I thought that was a mistake. We should have stuck with the team that beat Perpignan and Agen. Patrice missed a tackle on Galthie for that try and gave away a few penalties. But Guy makes very few mistakes, so who am I to question his selections?

The reception picked up as the night wore on. You don't get many opportunities to sing in France, so when I was asked I belted out *Stand By Me*. They loved it, the band picked up on it straightaway and they shouted "more, more". I did an Oasis number then, *Today Is Gonna Be The Day* and all the lads joined me on stage.

It's funny. You can have a great season, win 23 matches, lose only six, and yet because it all ends in defeat in the final of the French Championship, you feel miserable for days. At least the whole squad had a good end-of-season blow-out. We went to the Moulin Rouge, from where I went across the road to an Irish bar, called Sullivans. This was where I first discussed with the barman the idea of an Irish bar in Toulouse.

In my view, the biggest lesson the club should learn, with the benefit of hindsight, is to postpone any civic reception or celebrations until the French Championship is completed.

Season over. Still, I returned to Dublin a happy man. Myself and Paula were married in Mauritius on June 20th. Neither of us believed in rushing into things. We'd decided that a traditional wedding wasn't for us, given we'd already had two kids and bought our house. A friend who worked in a travel agent suggested a five-star hotel in Mauritius where you could combine a marriage ceremony along with a holiday. We went for a week, chilled out on the beach where you could have your beer and a sandwich brought to you. Got a bit of a tan. Went to Port Louis in Mauritius for the correct papers, arranged a priest and planned for the wedding day.

Errol, my brother and best man, his girlfriend Ciara, Paula's best friend Marie Ellis and her husband Mark, as well as Paula's sister Jacinta and her husband Lofty, travelled over. While my mother looked after the kids.

We wanted it to be small, intimate and easy-going. On the big day, I sunbathed until mid-day, drank a couple of beers with Errol, Mark and Lofty, was back in my apartment by ten past one for a shower and a shave, on the beach at half-one, and married by 2.00pm.

I wore a pair of sandals and a Hugo Boss suit I'd bought on the journey out. Because it was so casual, Paula had bought a suit rather than a wedding dress, but the day before our wedding, while going out for a run, I met some designers from the apartment next to us. When they asked me what we were doing in Mauritius, I told them we were getting married the next day.

They were with Storm Wedding Dresses, based in Glasgow, and had six models with them for a 'shoot'. They explained they had 50-odd dresses and suggested Paula try on a few. When I asked Paula later if she'd had any joy, she said that none of them had fitted; they were all size six or eight.

Oh well, we agreed it had been nice of them to offer.

Of course, the next day Paula arrived on the beach in an absolutely stunning dress worth about ten grand, and a crystal handbag that one of the designers had lent her. She looked amazing.

We invited the designer, and another couple who were being married that day, to dinner. The hotel set up a marquee on the beach next to the restaurant. A long table, for 12 people, was lit entirely by lamps and candles.

The ocean washed up ten feet away. The weather was perfect and you couldn't have asked for more. Unlike many weddings I've attended, or seen at close hand, it was stress-free. Just a dream wedding.

Back in Ireland, we organised a reception party in the Springfield Hotel, where we'd first met all those years before, working for the Hannigans. They provided a function room without charge and a fantastic deal on the food. We had a band and a DJ, and it was more like a 21st. We invited anybody and everybody. A lovely night.

Our new life, my new career, were up and running. We were champions of Europe. Paula and I were married at last.

Life was good.

EMILE NTAMACK
FORMER TOULOUSE AND FRENCH WINGER.

"I like Trevor, because he's got a big heart.

In his first season in Toulouse, we all knew that Trevor had the 'fighting Irish spirit'. And when he spoke to the team during a warm-up... Well, I may have been the captain, but Trevor was leading the way. I couldn't believe it! Here was an Irishman speaking French. And I thought 'Ok, we are French, we have fighting spirit too.' He spoke from his heart, and inspired us.

He arrived as a stranger, but soon, everyone is saying 'We should play like Trevor'. He is an example to us all. A leader. Everyone was saying this. Even the coaches would say 'Look at Trevor. He is a Professional.'

He had this aura. An incredible man. And he was good for the team. He showed us another side – that we had to keep working and trying every day. Toulouse has many faces, but he added another face.

When Toulouse is moving the ball, they are incredible. But against a great defence, or if game gets rough, we can have difficulties. Trevor gave us the means to overcome this.

With Trevor, we had another weapon. In tough games, he showed us the right way. No team can have 15 Frédéric Michalaks, or 15 Emile Ntamacks, or 15 Trevor Brennans. But if you have the right balance, the result is good.

Everybody knows the man on the field, this warrior. But he is a good man in life, too. He has visited my home with his family. To me, he is no stranger. He is a Frenchman. He is *Toulousain*. Now, he has his pub, and I hope that he will stay in Toulouse.

Of course, all his family live in Ireland. But everybody here loves him, and I think this is his real home."

CHAPTER 14

C'EST LA VIE

ON LIVING THE LIFE IN FRANCE

Integrating ourselves was a little difficult at first. When you were invited to someone's house for dinner, you quickly learnt not to bring gifts; a bottle of wine, flowers or a cake would be sufficient. They're more frugal, and more authentic. Not speaking the native tongue, your language can be a bit stilted, but that was easier for me than for Paula.

The invites were usually from people involved in the club, and I was working in an environment where learning the language was easier.

I also struggle with my own company. I like to get out and about, and meet people. Had Paula and my roles been reversed, I'm not sure I could have taken more than a year out here.

WE RETURNED FROM OUR WEDDING TO OUR NEWLY BOUGHT HOUSE IN Castelginest in June 2003, and to a burning hot French summer. There were 10,000 heat-related deaths in France that year. That was followed by a deluge of autumn rain and floods which forced 10,000 people from their homes in Marseilles alone.

Maybe there's a better water drainage system in Toulouse, but we didn't have it too bad. My ma had been trying to reach me for days and when I twigged why I really wound her up. "Jaysus Ma, I'm surprised you got through to me. We've had to move upstairs and the fire brigade are going around handing in bread and water. I can see the neighbours across the road up on their roof." I had her going for a good while!

In August, Liam Toland and the legend that is Gary Halpin had driven 900 kilometres on their bikes in one day from Normandy. They stayed for five days. I cracked open the barbecue and had the blow-up swimming pool filled for the boys. Gazza told jokes and had us in stitches – so much so that the neighbours wanted to come in and join the party.

The old mates are the best, but I'd never been happier than in my second year in Toulouse. I'd come to love the French way of life. Castelginest has given us a nice village lifestyle, with its little café and three or four boulangeries, two schools, a college across the road from the house, and – typical of any village here – all the sports facilities you could want. There are three football pitches right in front of the house where I sometimes go for a run or have a kick around with the boys.

We felt more settled that year, and I felt more settled in the team. I was 29, and Ireland was still very much in my thoughts. I followed the team's progress and all squad, and team, announcements closely. I still wanted to play for Ireland, I still hoped.

Although the winters can be every bit as harsh, you are guaranteed six months of sunshine a year. With each passing year I became more recognisable wherever I went. You can walk down a street and some fella will run across the road, drag you into a bar to sign a Toulouse jersey, and give you a free beer.

When walking along a street one day with Liam Toland, he couldn't believe it when a man wearing a lovely, crisp white shirt, black trousers and black loafers approached me and said "Brennan, Brennan, can you sign me? Sign me."

"Sign what?" I said.

"Can you sign me?"

I said "What do I sign, paper?"

"No, my shirt."

So I write "Bonne chance, Trevor Brennan" on his new white shirt. I try to add a personal touch.

Your euro goes a lot further over here. In most little café bars or bistros you can have a starter, main course and a dessert for about eleven euro. We can eat out three or four times a week if we want to. When given a table, a plate of jambon, a basket of bread and a glass of wine could be sent over. Or an aperitif on the house. If family or mates are with me, they are dead impressed. If I'm in the village to buy a paper and have a coffee in the local café, it might only be €1.80. I'm told it's on the house when I attempt to pay.

The French have their down side, of course, like any people. I hated the way they drive and I still do. Zebra crossings are decorations. They're aggressive, they're unfriendly, they're bad-mannered. To be honest I find the same in supermarkets, where they also jump queues. I have a love-hate relationship with French people depending on the situation and the place; anyone who comes on holidays to France understands what I mean.

Against that, they've very generous, helpful and kind. If I had to get work done on the house, somebody invariably knew somebody who could help me out. Being a Stade Toulouse rugby player had many advantages. Not only could I avail of the various club sponsors, but people went out of their way to help me. And that warmth is still there.

Integrating ourselves was a little difficult at first. When you were invited to someone's house for dinner, you quickly learnt not to bring gifts; a bottle of wine, flowers or a cake would be sufficient. They're more frugal, and more authentic. Not speaking the native tongue, your language can be a bit stilted, but that was easier for me than Paula. The invites were usually from people involved in the club, and I was working in an environment where learning the language was easier.

I also struggle with my own company. I like to get out and about, and meet people. Had Paula and my roles been reversed, I'm not sure I could have taken more than a year out here. It helped too that anything they put in front of me, I'd eat it. I'd never eaten rabbit in my life but, what the hell. The same with foie gras, pigs' legs, whatever. But Paula is a vegetarian.

Once we took about a dozen friends and family to a famous steak restaurant in town called Chez Carmen. It's the oldest steakhouse in Toulouse, opposite the abattoir. We all ordered steaks except for Paula when I said to the waiter.

"Ma femme est végétarienne."

"Végétarienne? Magnifique, pas de probleme. Je fais quelque chose."

"Merci. Bien, bien."

I turned to Paula and re-assured her. "I told you they'd be able to do something."

The steaks arrived along with a plate for Paula.

"Madame, la végétarienne… voila."

And he put down a plate of chips, without so much as a tomato or a green leaf of any kind.

The World Cup in Australia meant that we were without our internationals from June 8th to the last week of November. We played seven League Cup matches and won two out of three Championship games without the boys – and squeezed in a visit home for Ronnie's wedding in November – but when they returned they brought something back to the club immediately. Just a presence that had been missing.

In the boys first game back, we beat Narbonne 25-5 away. Coming off his World

Cup semi-final disappointment against England, Freddy Michalak was awesome.

He executed the exact same cross-kick for a try as he had done against Ireland in the quarter-final. His touch kicking and place kicking were first class, even when the 3-4,000 Narbonne fans started chanting 'Jonny Wilkinson, the best out-half in the world' to try and put him off. He also scored a brilliant individual try from halfway. He's some player.

A torn quadricep kept me out of the opening Heineken Cup game away to Edinburgh, which we lost. We were less than convincing beating Leeds 16-3 at home. Fabien Pelous' illness meant I was switched to second row on the day of the match. That weekend, Rory came over with my brother Errol and his wife Ciara. By Sunday morning, we were all in need of a cure. As the tablets didn't work, the father suggested we all go to Lourdes for a miracle cure.

Myself, Rory, Errol, Ciara, Paula and the two kids headed off on the hour-and-a-half trip down the M62. None of them had ever been to Lourdes before but it was about my sixth visit. I was beginning to feel like Padre Pio.

Our first Christmas in France was probably good for my wallet and my head, if not so much for my body. The holiday period is a busy time in the French Championship. The first of three games was a 1,200 kilometres round trip by coach to Grenoble, at the foot of the Alps, for a Friday night game. We won in front of a 12,000 capacity crowd.

One of the boys had grabbed two bottles of whiskey and a few bottles of coke, as well as a few glasses, from the post-match reception. There was a game of cards and a bit of a sing-song at the back of the coach. The boys knew the first three verses of *Dirty 'Oul Town*; my target was to teach them the remaining three by the end of the season. However, two bottles of whiskey between 20 fellas can last only so long and soon the spirits dried up too. We arrived home at 6.30am.

The next day, I bought the turkey and ham in the local market, but by the following Thursday, Christmas Eve, the smell from the fridge wasn't too good. I rang the brother, an ex-butcher, and he advised me to chuck it in the bin. So we had ham and veg but no turkey on our first Christmas Day in France. It transpired that the seal on the fridge had broken; the ma had a right go at me for buying a turkey five days before Christmas Day.

We beat Perpignan on Christmas week to draw level with them in our pool in the French Championship, after which I met up with Mick O'Driscoll for a few beers. We made our way wearily to Biarritz on January 3rd with an under-strength team for a post-Christmas stuffing.

I picked up a dead arm from the first kick-off but, like most players in those situations, just hoped it would go away. I didn't want to hold my hand up to be taken off after just a few minutes. I don't know whether it was brave or stupid but I stuck it out for 80 minutes and suffered the consequences. At the Monday video session, it was pointed out that I had missed three tackles. But I hadn't the courage to tell Novès that my shoulder was hanging off. Pas d'excuse.

Because of the World Cup, four rounds of the Heineken Cup were run off in January. We resumed our campaign at home to the Ospreys on a near waterlogged pitch. Jean-Baptiste Élissalde, who's not much bigger than Peter Stringer, was advised by the boys that he'd need armbands – as some of the puddles on the pitch were like lakes. The requests to the bag man were a little different too. Normally it's for shin pads and bicycle shorts, but some asked him for life jackets.

To gain a bonus point win was an achievement, but the stand-out performer of the night was Gavin Henson. Or more to the point, his stand-up hair. No matter what happened to him, every hair was still upright by the end of the game. The lads wanted me to find out what hair gel he used as they reckoned someone should market it.

Toulouse is definitely a funny old team. People often ask me why French teams are so unpredictable, and I have to admit I'm none the wiser after being with them for five years. We hadn't played well all season and went to the Ospreys for the return match a week later – at which point not one of the six French sides had won away from home.

We flew to Bristol in one of those small 50/60 seater jobs followed by a two-and-a-half hour bus journey to Swansea as we hit peak traffic. The lads were pissed off, and slagged off the club management for doing things on the cheap. The next night was cold and wet. All the old excuses were there. Yet we had a bonus point by half time. We played the way we had trained the previous Tuesday.

It was punishing stuff. We'd play for two minutes, then break for one minute. We did this 12 times, then took a three minute break. All told, we did this 36 times. I thought I was going to die. The emphasis was on keeping the ball off the ground. The coach didn't want slow ball. He wanted us to keep it alive and offload in the tackle. This was the Toulouse style of play, and that night in Swansea, it clicked.

Away to Leeds, we were level 3-all at half-time when Guy reminded us that we could still go out of the Heineken Cup. We dug deep for four tries in the second-half. I didn't cover myself in glory when interviewed by Sky Sports afterwards.

First question: were you happy with the win? Yes. Were you happy to score four tries and get a bonus point? Yes. Final question: what did the coach say to you at half-time to turn your performance around? Pause. Response: "Get your effin' fingers out of your arses, lads." It's never a good idea to curse, especially on television. Plonker Trevor!

We knew we needed another bonus point at home to Edinburgh to earn a home quarter-final, and that kind of pressure, especially at home, brings out the best in the lads. We won 33-0, to earn a quarter-final in Le Stadium against Edinburgh again.

That was the season I had my one and only call-up to an Irish squad in five years with Toulouse when Victor Costello was a doubt for the match away to England. On the team bus en route to Beziers for a championship game (which we lost by a point), I checked my messages and was stunned to hear the voice of Joan Breslin from the IRFU.

"Eddie wants you over for a training session on Sunday."

I was in shock for a while, but that plane journey couldn't come quickly enough. When I arrived at the City West Hotel, the first person I ran into was Shaggy (Shane Horgan). It was a funny feeling being back in an Irish training camp.

He showed me around the hotel, where, to reach your room you'd need a two-day camel ride. Things had certainly become more professional. I was particularly impressed by the amount of video analysis done by Mervyn Murphy. And England did play pretty much as the lads had been told they would.

Niall O'Donovan handed me a ten-page folder, all A4 pages, of the line-out options. "What's this Niallo, are you taking the piss?" There must have been 140 line-out options, even though you might use just ten in a match.

I nearly made the game too. Vic picked up an ankle injury in training and Eddie O'Sullivan told me to stay on for another day as cover. Vic was okay though. At the airport, the rest of the lads went through the departure gates for London whereas I returned to Toulouse. I watched them beat England in the Killarney pub.

Our Heineken Cup quarter-final in front of a capacity crowd against Edinburgh was the usual Toulouse story. We underperformed for the first 40, at the end of which we led 10-7, but the second-half was much better. Guy Novès emptied the bench – he always uses his replacements well. We won 36-10.

We returned to camp on Monday. Freddy Michalak, being the showman he is, wore an Armani suit for a sponsor's lunch, but first had to have some physio. He was also wearing black socks and black knicks, which made the deep heat less visible when Yannick Bru applied it while Freddy was in the shower.

We all pretended to mind our own business as we chatted and waited. Slowly but surely he became more agitated and suddenly parts of an Armani suit were thrown to the ground as Freddy raced back into the shower to try and cool himself down.

That night, a neighbour asked if I'd visit a friend of his in hospital who had been in a motorbike crash. The injured lad was only 17 but had suffered brain damage. As he is a big Stade Toulouse fan, I brought him along some posters and t-shirts. Seeing him was a reminder of how grateful we should be for our health.

In the build-up to the Heineken Cup semi-final, the squad was given an exhibition of weight lifting by the Maka brothers. They have freakish natural strength. When I came into the gym that morning, a crowd of about six or eight players had gathered around the weights bench in the corner, going "Ooh la la." Izzy was warming up with 140 kilos and Fino the same. I'd be lucky to do one max bench of 140.

Then they packed on another 20 kilos, then another 20. Finau does 180, Izzy does 180 and then 200 kilos. By the end the whole team was watching this in awe.

When you think that Izzy's own body weight is 140 kilos, lifting 200 is quite amazing. Needless to say, it was the talk of the club for the rest of the afternoon.

It didn't help that the only two English speakers in the squad when I joined were the Makas. Because they were useless! At lunchtime in the club canteen, I'd join them at the table and they'd be chattering away in Tongan.

I'd interrupt them by saying "It's bad enough dealing with these Frogs speaking French without you two speaking Tongan."

"Oh yes, sorry Trev. It's just our way."

"Well I don't give a shite now lads, speak English as you're sitting here at the table with me." But I'd have to keep telling them.

The Makas are the youngest two of a family of twelve boys and four girls. They were reared by their grandparents in Tonga for the first few years before being brought to New Zealand after their parents had settled there. Their father worked in a tyre factory but died of cancer when Izzy was 16 or 17.

Izzy played for the New Zealand schools and won four caps for the All Blacks. Finau probably could have played for the All Blacks as well, and has been asked plenty of times by Tonga. He declined in the hope that he would play for France when he qualified in 2006 through residency. He finally opted to play for Tonga in the 2007 World Cup.

I've never seen either of them in a fight. They're strong, but gentle and passive, and don't smoke or drink. Izzy drove me and my kids one day and I had to ask him to turn the music off. He was listening to this mellow Tongan music, "Wakatee-keetoo boo... tiki tiki..."

He's one of the nicest people you could meet. They live quite frugally, and both send money home to their mother, brothers and sisters. They've already bought a house in New Zealand to accommodate their mother and the families of three of their brothers and sisters.

In Tonga, Izzy is regarded as something of a king. Whenever he went home in the off-season they used to 'spit a pig' for him nearly every night. He always turned up for pre-season late and overweight. He'd have his own training programme, mostly of laps around the pitch. You wouldn't call it running, more waddling. The coaches would tick him off, but he would just say "yeah, yeah." He's just incredibly laid back.

Finau is a different character, more outgoing and more talkative. Izzy is a natural number eight, whereas Finau is a six or seven; a big, strong hitter. Neither of them are lineout options because you'd need a JCB to lift them. Messing in training one day, four of us couldn't lift Izzy, who reckons he was dropped from the All Blacks because he wasn't a lineout option. But could he lift!

Izzy went to play in Japan in 2006, and he's been missed. We didn't have a natural number eight in the two years after he left; loads of sixes and sevens, but no eights.

At that time of the season, the superstitious French mindset becomes more noticeable. For big games, some of the coaching staff are known to 'bless' the pitch.

The blessing consists of pouring holy water from Lourdes on the try lines at either end of the pitch.

Four days before we played Biarritz, our physical preparation coach, Zéba Troaré, started handing out lucky charms; as he had done at around the same stage the year before.

His bag contained around 40 bronze masks, each the size of a key ring, and 40 bracelets. As you took a bronze mask from the bag you had to say a little prayer, effectively asking the mask to grant you a wish. The bracelet had three colours: bronze, gold and silver, representing the earth, fire and air.

His father is the Minister of Sport in Burkino Faso, and he's from a village called Teukogo, of about 30,000. Traoré competed in the 100 metres at the Barcelona Olympics in 1992 and is the physical preparation trainer for both the club and the French Olympic athletes based in Toulouse. Each year around this time, some of the lads put salt in their socks, or wear lucky underpants that look like they were fit for the bin years ago.

My uncle George, my mate Peter Smith, Bull McKeogh, Ronnie, my father and a few more came over for the semi-final. Paula went back to Ireland for the weekend with the boys, and the lads stayed in the house. I remember ringing the little bar in the village the night before the game asking the owner how they were getting on. He said they'd started singing; that they'd had sixteen 'demis' each – which was eight pints – and none of the locals had ever seen this before. He'd taken a month's takings in one day!

The day of the game in Bordeaux was an April scorcher. Guy Novès speaks to everyone individually in the dressing-room before every match. When he took me aside he started pushing me, pulling my jersey, and then punching me in the chest.

"If they start pushing you, don't react. If they start pulling you, don't react. If they start punching you, don't react. Trevor Brennan, il est mort aujourd'hui."

In other words I was to lie dead on the ground rather than react.

It was very tough, very physical, and our defence won it for us. Izzy came on as an impact replacement and was exactly that. He was on fire that day. Serge Betsen, poor old Betsen, fractured his cheekbone and broke his jaw in trying to tackle Izzy. He missed the rest of the season. Izzy ran clean over him to score the decisive try and we won the game. I was happy with my own game too. I'd made a high tackle count and a zero penalty count.

Bordeaux is only a two and a half hour drive from Toulouse. The sun was splitting the heavens. I was given permission to go home in a convoy of family, friends and supporters in cars festooned in stickers and flags. We stopped at a petrol station where several hundred supporters had congregated in the picnic area and were chanting "Tou-lou-sain. Tou-lou-sain." They mobbed me and good-naturedly shook the car. The Stade bus stopped at the same station, and the players climbed onto the roof for an impromptu sing-song.

Twelve of us went out for a meal that night to El Teatro, which also had a disco with live music on another floor. At about 2.00am, when we were ready to leave, a supporter who owns another night club sent over four bottles of champagne. So, needless to say, we stayed just a little bit longer.

That night, I rang Alan Gaffney at about 1.00am to wish him the best of luck in Munster's semi-final the next day against Wasps. I'm not sure he appreciated it.

"Best of luck now Gaff in that match tomorrow, right? Genuinely, I really hope you win, right? Honestly, I hope you do it!"

"Alright Trev, thanks very much mate." he said, adding "Listen go and get the head down kid."

I was genuinely disappointed for Gaff and the Munster lads; players like Quinny, Foley, Wally, Rog, Stringer and Hendo, when they lost to Wasps. After losing to us in the semi-final 12 months before, I felt it would have been justice for them to get to the final. I thought they deserved it.

Admittedly, it probably took a little pressure off me. I would have been inundated with requests for interviews from both the Irish and French media, and also for tickets for that final. Instead, because of their defeat, I could have got hundreds of tickets from Munster supporters who'd bought them in advance.

The Irish Women's rugby squad came to Toulouse, and as well as a good sing-song with them one night in the Killarney, I showed them around the club. Axel's sister, Rosie Foley, bought an extra large Toulouse jersey. When I asked her who it was for, she said it was for her father Brendan. I said "I'd love to see him walking around Limerick in that."

The seasons here are much more punishing, and by now we were on a tread-mill. My first game against Brive was, as the boys had warned, probably the most physical game I'd ever played up front since joining Toulouse. Trailing 9-6 at half-time, we won 29-9. But our preparations for the Heineken Cup final weren't helped by our next game – at home to Stade Francais.

When we arrived in the ground it seemed like there were about 18,000 Toulouse fans to 1,000 Stade Francais supporters. The atmosphere was electric. It was 9-all at half-time; another very physical game up front. We were close to their line three times near the end but Stade Francais held on to win 22-16. They were becoming a bit of a bogey side. Everyone was bitterly disappointed because it was a game we had targeted. The defeat meant we would have to beat Biarritz home and away to qualify for the last four. What's more, those games had been scheduled for the Wednesday and Saturday immediately following the Heineken Cup final in Twick-enham.

I bought about 30 Heineken Cup final tickets for family and friends, and the Red Army was very visible around the ground when the coach arrived at Twickenham that day.

'All right, Brennan, best of luck today. We're all with you."

"We'll be shouting for you, Brennan."

That final against Wasps was probably the most expansive game of rugby I've ever played in. Our offloading, support play and continuity was magnificent.

We had done a lot of video work analysing their rush defence and decided that the best way of cracking it was to keep offloading in the tackle. Keep the ball alive and moving as much as we could. We played everything off the top of line-outs. We met them head on too, and tore into them defensively as they did to us. We earned a few good turnovers. We targeted their big ball carriers, like Trevor Leota, Lawrence Dallaglio and Simon Shaw.

Ironically, of the three Heineken Cup finals in a row that we played in, that was our best performance. We should never have lost that day. Unfortunately for us it was probably the best defensive performance Toulouse ever came up against in my five years there. I think much of that is down to Shaun Edwards, their defensive coach and former Great Britain rugby league player.

Even so, Guy had made very good use of the bench, and Izzy Maka had turned the game around. There looked to be only one winner in my view heading towards extra time at 20-all. But in the last play of the match, Clément Poitrenaud was guiding the ball over his own line for a 22 drop out when Rob Howley chased up his own grubber kick and pounced for the winning try. There was no time for the restart. Game over. It was terrible.

No-one blamed Clément. We all had a part to play in that defeat, myself included. I missed a few tackles, and one on Alex King about 30 metres out led to one of their tries. I blamed myself. Besides, it should never have come down to that last play.

I was disappointed with myself too, for not going into their dressing-room to congratulate Warren Gatland. When Munster had lost to us the year before, Quinny, Foley and a few of their boys came in to us and wished me well. They were big men to do that. I remember Gatty was dragged onto the pitch by Dallaglio and Edwards, and he was in his own zone, having his picture taken and celebrating.

I went in to our dressing-room and consoled Clément, who sat in the corner crying his eyes out. When I asked a few of the Wasps lads later where Gatty was, he was still at the press conference.

A large crowd outside the dressing-room area clapped us onto the bus. I wanted to get drunk and forget about it. I thought about some things, like not having my normal boots. I'd left them behind in Toulouse and had to get a brand new pair from one of the Papies in the club who look after all the gear.

Another custom of mine is never to go onto the pitch for the walkabout.

Some players do, in their suits or tracksuits, and kick or throw balls around, or talk amongst themselves or even with some of the opposition. I would have in my early days, but in the last six or seven years of my career I stopped.

I liked staying in the dressing room; withdrawing into my own zone; getting my strapping done; thinking about the game; not being distracted in any way. For example, if you walked the pitch beforehand, and met Mick Galwey, Quinny or Claw, you couldn't but say hello. But, for me, in those 80 minutes nobody is your friend.

However, on that day I did. Maybe it was another sign of bad luck. David Gerard came into our dressing-room to tell me I had to go out, there was something I had to see. I went out through the Twickenham tunnel and saw a 20 foot tricolour. "Best of luck Trev." I laughed when I saw it, and waved toward the crowd who held it.

Afterwards I thought about all these little bad omens. French players can be a bit too superstitious themselves, and I thought about some of the lads staying up late for a séance with an ouija board.

I was looking for excuses. My head was going mad. This defeat was really driving me nuts.

We had to play Biarritz back to back on the ensuing Wednesday and Saturday. No-one gave us any chance of beating Biarritz away. We hadn't won there in years. Few away teams do. But out of the disappointment of losing that final to Wasps came a huge desire to get something from the season. And as I've seen in my time here, when Toulouse backs are against the wall it usually focuses the mindset. I started the game at number six. Everybody stepped up to the plate, and who else but Clément Poitrenaud scored two tries in a Man of the Match performance. We beat them again in Toulouse on the Saturday and reached the semi-finals.

We played Perpignan in Montpellier, which was much closer for their supporters to reach. Even with this, the Perpignan supporters arrived in unusually large numbers. They arrived in strength the day before as well, judging by the noise outside our hotel. Driving by in convoys, hooting their horns, chanting our names, and even setting off the hotel fire alarm during the night. They kept us awake until the early hours. Groups stationed themselves outside and played music loudly. I went to the curtains a couple of times and was tempted to go down, but there were too many of them. And, of course, any sign of life from the rooms only encouraged them.

It was a mixed night's sleep and was the talk of the squad the next morning.

"C'est fou. C'est fou." It's crazy. It's crazy.

It was one of those infuriating, frustrating games. They went ahead early on and we spent the whole game chasing the lead. We had a long range penalty late on to win it but lost 18-16. Afterwards, I went into the Perpignan dressing-room to wish Mick O'Driscoll the best of luck. Not easy.

To play such great rugby, to reach a European Cup final, to lose that so cruelly, to dig so deep to reach the French semi-finals against all odds, and then to lose that by a kick, was one of the biggest let downs I've ever experienced. I think the team was good enough to beat Stade Francais in the final that year. Of all the seasons, that one really knocked us for six.

It was, in many ways, a successful season, and yet it was a failure when it mattered. It happens, to Toulouse and many other good teams, in rugby and plenty of other sports, and it usually happens to good sides. Look at Munster's years of heartbreak in the Heineken Cup. With another bounce or kick of the ball, we could have won both the European Cup and Le Bouclier de Brennus. We won neither. That's life, that's sport. But the more ambitious the club, the more disappointing it is.

I spent the whole summer thinking about that Heineken Cup final and the French Championship. We stayed in France, to acquaint ourselves better with the country. I went to the Féria; the bullfighting in Fenouillet in Toulouse.

I'd never been to a bullfight before. Didier Lacoix organised the tickets and, to my surprise, I discovered they were just behind the wooden fence, in the front row. This is where the bullfighters warm up and where, occasionally, a bull has a run at the fence!

I was astonished that the bull was half dead before the matador came out with his red blanket, having being run ragged and spiked several times by the picadores.

Later that evening Malcolm O'Kelly rang to say he was on holidays in Toulouse with his then girlfriend, Stephanie, now his wife. I told him to jump in a taxi and join me in Fenouillet, kick-starting a long night.

By the end of the night, myself, Mal and Stephanie were playing drinking games with some of the locals. This involved drinking beer drained through a sock, out of a dirty runner and a few others I'd better not mention. Passing by one of the tented bars, I could hear the noise of the French Championship final on a screen inside and had a quick glimpse. Stade Francais were running away with it but I couldn't bring myself to look for more than a couple of minutes.

We ended up in the Stade Toulouse bar where we bumped into the president of the club, René Bouscatel. He was impressed to meet Mal and began questioning me about his contractual position with Leinster and Ireland; his age; the whole lot. He was interested in signing him.

About an hour later myself and Mal somehow ended up doing a dance on the bar with our shirts off.

At the time I'd thought it a great night, but now I was saying to myself "Balls, never again." And I think Mal messed up his chances of ever playing for Toulouse after his performance in the bar that night!

Spending my first summer in France – I went to St Tropez, to Toulon and other places – I couldn't believe how much I was recognised. It hit home with me how big Toulouse were, and how well respected they are as a club all over France. Especially across the south.

❖❖❖

IN MY FIRST YEAR IN TOULOUSE, I ONLY EVER DRANK IN THE KILLARNEY, OR occasionally Mulligans, even though they are a bit out of town. A Paddy on Tour. Yet even those two genuine Irish bars, like everywhere else in Toulouse, would never show a game of soccer, much less an All-Ireland final. Plasma screens in pubs just wasn't the done thing. And this in a town of 800,000 people, with many Irish, British or English-speaking people amongst those employed by Airbus.

After the 2003 French Championship final in Paris, I crossed the road from the Moulin Rouge into an Irish bar, where I met one of the owners, an Irishman, George McIlroy. A busy bar with plenty of plasma screens showing sport, he said they were thinking of a similar venture in Toulouse. The germ of an idea was sewn in my head. This would definitely work in Toulouse.

As the summer went by, there was no word from George. I had spoken to Beamish before going to Ireland for my summer holidays. When I returned I had a chat with a girl called Colette Buckley, who worked in the Killarney. A lovely girl from Tipperary, and a hard worker, she had been in Toulouse for six or seven years. She and her boyfriend Dave, who worked in Airbus, had heard that I was thinking of opening an Irish bar in Toulouse. They said they would like to become involved themselves.

Beamish know what pubs might come on the market, and that this pub had been closed for over a year. The owner Patrick had relocated to La Bege, the equivalent of a UCI cinema, which could provide 600 meals a day – whereas there was no parking around this place. We bought a 99-year lease for a relatively bargain price.

Our funds were tight enough, but we did most of the donkey work ourselves. I spent the summer of 2003 with Dave, Colette and a few other Irish expats who helped us; breaking up floors, pulling down ceilings, chipping at the walls, knocking down tiles, filling skips and bringing all the rubbish to the scrap yards. It was a good three months' hard slog before the Irish Pub Company arrived. The floors and all the beer pipes had to be laid, the walls to be plastered, dry-lined and painted, the ceilings to be suspended and the air conditioning installed. When all that was done, the IPC sent their fitters to Toulouse for three weeks, working day and night to furnish the bar.

We didn't want to call it Mulligan's, Dicey Riley's or whatever. We considered The Corner Bar or Brennan's Bar, before agreeing, originally, on The French Paddy. But one night I came home and my wife told me she had read a book of Irish folklore to my son Danny and one tale was about an Irish goddess called De Danu.

Paula did some further research and it transpired that De Danu had been a goddess of water in the 13th century. The bar is beside a river and we also needed a name that rolled off the tongue for the French. I ran it past Colette and Dave, and we had our name. I should really have a brief history of the name inscribed on the wall or framed.

We haven't looked back really. It's even better than I pictured it. We couldn't possibly have imagined it would do as well as it has. The Heineken Cup, and especially the visits of Munster and Leinster, have been a godsend. They filled the Kyriad Hotel across the road and then filled the bar. They have their Irish breakfast, play their bodhráns and never cause an ounce of trouble. It was like an old style lock-in.

The same with the Llanelli, Edinburgh, Leicester, Wasps and Northampton fans. When Leinster came here in 2006, they filled the street and the bridge across the road, stopping the traffic up and down. So I'm reliably informed, anyway! I didn't want to show my face after the devastating defeat to my old team.

The summer months will be quieter with the rugby and football seasons closing down, as the locals migrate to the coast for their holidays. Before the World Cup came to France in 2007, I'd been a hands-off owner, but due to my enforced absence from Stade Toulouse, I have become more hands-on.

Paula says all sports people are essentially selfish, and she's right. I've been used to playing and partying every weekend. Paula says I can still go to Toulouse games, as long as I take Danny with me and no doubt, Joshua too, before long. A few weeks ago I took him to a home match, and afterwards Dan came with me to the pub to collect glasses.

"Now Da, be careful you don't drink too much. Ma says we can't be home too late."

The Bairns

Daniel was born on September 23rd, 1998, a day after my 25th birthday. I was training with the Irish squad and based in the Glenview Hotel when Paula rang me.

"I've been in for a scan and the doctor says I'm having the baby tomorrow."

"You're what?"

"I have to be induced."

So I called to Gatty's room and said to him "I have to go into town tomorrow."

"For what?" he asked.

"My missus is having a baby," I explained.

"How do you know?"

"She told me, she said she has to be induced."

So he said "Go head, you couldn't miss that."

The next day I went in to the Coombe with Paula. She was allocated a room with six other women of whom only one, I think, was Irish. We went public rather than private. Your first child is a beautiful and moving experience. I practically delivered Daniel with the nurse, because they were shorthanded, due to two more deliveries happening at the same time.

After his safe delivery, I was given a shopping list – babygros and so forth. Then came the phone calls to all the family and friends. I enjoyed an absolutely brilliant night with my family, Paula's family and friends, before going back to Alan Graham's house where he concocted a few cocktails.

I woke up the next day not feeling too well, but at least the Irish squad was no longer in camp. The following night, the 24th, I went with Victor Costello, Denis Hickie and Emmet Byrne to an annual charity event for cancer research organised by the auctioneer Pat Gunne.

We bought a horse for a day; £2,000 between four of us. It was trained by Dermot Weld. I haven't a clue what's happened to the animal since then. At least it was for a good cause. It was a good night too, I slept on someone's floor and when I visited Paula in the Coombe the next day, I think I pushed her out of the bed into the visitors' chair while I slept for about three hours. Having shared a room with other new mothers and screaming babies during the night, she was wrecked herself, and I don't think she was too impressed.

We chose the name Danny, or Daniel Damien; the second name in tribute to my brother. I loved the song *Danny Boy*. Paula loved it too and I'd often sung it at parties. I'd had it in my head from the word go, and thought it was a strong Irish name.

He often says to me "How come there's so many famous people with my name, like Daniel Carter, Daniel Day-Lewis? Why have I got such a famous name da?" He loves his name.

He's an amazing kid, who seems way ahead of his years. He learned to talk quickly. He's great with numbers, loves playing and is very outgoing. He can talk to anyone about any topic.

He loves sport, and loves his food too; always has. He doesn't play rugby. I tried him at about five, but I think he was just too young. He plays hockey with friends from school, and does judo too. I suppose, like most families, we were that bit harder on Danny. We let Joshie away with murder, but it was the same when I grew up. Poor Ronnie had an awful time. We screamed loudest but Ronnie was blamed. And likewise, poor Danny was probably wrongly blamed too. But I'm becoming wiser about that other little fella, because he screams for everything.

Joshua, or Joshie, was born on November 28th, 2001. That time we went through books of names and had plenty of options. I liked the album *The Joshua Tree*, and admired Josh Kronfeld as a player. It was also unusual. I didn't know too many people called Joshua, so there was no-one to put me off the name.

Joshie was also born in the Coombe. I did celebrate with family and friends, but more quietly, because I was minding Danny, and it was the middle of the rugby season. He's very similar to myself; absolutely mad. He's always on the go, wiry and hard, but never stops crying. He's also good-natured. Himself and his brother kill each other, but despite the three year age difference, Joshie is well able for Dan. He winds him up, but Dan always holds back.

Unlike Dan, he has no interest in school, and has little interest in sport as yet. We hope he will, not least because he's so competitive. If they simply kick a ball against the garden wall, he has to win. If he doesn't win, he comes in bawling, then goes out again five minutes later.

He's his own man, but if I could pick a sport for Josh – although Paula won't let me – I'd put him into a boxing club straight away. He's really tough. People say he's a replica of me at that age, a mini Me. I think his character is like mine too, but I'm delighted to have him. He has his good points too!

We worried that he might be a little jealous of the third boy, Bobby Valentine, who's six years younger, but he isn't. He's very loving and caring towards him, he wouldn't let anyone harm Bobby, and he's always minding him.

For Bobby's birth, it was different over here. Because of the French healthcare system, Paula had a room all to herself. Probably like one in the Blackrock Clinic; shower, toilet and her own mini kitchen. The Coombe was fine and they treated us brilliantly, but it's tough sharing with six or seven women and their babies.

I suppose it didn't do any harm that the hospital director was a Stade Toulouse fan. He even sent Paula flowers and made sure she had the best of everything. It seemed like another world.

They have incredible medical back-up – check-ups, scans and blood tests every month – all the way through the pregnancy. I thought it was pretty top-notch stuff.

Because the Six Nations was on at the time of Bobby's birth, there were about 21 of us left in the club – players not involved in the Six Nations, doctors, physios and so forth. I invited them all to the bar.

We had a bit of a meal, laid on two kegs of beer, and we definitely wet the baby's head!

When the boys returned from Six Nations' duty, they heard about the night and wanted to re-enact it. So about 28 of us threw €40 apiece into a kitty, laid on another meal in De Danu, and a few kegs in the bar to kick-start another night. Every player made it except Fabien Pelous, who had something else on, and Gareth Thomas.

We're trying to acquire an Irish passport for Bobby. We see him as being Irish. He was born on Valentine's Day, 2007, so that explains his second name. He is Bobby, not Robert. I always like the name Bobby – I'd played with Bobby Casey. Of all the names we'd gone through, I was given the choice if it was a boy, and Paula the choice if it was a girl. I liked Valentine as well, as one of my team-mates is Valentin Courrent. We're very lucky with Bobby. Whereas the other two were wild, and cried plenty in the early days, we sometimes forget he's there. He cries only when he's hungry, like any baby.

None of our kids were really planned but we're delighted with them all. That's probably the last of it now. We were happy with two, but we're even happier with three!

CHAPTER 14: C'EST LA VIE

WARREN GATLAND
EX-WAIKATO AND ALL BLACK HOOKER, FORMER COACH OF GALWEGIANS, CONNACHT, IRELAND AND WASPS, CURRENTLY COACH OF WAIKATO.

"What I loved about Trevor was just his passion. Everything about Trevor was heart-on-the-sleeve, both on and off the field. You knew when he was playing he'd give you 100%, and you knew if he came off the bench he'd give you 100%. And if he wasn't in the 22, he was the one guy cheering the loudest and shouting for the team and being happy about the performance if you won.

Those are the sort of qualities that you want in a guy in your squad. I think he had the ability to galvanise a team with his sense of humour and his ability to have sing-songs and bring the guys in the squad together; I think that was also one of his strengths.

As a player, he was tough, physical and uncompromising. You put the biggest, toughest guy in front of him and he'd be the first in line to tackle him. To be honest, it probably took me a little bit of time to appreciate him.

I suppose I would describe him as a Munster player playing for Leinster. He should have been born in Limerick, because to me he epitomises what Munster rugby is all about; being passionate, uncompromising and loyal.

I've huge amount of respect for him too. I remember in the second test in South Africa he was on the bench, and there was quite a lot of niggle and fighting. I was accused of sending him on the field to provoke more trouble, but my implicit instructions to Trevor were "Whatever you do, do not get sent-off. Don't get involved in anything." And in fairness he didn't.

In hindsight he should have won more than the 13 caps he won when I was Irish coach. He was probably a bit unlucky in terms of playing in France. He didn't have the exposure he would have had when he was playing in Ireland. But if you look at it, he was starting every week for Toulouse at the time they were probably the best team in Europe.

Even when we (Wasps) beat them in the Heineken Cup final, they were probably a better team than us. We took a couple of tries and defended well, but I watched them a few times and thought 'you've got to be pretty good if you're starting every week for that team. You've got to have some respect.'

And I thought to myself that he was the sort of guy you could have had in an Irish team fulfilling a number of roles. He could have started for you, he could have come off the bench, he could have been your six, or your lock, or your lock/six cover so that you could carry another loose forward.

In a World Cup, he's the sort of guy you'd want in your squad to fulfil that role.

I've a huge amount of respect for him as a bloke. There's nothing pretentious about Trevor. He told you what he was thinking and he gave you what he was thinking, you had to admire that.

As a Kiwi, there were a number of things I could relate to; not everything in his life was easy. He'd worked at some odd jobs and worked his way up; not everything was a bed of roses for him to come through and make it. In a middle-class dominated sport, as it is in Ireland, I think it takes a lot to do that.

I know now that if you turn up somewhere and you see Trevor in a bar, you'd have a few pints and reminisce about times. For me, that's the most special part about being involved with a team.

There are certain people with whom you wouldn't do that, but Trevor is definitely one of those guys. You might not see him for a number of years, but when you eventually get to go out, you'd enjoy his company all over.

And there'd be mutual respect, I suppose. You'd both have a good time."

CHAPTER 15

VICTOIRE ENCORE

UP FRONT AND PHYSICAL

Rugby isn't like soccer. It's gladiatorial. First and foremost it's a physical fight. It's full-on, it's dogged. That's what rugby is about. You can be friendly and be best buddies and be shaking hands after games ... and sometimes you can't.

THE HEINEKEN CUP: WIN NUMBER TWO

The full-time whistle was a fantastic feeling. For me personally, it was better than winning two years before in Lansdowne Road, when I had led the team onto the pitch and experienced all the other emotions involved in returning to Dublin with Toulouse. In putting the final against Wasps to bed for the first time in 12 months, it also made the win over Stade Francais as satisfying as any in my career.

GUY NOVÈS DIDN'T JUST SAVE MY CAREER. GUY NOVÈS SAVED MY LIFE. In November 2004, we played Castres away in a televised Friday night game. I'm told it wasn't a bad game. In the 66th minute they had just kicked a penalty to move 18-17 ahead. In a temper, I took off my head gear (always a signal that things weren't going right) threw it over the sidelines and said to myself that from this kick-off I was going to make a big hit on somebody. That was the last thing I remembered when I woke up in hospital.

That night Christian Gajan, the coach of Castres, came to visit me and arranged to pick me up the next morning and drive me back to Toulouse. On the way back, we stopped off in his house and he asked me if I wanted to see the incident. I said I wasn't too sure but why not? So as we watched it, his wife made me breakfast. I have to say, I haven't seen too many knock-outs like it. And seeing it on the video made me appreciate how lucky I was to be there having breakfast in his home.

Jacques Deen, Castres' South African number 8, had gathered the restart. I was the first one up to make a tackle. He didn't slow down, and I didn't slow down. At the last second he dipped his shoulder, which caught me on the bottom of the jaw, and his forehead on the side of my temple.

The two of us dropped like logs; my head bouncing off the ground. He was out for a minute and when he got up he was a bit shaken as well. As for me, picture the scene in *Jerry Maguire*, when Cuba Gooding Jnr, i.e. "Show me the money!", scores a touchdown, but collapses, apparently unconscious. The only difference was that I was out for about five minutes longer. And when I stood up, I didn't dance.

I was out cold for eleven minutes, and had swallowed my tongue. Both the Castres and Toulouse doctors were in the dressing-room treating our young hooker Virgile Lacombe, who'd come on as a replacement and suffered a neck injury at his first scrum. If you watch it on video, you can see Vincent Clerc turning away in horror.

Luckily, Guy immediately took it upon himself to come onto the pitch and force my mouth open. His wife is a doctor, so he knew what he was doing, and he managed to force my teeth apart and pull my tongue out of my throat. I bit down on his thumb so fiercely that he still carries the scar, and every now and then pushes his thumb into my face as a reminder. I have literally marked him for life, but I probably owe him my life for that.

It turns out we lost the game 21-20. They kicked a drop goal in the 14th minute of injury time and had our prop Patrice Colazzo sent off. We'd had mixed form up to then, beating Stade Francais for the first time in four attempts in my first three seasons here. Vincent Clerc's injury time try gave us a bonus point in a 32-16 win. It had been a sell-out for weeks and was, as expected, all-out war. It was like we'd won the championship against Stade Francais. But the following week we lost at home to Narbonne.

The mandatory two-week rest for concussion at least meant I could go home for the first time in over a year. My good friend Alan Graham picked us up at the airport; lunch was in the father and mother-in-laws, Paddy and Kate Kennedy, followed by dinner in my parents' house. When I told my mother I was coming home she said "son, what do you want for dinner?" I said "Me favourite ma, bacon and cabbage."

Well, the ma didn't let me down. It was like Christmas Day. The good table was set, crystal glasses out, the best knives and forks, and a couple of bottles of vin rouge from her last trip out here. The house hadn't changed much except that downstairs had become a shrine to Trevor Brennan. The only thing missing was a plaque outside "Trevor Brennan born here, 22/9/1973, weighing in at 10lbs...". On his previous visit to Toulouse my da had picked up a poster, about the size of a bus stop sign, of me catching a ball in a line-out. He took it from a sponsor's tent and had it framed, about 4' high by about 3" wide on display in the middle of the sitting-room. The poor mother is driven mad.

The day Ireland played Argentina was like a trip down memory lane. It began by watching my nephew Matthew play for the Barnhall under-eights that morning. I must admit to becoming a little emotional then, thinking of my brother Damien, and also at Lansdowne Road in the afternoon when watching the lads during the National Anthem. It brought back some old memories and I thought to myself "I'd love just one more chance to put on that jersey and stand there for the anthems."

After Ronan O'Gara had kicked Ireland to a last-ditch win, myself and Paula went to Roly's Bistro for our first ever meal there. Then we met Victor Costello and a couple of old friends in Smyths in Haddington Road, before heading into the Shelbourne Hotel to meet up with a few of the lads.

Omar Hasan helped to wangle us into the function room for the post-match meal where he and Agustín Pichot gave Eddie O'Sullivan a good-natured grilling for not picking me. Myself and Eddie chatted for a while. We spoke about the French being hammered by New Zealand. He said he wished they'd play like that in the Six Nations. He asked me how I got my two tickets and I told him they were actually in his name, through his agent John Baker. He laughed, so I said I wouldn't mind the same two tickets again for the next match.

With that, it was back to the treadmill. That season the French Championship was expanded to a home-and-away, 16-team league, with play-offs. This increased the regular season from 20 to 30 games. To make room for these extra matches, we played twice a week throughout August.

Maybe it's the way the game was developing. Maybe it was just that I was getting older. But with each passing year, even the pre-season seemed to get harder. The year before had been a disappointing season, losing that Heineken Cup final and the French championship semi-final. So we set our goals even higher for the 2004-05 campaign.

They say no team comes back hungrier than beaten finalists, and all season long, what happened in Twickenham against Wasps was at the back of our minds. We began with a lucky 9-6 win away to Llanelli in a hurricane – Gareth Thomas' first European game for Toulouse since joining us that season. Then we beat Glasgow at home, but slipped up away to Northampton.

Normally we would train first and look at the video later on the Monday morning at about 11.30am. But this was to be no normal video session. It started at 10.00am and all the players were joined by the coaching staff and the president of the club.

Our head coach, Guy Novès, went through the faults in the performance. It was definitely a game we could have won, and won well; knock-ons and basic handling errors close to the line costing us. He wanted to know why this was happening, why players were doing this. Omar Hasan was sin-binned for ten minutes, in which time Northampton scored ten points. He said this was totally unacceptable.

At the end of the session, the president – René Bouscatel – gave a speech explaining how Europe was very important for the club's coffers. The gate receipts from the home quarter-finals in the previous two years, prize money from ERC and sponsors' bonuses had enabled Stade Toulousain to build virtually a whole new 20,000 seat stadium at the Ernest-Wallon. Along with new offices and new corporate boxes. That season they added a newly built gym, and knocked down the old sponsor's tent to replace it with a new, state-of-the-art, air-conditioned tent which holds over 3,000.

The club have also built a new all-weather pitch at the back of the stadium at a cost of €400,000, and a training area alongside that pitch. There's also a new club shop in the stadium, new bureaus, a new centre of information for young, up-and-coming players, a new car park and there are plans for a new running track.

The president explained that the club was supplying the best of everything to get these results. That the team couldn't continue losing matches like last Saturday's, and that a home quarter-final was vital to the continuing growth of the club.

That concentrated the minds. We beat Northampton at home the following weekend,. In January, we completed back-to-back bonus point wins away to Glasgow and at home to Llanelli, scoring 83 points in the two games. This earned us a home quarter-final against Northampton, which we won 37-9 in Le Stadium.

On the Sunday after returning from Glasgow, I had been invited to the Salle de Fêtein the community hall by the town mayor. I went out for a run at about 11.30am and, upon arriving home, there was a strange car outside the house. Alain Servat, the caretaker of the college in Castelginest, had turned up to say I was late for the presentation. I was to receive a medal, and everybody was waiting for me.

It turned out that some 200 people had been invited to an awards ceremony where a 20-piece orchestra played. The mayor called up a man who had lived in Castelginest for 60 years, then a guy who'd fought in World War II and a girl who, over the previous ten years, had done huge work for local charities.

I was asking myself what I was doing there, and why the hell they were giving me an award, when "Trevor Brennan of Stade Toulousain" was called up to a huge cheer.

I'd supplied a local rugby club with some furniture, run a few raffles and had jerseys signed, but nothing that I would see as meriting an award alongside a fella with 60 years' service or a World War II veteran. It's the everyday stuff you'd do as a sportsperson.

"So how long have you been here Trevor?"

"Eh, just over a year."

I felt a bit embarrassed.

The week before we were due to play Leicester, we met Castres again at home in the French Championship. There had been some quotes from both camps in the newspapers in the build-up to the game, which was quite fiery. On a few occasions Guy shouted at me from the sidelines.

"Trevor, calme toi, calme toi, la semaine prochaine, c'est plus important." The match next weekend is the big one. At half-time he re-enforced this message to me.

Within a few minutes of the start of the second-half, Guy shouted at me again. I thought to myself, 'Jaysus, will he ever shut up. I got it in the dressing-room, I'm getting it throughout the match, I'm getting it again now.' So I turned toward the dug-out and shouted back,

"Guy, f*** off."

I could see some subs and the coaching staff just staring at each other and Guy looking at me with an expression which read "Are you telling me to f*** off?"

Soon after this, just in front of the Castres dug-out, poor little Élissalde got into a row with one of their locks, the French international Lionel Nallet. A 6' 5", 120kg lock against a 5' 8", 73kg scrum-half. I made my way over, as I do, to pull them apart. I grabbed Nallet by the neck and said:

"Pick on someone your own size."

I could hear Guy screaming "Trevor. Non. Non. Non."

With that Nallet punched me. I kept a hold of his collar and said:

"Is that the best you can do? Encore."

Sure enough, he does, not once, but twice more. I could feel the blood trickling down my face and my fist clenching by my side. Guy was screaming "Trevor, non, s'il te plait. Non."

The referee and other players arrived to break it up, Nallet was yellow carded and I was taken off to have a few stitches. Some of the lads told me that Guy wasn't very happy with me for telling him to f*** off. When he spoke to me in the dressing-room he congratulated me for my reaction to Nallet.

"You're a bigger man than I thought you were."

"Guy, I just wanted to say I'm sorry for telling you to f*** off."

He smiled slightly and replied "F*** you too," and walked off.

I was worried, and immediately asked Jean-Michel Rancoule "Is he alright?"

"Oh, he's alright yeah."

I never did it again, and for the next few weeks Guy cited me as an example to the other boys of the need to keep our discipline, how he'd seen a big change in me over the years, and that if I could do it, anybody could.

Leicester Tigers v Stade Toulousain has a ring to it. Two giants of the European game. The only two two-time winners of the Heineken Cup, and perhaps the two biggest clubs in France and England. This was to be the first rugby match in Leicester's football ground, the Walkers Stadium. Our biggest game of the season so far, by a mile.

As usual we had our first team meeting on Monday. Guy ranted and raved about Leicester, about losing the final to Wasps the previous year, about the World Cup winners in their squad. This would be France versus England, with the odd Paddy and a few assorted internationals thrown in.

Personally, I hate giving the opposition too much respect so I kind of switched off for a while. He asked Romain Millochlusky if he was up for the challenge of playing Martin Johnson, would he cope with the pressure? Martin Johnson would be mentioned more often than any other player that week. Martin Johnson, the World Cup winning captain, the four-time winner of the Premiership with Leicester, twice European Cup-winning captain. A serial winner. You have to respect what he's achieved. He's probably the greatest rugby captain of the professional era. A brilliant second-row, and as hard a player as rugby ever produced. For us this week, he was a legend and an agent provocateur.

Looking a little embarrassed, Romain said yes. He's a hard-grafting youngster but very quiet off the pitch. Then all of a sudden I heard my name mentioned and my ears cocked at the words "caviar and Martin Johnson". Guy was saying that players such as Trevor Brennan were like caviar to Martin Johnson. Hmm. I said nothing. I wasn't asked to. He was speaking to the whole room.

After the meeting I went to the physio for treatment on the leg injury I'd been struggling with since a bad 'shoeing' in the Clermont Auvergne game. Guy appeared in the physio's room and asked if I'd understood what he'd said when he was talking about me and Martin Johnson. He was putting his fist up to my face and pushing me now; the usual. Testing me to see if I would snap. If Johnson does this and does that, what will I do?

"Will you get sent off? Because you know we can't afford to have you sent off."

"Tu connais Diego Maradona?" I asked him.

"Oui."

"Well, on Sunday I will be Diego Maradona," I told him, and I rolled off the bed, landed on the ground and feigned injury.

"That's the Trevor Brennan I want," he said, looking down on me on the ground and left the room pointing two fingers into the right side of his head, whistling a couple of times, and saying "Craz-ee Irishman."

Unable to join the lads in the runs, I did some bike work and weights for the next couple of days, joining in the light team run on Thursday. Friday was a day off, so I had a lie in. I brought my Sky Box and remote control to the shop where I had bought them, as the control wasn't working. I met the ERC commercial manager Diarmaid Murphy for lunch in the bar – who sorted me out with some tickets for the game – then dropped him off at the airport and returned home.

"Where's the Sky box and control," were Paula's first words. Merde. "How am I going to watch the match?" she asked. The shop was an hour's drive away through traffic on a Friday evening so I gave the lie that it would take two or three days to fix it. She wasn't having it. So I was made ring the shop and was told it was ready for collection.

When I got there, the fella in the shop asked me if I had a dog. I said "No, why?" He explained that the control looked like it had been chewed by a dog. He asked me if I had kids.

"Yes, two."

"Boys or girls."

"Boys."

"That explains it," he said.

That night I spent four hours painting the spare bedroom downstairs. The life of a professional rugby player. Half-way through, I was taking a tea break with a couple of choccy biscuits, when Gareth Thomas rang. I've made countless good friends through rugby and none better than Gareth (aka Alfie). But he couldn't scratch his arse by himself. He wanted to know if we needed our suits for this match.

"Jaysus, Alfie." I said, "For such a big game? Of course!".

Saturday came, and Paula and Daniel waved me off (Joshua was still in bed) as I headed to the club for breakfast. Alfie asked me if I had a suit carrier? 'Merde,' again. I'd forgotten the suit. I rang Paula, who had half an hour to come to the rescue with my suit. She made it just before we left for the airport.

It was a spanking, brand new 50-seater plane. The plastic was practically still on the seats. It even had the Stade Toulousain logo on the emergency exits. The air hostess informed me that it was the plane's first commercial flight. Alfie, sitting to my left, talked about the fresh new smell of the leather seats. "Fabulous," he said.

We arrived that afternoon at the Sketchley Grange Hotel. A day ahead of the semi-final and a couple of hours before our team run at 4.30pm in the Walkers Stadium. It's an old country house-type hotel in the middle of nowhere, with no distractions. No lads heading off to coffee shops. Everything was centred around the hotel. With some time to myself, I was thinking of my old club Barnhall. That afternoon, they were in a play-off at home to Clonakilty to stay in Division Two.

The previous Tuesday, I'd taken time out to write to them on Stade Toulousain headed notepaper, telling the boys the importance of the club to me. I recalled that I'd played there from eight to 18 before moving on to Bective Rangers when Barnhall were still a junior club. They'd won six promotions in six years before I'd come back to play for them in Division Two. "You have to do it for the jersey today lads."

I had faxed it over to Ian Morgan, aka Moggy, who was then in his ninth year as coach. It had been a tough season for them. The Burkes, the mainstays of the first team throughout their rise to the second division, were no longer its backbone. The eldest, Conrad, had retired at the end of last season; Brendan, who had played in the same under-age team as Damien, had been out injured for most of the campaign, and another brother, Owen, was also injured.

Yet another in the clan, Declan – also blessed with the Burkes' speed genes – had the makings of another great winger, but he'd gone to Australia. Actually, in the year I went back, Eoin wasn't there for that season either. Just Conrad.

When Conrad was working in Amsterdam, the club had flown him home every weekend. Even when Eoin was in Australia, they flew him home for two or three games. That's a measure of their importance to the club, and what they've given to Barnhall. A Barnhall team without a Burke was like bread without butter. Fantastic players and a great sporting family. Conrad retired prematurely. He definitely had another year or two in him and could have gone higher too.

Writing that letter made me quite reflective during this semi-final week. But Leicester v Toulouse was as big a game as club rugby could throw up, and all thoughts of Barnhall receded rapidly when we arrived in the Walker's Stadium that Saturday afternoon for our captain's run. These are always strange affairs. The calm before the storm. Our voices echoed around the empty ground. The next day there would be 32,000 supporters there. I couldn't help but gaze around and think about last year's final defeat. Guy made his customary little speech before handing over the reins to Freddy Michalak.

It was Freddy's first 'captain's run'. After Thursday's announcement that he would be captain, Freddy joked that he'd have a champagne celebration in the local night club, The Factory, letting on it was all a big laugh. That was his way of saying 'I'm still Freddy Michalak'.

We'd discussed what we'd do. Normally we'd do a lot of line-outs and scrums. Should we do a few laps? Freddy's attitude was one lap around the pitch and then some touch rugby and a bit of a laugh. He took all the nerves out of the occasion. Nice and relaxed. Typical Freddy. Sometimes the appointment of a new captain can change the relationship between him and the rest of the players. But not with our Freddy.

Backs were doing line-outs and mauls, forwards were running the backline; the whole thing was a laugh. The coaches didn't look happy on the sidelines. But it's the captain's run. They couldn't get involved. It was Freddy's call. We played touch, did a bit of stretching, did a bit of cat and mouse (where someone's a cat and the rest are mice), climbed up the posts and swung out of the bars.

When we came together at the end of the team run I wound the boys up by telling them that the Irish media had quoted John Wells as saying that we were bad travellers; had a bad scrum, our line-out was no good (which, if he had said it, wouldn't have been a million miles from the truth at the time) and that he was looking forward to Leicester's fourth final.

"Did he really?" they asked. So I told them I'd had loads of calls and texts about it. They were fuming, but I wanted to wind them up to get the best out of them.

Back in my room I rang Ronnie, the brother. Barnhall had won. Everyone had played brilliantly. There had been 3 or 4,000 people at the game. Moggy had photo-copied my letter and given a copy to seemingly everybody. It had been the talk of the club. I don't know if it made any difference, but any little help for my old club made me feel I'd contributed something.

Just as I was feeling good with the world, I suddenly had a bit of a panic attack when I couldn't find a rucksack which contained all my match tickets, my mobile phone and a book.

"Alfie, did you see my rucksack anywhere?"

"What rucksack, Horse?"

"Ah Jaysus, I think I've left it on the plane."

Now I was in a cold sweat. I had visions of the da and the boys arriving and me with no tickets for them. And it was a sell-out!

The bus driver had locked the coach and was staying in a B&B up the road. I even tried forcing open the door. I'd just about given up on it when Jean-Luc Braemor, right hand man to the club president – who looks after hotel bookings, organises coaches and the like – called to my room with the bus driver. He'd located him after contacting every B&B in the area. He opened up the coach and there was the bag underneath where I'd been sitting.

I was whacked by this stage. When I turned off the TV, Alfie turned it back on again and begged me to let him fall asleep first because of my snoring. Apparently it can be like sleeping next to a train station. But it would be another sleepless night for Alfie. Me, I slept like a log.

The father arrived at the hotel in the morning to pick up his tickets. He'd come over with nine mates and a bottle of 12-year-old whiskey for Jean-Luc – source of the tickets. He was chuffed with the whiskey and said there was no need for it.

Kevin Corcoran, a good friend of the father's and myself, travelled with Alan Graham, Chris Gallagher and a Kildare captain, Enda Murphy. A few of them were looking the worse for wear as they'd been out celebrating in Barnhall the night before.

We'd been totally written off even by the French media, so far as I could tell. It was a nice, warm, sunny day; perfect for a French team in April. Inside, the team meeting was relaxed. Serge Lairle and Philippe Rouge-Thomas are Guy's assistant coaches, and Serge congratulated us before we had even played the game. It was no mistake that we were there; it had been a long road; eight months of days and nights training and sweating in the gym and on the pitch; all the knocks and cuts that we'd taken along the way.

And it wasn't just the 22, there were players back in Toulouse who had helped to get us there but couldn't make this trip. We weren't to forget them, players like Nicolas Jeanjean, whose season was over after sustaining a leg fracture. Serge's attitude, unusually for him, was for us to go out and enjoy ourselves – because we had worked hard for this day.

Guy then said his few words. Again he mentioned me and my discipline. He knows I have a temper, that I play on the borderline. Although I had received relatively fewer yellow cards playing with Toulouse, French rugby is that bit more physical. Touch judges don't put up the flag as quickly as they do back home. Whether it's good rucking or a punch, in France they're more inclined to see it as part of the game.

"Pas de probleme aujourd-hui, Guy," I assured him.

We arrived about an hour and ten minutes before kick-off. Guy doesn't like us to arrive too early. I did my usual routine, staying in the dressing-room until the ref called us out.

There is a long corridor from the dressing-room to the pitch. The 23rd and 24th players, David Gerard and Patrice Colazzo, along with the coaches, the doctors and the rest of the staff formed a tunnel and clapped us out. Which is not normal. "Allez les gars." Hearing all these voices before Leicester joined us in the corridor was a great lift.

Tunnel vision too. Normally teams run out on to a pitch separately; the away team first. Then the home team emerges to a massive roar. So you might see them down the corridor, that's all. But for this European Cup semi-final the two teams come out together, same as for internationals. On occasions like this I never look across at my opponents, and didn't when Leicester lined up alongside us. It can break your focus.

Just head down or look straight in front. Two years ago, at the European Cup final in Lansdowne Road, I didn't see anyone. I didn't even see Perpignan beside me – or anyone behind me. I was looking only in front of me. Ken Ging said later that he said hello to me, as did Roly Meates. But I wasn't aware of either of them.

Normally you just don't want any distractions, because you have in your mind what you want to do from the kick-off, the first hit, the first tackle. You don't want to see anyone. When we played Munster two years ago in the semi-final, I heard my name but I never looked over.

Rugby isn't like soccer. It's gladiatorial. First and foremost it's a physical fight. It's full-on, it's dogged. That's what rugby is about. You can be friendly and be best buddies and be shaking hands after games ... and sometimes you can't.

We had about 1,000 supporters there, and in fairness to them they made quite a noise. It was every bit as physical up front as I'd expected. They ran everything at us, especially through their number eight Henry Tuilagi. Their line-out maul and their pick and drive game were strong. After we scored an early try, we spent the rest of the first-half defending.

Everyone played well, but we had some luck too. Leicester had overlaps on three or four occasions, but knocked on, or the ball didn't go to hand. I played second-row alongside Romain Millochlusky. He was having a big game. Guy's words were working. Jean Bouilhou's selection at six was no harm either. Our line-out had been struggling, but that's his speciality and he helped sort it out.

But Bouilhou would sustain a dislocated elbow. After he went off, our line-out fell apart. I was moved to take Gregory Lamboley's position in the middle of the line-out. Greg went back to Jean's place. And Izzy (Maka) isn't really a line-out option unless you have a crane, although he did win one ball.

A defensive effort like that goes by in a bit of a blur. It's just all hands on deck. It was only when we looked at the video of the game on the following Monday that we saw it in detail and could appreciate it. There was a moment when Clément Poitrenaud made a big hit on Harry Ellis at the base of one of their rucks, and he wouldn't be known for his physical play.

Everyone in the room looked at Clément and Guy Novès just said "Bravo, Clément. Bravo." He came up in the defensive line a few times to make hits that day.

Still, we had a couple of let-offs and at half-time we knew we'd have to do more if we were to win. Guy Novès told us to play more rugby and stop the kicking game. We weren't playing our normal running rugby. We had become too defensive mentally, and when we had the ball we were kicking it away, then defending again. "Go out and enjoy the next 40 minutes," he told us. "You're not here by chance, you deserve to be here."

That lifted a few heads and we scored two tries in the second-half. Izzy made a good impact and so did Gareth – the two combining for Freddy's match-winning try. Guy had gone on about Martin Johnson again in the pre-match talk, and so when niggles broke out once or twice, I stood off, took a back seat and watched unless I was really needed.

Towards the end Johnno was talking to the referee, Alain Rolland, after every decision. He is hard and tough, but I was glad I didn't get into any confrontations with him. I just wanted to concentrate on rugby. Put myself into tackles and scrums, hit rucks and mauls.

I was frustrated not to get my hands on the ball a little more. That game was a big opportunity for me to show how much I'd improved since the move to France. But certain games just don't go your way. I'd normally be used as a runner off nine or ten, breaking gain lines. But we didn't have the platform to get our running game going.

We scored three tries off kicks by them, and it's a big mistake to not make touch – because French teams will counter-attack. It's not like the Premiership or in Ireland. We won 27-19. By beating Leicester in their own city, we'd removed that monkey of being bad travellers off our backs. We'd also beaten a team containing nine Lions, which gave me personal satisfaction, and the team belief for the final. Clément Poitrenaud laid the ghost of the previous year's final against Wasps to rest. I think they targeted him early on, but he caught some lovely balls and counter-attacked well when he had his chance.

I met up with the da and his nine friends afterwards for a quick drink in their hotel across from the Walkers Stadium. We had an hour-and-a-half journey to Birmingham. The plane was delayed by 90 minutes and we didn't arrive home until 1.30am. About 1,500 people were there to greet us and cheer us through the airport as if we'd already won the Cup.

There'd been no drinking, so I rang my bar, De Danu, and about a dozen of us had a few late drinks there. It was perfect. No big crowds, and no sing-song; just a few quiet pints chilling out. I had a long chat in the corner with Fabien Pelous.

I'd been playing against one of the giants of English rugby, and now I was listening to a man I consider the undisputed giant of French forward play. Like Novès, he has an aura about him. When he talks, you listen.

He's the ultimate professional, the ultimate captain. He leads from the front and would never ask a player to do anything that he wouldn't do himself. Sometimes Fabien doesn't say anything at all in the dressing-room, leaving me or someone else to do the talking.

But come game time, Fabien will put in a massive hit. Or if there's any physical stuff, Fabien will be the first to confront an opponent. He never backs down. I suppose he plays on the edge, and like Martin Johnson, he's had his fair share of red and yellow cards. Like Johnson, he has a presence. They're both hard men, on and off the pitch.

Rugby is a confrontational sport, all the more so when these guys started. Fabien admits now he received and gave stuff that wouldn't be tolerated any more. Fabien made his test debut in 1995 at the age of 21 in a crazy French pack.

Nobody at Stade Toulousain trains harder. He mixes with the boys but he doesn't say much, and he watches everything. He's similar to Guy Novès. Listening to him discuss the semi-final, and my own game was fascinating. I was a bit frustrated with my own performance but he congratulated me on what I'd achieved. This would be our third Heineken Cup final in a row. He pointed out how well things had gone for me and how delighted he was for me.

He stressed the importance of a good squad, where each of us brought something different. I brought a bit of madness, a bit of bite and a bit of spirit. He felt that on the day, I had stepped up to the plate; that the younger players looked up to me. Fabien said I made my tackles and brought a vocal presence that he would normally bring, especially in the dressing-room before the game. He cited my comments about this being Stade Toulouse weather as an example, and my telling them to just go out and play our normal game; to remember losing the final last year and the hurt and the pain that had caused us. True enough, I had probably been the only player who had talked before the game. It can be a quiet squad.

But still I didn't have the skills of most of them, I said, or things which other players bring. That's what makes a good team, he said. There can't be two Freddy Michalaks; Élissalde brings his game and his kicking; Poitrenaud brings his counter-attacking; Isitolo Maka brings that ball-carrying and ability to break defensive lines. That's what makes Toulouse, he added. And the more we bring it all together, the better we play.

This was making me feel even better than the couple of pints. It was late, about 4.30am by the time I reached home. But it's difficult to sleep after a match as big as that, and such a long journey home. You need the time to unwind. Away from the workplace, as a group, French squads don't tend to socialise too much – except for the few hours after a game.

I was tired for the next few days. Sore too. I'd strained my thigh and wouldn't be able to do much training for a while. Summer arrived in that last week of April; the temperatures hitting the mid 20s all week. We had a dress rehearsal with Stade Francais in Paris on the following Sunday. I'd be lucky to make the bench. The players would have to rest up, and play through tiredness and pain, for the remainder of the season. But with two big trophies to play for, that wasn't an issue.

We'd lost to Stade Francais, who'd be our Heineken Cup final opponents in Edinburgh, repeatedly in the previous three years. They usually did a number on us up front and stifled us with their forward play and defence.

However, our build-up was better. They arrived two days before the game and there was a wedding in their hotel, so they had to change base. We arrived the day before the match. Bam, bam, bam. Gone. Just the way I like it.

Match day came and the atmosphere in Murrayfield was electric. I was surprised at the amount of red and black in the 50,000 crowd. Before the game Guy went around to every single one of us, looking us in the eye and selectively picking out something about our games. He said that discipline would win this final, and he was right.

I know it wasn't a great game, partly I think, because we just know each other too well. With the extensive television coverage in France, the video research by both teams on each other is just incredible. Stade also took no risks, and what rugby was played, was played by us.

We trailed 12-6 at half-time and the second-half flew by. When their out-half David Skrela lined up a drop goal at 12-9 to them in the last quarter, I managed to charge it down. Jean-Baptiste Élissalde's fourth penalty made it 12-all after a big burst by Finau Maka. I didn't realise it was so near the end. Suddenly the ref blew his whistle and we were into extra time. Then, from somewhere, we all found a surge of energy. We stayed out on the pitch, whereas they went back into the dressing-room. Maybe that showed we had the momentum and were hungrier to get on with it.

When Guy gave his team talk on the pitch, I admit I was thinking to myself "Not again. Not again. I can't lose another final. No, I just can't lose another final."

I thought of all my family, who had been in Twickenham the year before, sitting in the Murrayfield stand 12 months on, and how they must have felt. I wanted to win for them, to make up for the previous year. I wanted to win for myself, just to exorcise those ghosts. Any player will tell you, there's nothing worse than losing a final. And for me, there was nothing worse than losing that European Cup final to Wasps. We went into a huddle and said right, this next 20 minutes would be everything. We had them on the back foot, and now we would really go for them.

At the start of extra-time, Isitolo Maka rumbled up the middle and went to ground in their 22, where they gave away a penalty. With Jean-Baptiste off the pitch, Freddy took over the kicking duties as well as switching to scrum-half, to make it 15-12 to us. At the start of the second period, he kicked another to make it 18-12.

Guys were going down with cramp. When Finau Maka was on the ground with five minutes to go I shouted at him "Get up, the next five minutes of your life are everything." And that's the way it felt to me. When we went three points ahead I was pushing and shoving David Gerard to get the next kick-off again, which he did. All the subs made a difference, as Guy Novès said they would have to do if we were to win this match.

Everybody seemed to get more vocal in encouraging each other. Don't let anything go. Encore, encore. Allez, allez. Everything counted now. When Freddy landed that second penalty we knew the Cup was ours.

The full-time whistle was a fantastic feeling. For me personally, it was better than winning two years before in Lansdowne Road, when I had led the team onto the pitch and experienced all the other emotions involved in returning to Dublin with Toulouse.

I'd never played 100-plus minutes in my life and I was obviously delighted to last the whole game. I played the first-half at blind-side, but switched to the second-row when Fabien came off injured and was replaced by Jean Bouilhou early in the second. I felt it went well for me on the day.

I immediately picked out my father, my brothers, my uncles and my friends and I jumped into the stand. I was draped in a tri-colour and enjoyed the lap of honour with the lads.

I had a few beers with Alfie in the dressing-room before he headed off on Lions duty, and an hour later I was receiving a text from him saying he was having a beer on his own in the airport.

After the shower, the phone was hopping. I went through a sea of red and black to put my bag on the bus, but it seemed to be more red due to the number of Munster fans who had bought tickets in advance, hoping their team would be there. With the Toulouse players and supporters looking on curiously, I sang the *Fields of Athenry* with about 100 Munster supporters and it felt like I had my picture taken with every Munster fan who was at the match.

I said goodbye to the family and friends – they were heading off to the airport – and went to the reception. I felt on top of the world. When we arrived back at 1.30am, Blagnac airport was black. Everyone was chanting Guy Novès' name. He had left the trophy presentation to kiss his wife and son in the crowd, before a security guard had refused to let him back on the pitch. He was then frogmarched away by two Scottish policemen. The crowd chanted "liber-té, liber-té, liber-té,". "Free-dom, free-dom, free-dom."

It reminded me of the scene out of *Braveheart* when Mel Gibson is being executed and he shouts his last words "Free-Dom!" Guy got a fair bit of stick from the lads, and it was probably myself who had shouted "Freedom" at him, and lines like "I'm an innocent man" from the film *In The Name Of The Father*. Mind you, I did have a few drinks on board, and I knew he couldn't say anything as we'd just won the European Cup. You don't get chances to slag Guy too much.

Half the squad went to a disco, the others to the bar, and I suffered for two days. As is tradition in Toulouse, the trophy was put on show on the balcony at the Place du Capitole for about 8,000 people on Monday evening.

The next day I rang my mother-in-law Catherine. "Who's your favourite son-in-law?" I said, laughing. She said it would take more than a Heineken Cup medal to make me her favourite son-in-law.

She's a devoutly religious woman, and I'd asked her to light three candles for me, one for the first-half and two for the second. She said I hadn't warned her about the possibility of extra-time, and when we were losing 12-9 near the end she blew them out. Then when she returned to the television and saw that we'd drawn level, she lit the candles again and apologised to the Sacred Heart for not having faith. Her prayers were answered.

Unfortunately, Stade Francais had their revenge against us in the French Championship semi-finals in Bordeaux. That Bouclier was proving tantalisingly elusive. We were only denied a place in the final by a desperate, last-ditch, tap tackle on Florian Fritz by Jerome Fillol as he was going through with men outside him. We lost 23-18. It was terrible. In part, once again, I'd blame the post-Heineken Cup celebrations.

I just can't understand the whole business of coming back with the European Cup, having a civic reception, celebrating, the lads having a few drinks; and then you've to play a semi-final the following weekend. It just does not make sense. The whole timing is wrong. I know the politicos, dignitaries and VIPs, no less than the club, wanted to celebrate a fantastic achievement, and it deserved to be celebrated. But in my view, there is no time to celebrate winning a Heineken Cup in France – if you're lucky enough to win it – until the season is over.

As in the previous two years, it seemed as if we were being punished domestically for our achievements in Europe. Hats off to Wasps for doing the double of the Heineken Cup and English Premiership the year before, but no French team has managed that double in my time here, and that's partly because the system works against us.

Three successive European finals was a remarkable achievement in its own right, not to mention winning two of them. Nobody has ever done that. But the season had ended with that semi-final defeat to Stade.

"Life is Life, la-la, la, la-la." That song had been adopted by Stade Francais and all summer long if there was one song that made me walk out of supermarkets, pubs or restaurants, it was that bloody tune.

CLÉMENT POITRENAUD
TOULOUSE AND FRANCE FULL-BACK.

"I prefer first to talk about the man. The man is the most important thing. A few days ago he said to me, 'You are my brother' and I think that's true of what has happened to Trevor in Toulouse, the last five years. He is like a brother to all of us, and I'm sure we're gonna see Trevor after our career, because he really is a friend for life.

His greatest virtue as a player was his courage. He would die on the field for the other players. When it was difficult for us in some games, he was every time here for us and the team, and that is the most important thing in rugby. As a player with Toulouse, he always brought his fighting spirit. We needed it, because in France we love to play with the ball, but some times we forgot to tackle hard and to play strong. So it was good. It was very important to have a player like him in our team, because as I've said before, all the other players follow him. When it's hard, he would go first and all the others would follow him.

I don't understand why he never played with Ireland in five years with Toulouse. He was one of the best second or third-rows I've known, and I think it is important to have a player like him. Not only on the field, but off the field too – because every time he is positive.

When he plays, he is happy, and when he did not play he always encouraged the other players. In the first six months we had a good feeling in our team, that was this man and his approach with everybody. Trevor is special. I regret he finished like this. I wanted him to play until the last match with Toulouse, and be part of the big party with the public. Like the other big players who played with Toulouse.

ALAIN ROLLAND
FORMER LEINSTER AND IRISH SCRUM-HALF AND
CURRENT INTERNATIONAL REFEREE.

"I'd been around for a few years before he arrived on the scene. He had a good name for himself insofar as he was talked about as a very hard, tough, physical player. You always knew where you stood with him; sometimes that was a good thing, and sometimes it wasn't. In the early part of his career, he was so committed to the cause that he gave away one or two penalties, which, with experience, he may not have done. But as a team-mate, if you were going into battle, he would have been first on the team sheet because he would give it his all. And that was one thing about Trevor. I think that got him a lot of respect from other players.

He would have been very raw when he started with Leinster, but we were only then on the cusp of professionalism, so it was new territory for everybody. He was always so keen to learn that he'd almost listen to anybody. He'd take on constructive criticism too.

I can remember many times when we were sitting beside each other on the bus and he'd talk about personal things, about the brother and the family and stuff like that; I won't necessarily go into detail about what we chatted about. We chatted about a few things on a professional level. And on a personal basis too.

I look back and laugh on the night in Toulouse when I was called out of bed at 2.30am to help get the lads out of a police station, but it was serious enough at the time. I hadn't a clue what was going when the lads woke me at 2.30am. I jumped in a taxi and went down to the cop shop in Toulouse. Obviously I had the lingo. Jim Glennon and Cally hadn't been notified at that stage, but once I saw how serious it was, I sent for them as they needed to be there.

There was a bit of mistaken identity, a case of wrong place at the wrong time. Our problem was that we had a flight first thing the next morning. So we couldn't wait for a judge to make a decision on it. I had to persuade them to actually ring the judge in the middle of the night, and see if we could get dispensation to get them out early. After about three hours we did.

I refereed a few Toulouse games involving Trevor, including the Wasps v Toulouse Heineken Cup final, an extraordinary, phenomenal game. He played hard but he never really stepped out of line. I think there was one altercation when I did Toulouse at home against Edinburgh and play went into the sideline. I would generally refer to players by their numbers, but when he took exception to the physio for the Edinburgh team I said "TREVOR" and gave him a look as if to say there was no need for him to go there.

"Sorry Rollers, sorry Rollers." He was always very apologetic when it came to him being disciplined, and that wasn't very often. Fabien Pelous is a fantastic captain but there were also times in the heat of battle, when tensions were running high, and I could pull Trevor aside and say "Trevor, have a word with…"

And he'd say "No worries Rollers, leave that to me."

I wish him nothing but the best in his retirement. I thoroughly enjoyed my time playing with him; I always found him a fantastic team-mate. I thought he was a great guy and wherever his future takes him, I think he should stay in rugby. He's certainly someone who could put something back into the game."

CHAPTER 16

BITTER PILLS

ON LOSING TO LEINSTER

After another sleepless night for me before the game, we travelled to the ground with a police escort. One of the first people I spotted there was Roly Meates, walking around in his thoughts and his usual haze of pipe smoke. That brought back memories. Amid a few thousand red-and-black-clad supporters, there wasn't a chance to speak. Anyway, I was already trying to get into my zone. I was confident we'd do well.

We started quickly, but the referee wrongly disallowed a Vincent Clerc try for a non-existent forward pass. Sometimes a decision like this can change a game. Not long after, we let one through; O'Driscoll seemed to waltz untouched through our backs. Our back-row weren't pushing out as we were too busy putting up three pods in the line-out. Leinster had either done their homework or Contepomi had read it well. He had one of his best games in a Leinster jersey.

WE SPENT THE SUMMER OF 2005 IN FRANCE, VISITING THE BASQUE COUNTRY around Biarritz, San Sebastian, and French Catalonia before returning to Toulouse for pre-season training. The French have their own way of doing things. Nothing happens in August. Especially in the cities or the bigger towns. If it doesn't have a beach, it closes for the month. Bars, restaurants, shops. You name it, they close. And those that do stay open don't have any customers. Like ourselves.

You won't find a place to eat except fast food or a sandwich in a petrol station. If you arrive on a Sunday in August, your goose is cooked. As for Sundays in the other 11 months, you're really in trouble if you forget to buy, tea, milk, bread, butter, cigarettes or whatever. It's cold turkey until Monday.

September and October are more mushroom and wine season. A neighbour popped around with a big bag of mushrooms the size of footballs. You cut them and slice them and mix them with garlic. Lovely. Lots of French people have their own patches for picking mushrooms, also known over here as cepes, but will never reveal exactly where they are; they point vaguely towards hills or mountains.

You also see hundreds of men and women picking grapes for the first of the season's wines, with Beaujolais Nouveau usually first on the market on November 18th. It's invariably cheap, awful, and blows the head off you. They call it the workers' wine.

After four finals and two semi-finals in three years, I was as hungry as ever. Patrice Collazo, Christian Labit and David Gerard moved on. In came Yannick Nyanga, the outstanding French back-rower from Béziers; Gregory Menkarska, a very good scrummager from Auch and my old team-mate from Leinster, Aidan McCullen. A fluent French speaker with a great sense of humour, he settled in quickly and started the first five games.

Unusually in my time here, we won our first eight games; Toulouse's best start to a championship. Towards the end of 2005, Yannick was one of several Toulouse players to win awards. I went around to Gareth Thomas' house the night he won the BBC Wales Sports Personality of the Year award, as voted for by the viewers. In a year when he captained the Lions, led Wales to the Grand Slam and also won a European Cup winners medal, he was a shoe-in.

Yannick Jauzion won the French Championship Player of the Year, and was also picked on a World XV along with Yannick Nyanga. Jauzion is such a down to earth fella in every sense. He comes from a farming background in Agen and studies agriculture. He also works part-time in a bank on his days off. Nothing fazes him. To him, he's just doing a job, but what a job he does for us.

He weighs in at 106 kilos and is 6' 5". You could put him in the second-row. He's very quick, and runs great lines. It usually takes two or three people to stop him, and yet he also has a great gift for making offloads in the tackle. He constantly opens up gaps for other players.

Nyanga's work-rate is phenomenal. He tackles, tackles, tackles. He'll make four in a row in one phase of play. He's also a good line-out option for us, especially on defence, and he's very, very quick. As a bloke, he's also a good laugh. He's the new playboy of Stade Toulousain. Single, good-looking, black, 23. That says it all.

Guy also picked up an award from the English journalists for Services to Rugby. Only the third Frenchman in 20 years to win it after Philippe Sella and Jean-Pierre Rives.

And then there was The Horsebox, T. Brennan, who was invited to the 48th

Texaco Sportstars Awards as the rugby sports star of 2005. It was an unforgettable night and I was humbled to be in the presence of so many great Irish sports people. Memories are made from nights like that and I felt blessed again to be doing something I love for a living.

The da was bowled over by Ronnie Delaney, an athletics legend and Olympic gold medallist, coming over to our table and tapping me on the shoulder to congratulate me, and later wishing me the best for the rest of the season. A pure gentleman. And there aren't too many nights in your life when you can see old clips of Johnny Giles and get to meet him.

In Europe, we had the swagger and confidence of reigning champions, especially after reaching three finals in a row. For the fourth year running we earned the club a lucrative home quarter-final. I missed the opening 50-28 win at home to Llanelli, due to a stupid calf injury (only the third Heineken Cup game I'd missed in four years with Toulouse) We drew 15-all away to Wasps – when we should have won. We beat Edinburgh away, and then again at home, a week later. And I won my 50th cap in the Heineken Cup – 22 with Leinster and 28 with Toulouse.

My landmark was announced as I ran out onto the pitch and I received a huge reception from the 17,500 crowd. We won with a bonus point and afterwards I was presented with my 50th cap by Guy Novès in front of the Sky cameras. He grabbed my hand and went down on bended knee to present it to me. So I knelt down and gave him a big hug before proceeding to the dressing-room for an Irish jig while the lads clapped.

The week before we played Wasps at home, an under-strength team suffered our first home defeat in over a year to Bayonne. I scored a try and settled a private score with Richard Dourthe. But it's amazing how much a big match can act as a miracle cure for so many different injuries, because by Tuesday virtually everyone was fit to train. No-one wanted to miss a re-run of the final two seasons before, especially in front of a capacity crowd in the football stadium. On the Wednesday before the Wasps' game, I signed a contract for a fifth season with Toulouse despite an offer from Michael Cheika to return to Leinster. I felt my future was in Toulouse, and the decision wasn't just about rugby.

We beat Wasps 19-13, but fellas really had to put their bodies on the line; even the likes of Xavier Garbajosa almost played as an extra forward. Michalak made a superb start and our forwards really stood up to Wasps. Everyone, including their players, reckoned it was like an international for intensity and physicality.

Munster's Red Army had invaded the town for their Friday night win away to Castres and came in numbers to both our match and, for three successive nights, to De Danu. Even Wasps' players couldn't get into the bar and so the English pub across the road did a bit of business for a change. When I gave a rendition of *Dublin In the Rare Oul Times*, the Munster fans sang along – that was a first and probably a last – and they kept going long after I went home. If I was a Munster player I'd be so proud of them.

As Guy kept reinforcing all week, we still had to beat Llanelli away with a bonus point the following Saturday to earn that home quarter-final. And we did, by 49-42. We had to wait on the results the next day to see who we would be hosting. Leinster were visiting Bath in the final match, and had to win to get through. If they did, they would qualify as eighth seeds and therefore be playing the top seeds – ourselves. I watched the match alongside a few of the Toulouse lads in De Danu. We were all tucking into a full Irish breakfast when the game kicked off. Because Bath had beaten Leinster in Dublin, we thought they might do the same at home.

However, it didn't take long for Leinster to get on the scoreboard. The pace of their backline, and willingness to run from everywhere, cut Bath apart. So confirming that we would be playing my old team. Immediately I had mixed feelings about that. The three previous years we had avoided each other; now I'd have to play them in the quarter-finals, and all with 11 weeks to think about it.

Some light relief was provided when I arrived in training the following Tuesday. The boys were hopping mad, telling stories of things that had happened to them during the night. Over in the corner of the dressing-room, Freddy Michalak looked shattered but was laughing away to himself all the same. He'd had a long night...

***

It all went back to our trip to Llanelli the previous weekend. On arrival in Cardiff airport, one of the boys had emptied the contents of Freddy's bag onto the carousel. He wasn't happy about that. Before the match, some of the boys put deep heat in Freddy's boots and he had to go searching around for another pair. He was even less amused about that. Finally, when we arrived back in Blagnac Airport on the Saturday night, his bag had been nicked and reported missing.

By now, Freddy was fairly pissed off.

The lads feared there might be repercussions but figured they'd be safe, as he wouldn't know who to blame. Freddy narrowed it down to four possible culprits: Yannick Jauzion, Yannick Bru, Xavier Garbajosa and Jean-Baptiste Élissalde.

There had been a warning during a scrummaging session on Monday evening. Freddy has a mate in Domino's and suddenly a motorcycle delivery man was driving across the pitch delivering three pepperoni pizzas in the name of our forwards' coach Serge Lairle, along with a bill for €35. Nobody paid him but we got to have a slice of pizza before settling down to more scrums.

Freddy's dad is a builder, so he headed off, late one night, in his car – his boot filled with ready-made cement, concrete bricks and bags of dirt and rubble. He started off at about 2.00am at Garba's house, and began building a wall at the front door.

He'd reached about two layers of bricks when, due to the foggy night, he began to think he had the wrong house as Garba's car was parked in between the two houses. Abandoning his first effort he went next door and proceeded to erect a five foot wall, finishing the job with some satisfaction at about 4.00am.

Garba emerged from his house the next morning and – to his amazement – saw an unfinished two foot wall immediately outside his front door; more amazing though was the trail of footprints through the garden leading to his neighbour's house where a freshly constructed five foot wall now blocked his neighbour's front door.

He said nothing, hopped into his car and went training.

In the meantime Freddy had been busy until dawn. He had driven to Bru's house and painted 'Goby' – Yannick's nickname – in big writing all across the front wall. He then drove to Jauzion's house, jacked up his car, and swapped the wheels for cement blocks. He drove on to Élissalde's house and covered his car in muck and rubble.

Freddy who'd been a busy boy, looked both whacked and happy. "Listen lads," he said to them, "I'm a single lad with no kids and no responsibilities. Do what you like, but I'll always get you back." This one was set to run.

***

During the Six Nations, I went home for the brother's 30th birthday and then to Paris for the France-Ireland game. It transpired Errol had been celebrating his birthday a day late for the last 29 years. He and the rest of us thought it was on the 27th but he discovered the mistake when he needed a birth certificate for his marriage in December. Typical Brennans.

On returning to Leixlip, bacon and cabbage in the ma's was followed by a few drinks in the recently opened Courtyard Hotel. I gave the owner, Luke Moriarty, a Stade Toulouse jersey to hang alongside his collection of Gaelic jerseys from his native Kerry. Now he has a Cédric Heymans' French jersey after he put eleven

Toulouse players up for free at a charity golf day in Westmanstown in aid of meningitis and cancer research.

The eleven weeks passed and the Leinster quarter-final loomed. I'd used my diary in *The Irish Times* to refer all inquiries to the De Danu e-mail address. Let's just say I was a popular man. For a month I took calls from people I knew and didn't know at all, or people I hadn't heard from in years. They wanted to know the good restaurants, good hotels, how to get from A to B, taxis, buses, trains, timetables, match tickets... and then there were the e-mails to the bar.

"How's it going? We play tag rugby every week in St Mary's. We're a group of ten blokes. Do you think you could organise a match for us?"

Another "Hi. We play indoor soccer every Wednesday. Could you organise a hall for us to play in? Or maybe there's a team who would like a match?"

"Hi. Could you book five tables in the bar on the day of the match?"

"Can you get us 50 tickets?"

The list went on and on. Was I sorry I'd given the email address in the paper?

One day, as I was having an afternoon nap in between sessions, the house phone rang. At first I didn't answer. When it didn't stop, I thought I'd better answer, as it might be urgent.

"Hello."

"Howya Trevor. Billy Byrne (not his real name) here."

"Who?"

"Billy Byrne."

"How's it going Billy, what's up?" I asked, thinking to myself, how do I know this guy Billy Byrne... Maybe it will come back to me.

"I hope you don't mind me ringing you, but I would like tickets with the Toulouse fans. Ten, if that's okay. And I read in one of your columns in the *Times* about the restaurant in the market. We'd like to eat there."

I asked him politely where he'd obtained my number, thinking maybe he knows one of the family, or a friend.

He replied that he'd been on to directory enquiries in France looking for a hotel in Toulouse and, while he was on, had asked the kind lady for Trevor Brennan's house number. "I hope you don't mind."

At which point, I told him where to go, hung up and yanked the phone cable from the wall. This was the kind of stuff I had to put up with. I was also in demand from various journalists, radio and tv stations, for interviews – which I found rather hard to deal with. So I said no to most of them.

We booked into our usual hotel for two nights, instead of one, before the game.

Family and friends arrived in force, and told me the craic in the bar was mighty. Leinster had brought their biggest ever following for an away game, maybe six or 7,000 invading the city. Apparently, half of them were as interested in the bar as they were in the match. RTÉ and Sky Sports also called in to De Danu, and by all accounts it was a sea of blue everywhere.

Guy Novès kept talking about the Leinster stars, especially the backs, D'Arcy, O'Driscoll, Contepomi, Hickie... singling out Yannick Jauzion, Florian Fritz, Vincent Clerc and Cédric Heymans to ask them if they were up to the challenge. In my opinion, all that talk about the Leinster backs may have backfired a little. That said, it's Guy's way, and a successful way, of motivating players. I kept telling Yannick and Florian that they were the best midfield combination in the world.

By the time of the game I was totally drained. I never like being in camp for two nights. I was rooming with Aidan McCullen, another former Leinster player, who was 23rd man. Because of a crushed cartilage which would require an operation at the end of the season, I had only played one or two games in the previous six weeks.

RTÉ and all the Irish papers were on to me. I turned down most interview requests, except for one or two individual ones with French papers and with Brendan Fanning of *The Sunday Independent*. I tried to talk down the game as much as I could.

That week the demand for tickets, hotels and the rest, was the highest I'd ever experienced since coming here. I was running around the place doing things for people. The whole build-up got to me. I'm not trying to make excuses, but sometimes it's just hard to switch off. You're supposed to be professional, but sometimes you can't manage it.

After another sleepless night for me before the game, we travelled to the ground with a police escort. One of the first people I spotted was Roly Meates, walking around in his thoughts and his usual haze of pipe smoke. That brought back memories. Amid a few thousand red-and-black-clad supporters, there wasn't a chance to speak. Anyway, I was already trying to get into my zone. I was confident we'd do well.

We started quickly, but the referee disallowed what we thought was a perfectly good Vincent Clerc try for a forward pass.

Sometimes a decision like this can change a game. Not long after, we let one through; O'Driscoll seemed to waltz untouched through our backs. Our back-row weren't pushing out as we were too busy putting up three pods in the line-out. Leinster had either done their homework or Contepomi had read it well. He had one of his best games in a Leinster jersey and they scored some good tries – although some were soft from our point of view.

Early in the second-half, I felt I was just coming into the match when I was taken off. I'd been heavily strapped and was worried that if I got a direct knock on it I'd be gone. I had all sorts of padding and rubbing. I took it off nearing half-time as I was feeling a bit freer, although it definitely did affect my game. But that's the coach's call and he knows his stuff. It was very frustrating to then watch it slip away from us, in part due to self-inflicted wounds. And to only lose by six points!

Arthur Tanner made his way over to our bench when he knew the game was over, and they had won. He commiserated with me, but congratulated me on all I'd achieved over the years in Toulouse. I was gutted but appreciated the gesture and the sentiments. We embraced each other and I wished him and Leinster the best of luck in the semi-finals.

Of all the many wonderful friends I've made through Leinster – way too many to count – there was none better than Arthur. Not alone is he a brilliant doctor for the players, but for their families as well, if necessary. If he thought you weren't up to a game he'd tell you honestly "There's bigger things than this game." A very genuine, accommodating man, on and off the pitch. He's not just a doctor, he's more a friend to all the players. He's a doctor to the stars and could be so much up his own arse, but he's not. He's just Arthur, and will drink pints with any of the lads. Just a lovely, lovely man.

This encouraged me to congratulate some of the Leinster lads as they made their way around the pitch to thank their supporters. I hit the changing-rooms and sat there, shocked that we had just lost a quarter-final at home, and for the first time in Le Stadium. Various sponsors, TV crews and journalists came into the dressing-room for the next hour.

I watched players coming and going from the showers, taking off strapping, getting dressed, doing interviews. I just sat there, drinking my bottle of Heineken. Followed by another, and another… The Cup sponsors have rarely come in handier, and when I looked over to the corner I saw Freddy doing the same.

Some players tapped me on the head, and said "Sorry Trev, we let you down today." I'd obviously made this one a bit personal. I'd never done that before, not even when we played Munster, so they realised how much it meant to me. I contemplated going into the Leinster dressing-room to congratulate them but couldn't bring myself to do it.

Eventually, everyone had left the dressing-room except me, Freddy and Guy Novès. I felt bad, but felt even worse for Freddy, who had kicked badly throughout and who had thrown an intercept pass that led to a Cameron Jowitt try. Freddy was in a terrible state. I went over to him, put my arms around him and told him it was only a game, or something useless like that. What can you say?

He'd been booed off the pitch against Ireland in Paris and now again today by the Toulouse public. I was at that Six Nations match, when Bernard Laporte had called the Stade de France crowd 'bourgeois shits', and the Toulouse media and public really got stuck into the Parisian crowd for doing that. And yet here he was being booed off the pitch by his own club fans at home.

Freddy is a great friend. You couldn't meet a more genuine, nicer guy. I know everyone labels him a big star, like Brian O'Driscoll in Ireland, and he has the poster boy image, the diamond ear-ring and all the rest.

He's a little like the David Beckham of French rugby, because he's good looking. Girls would die for him, and he's young, talented and gifted.

But he's so different from his public persona. Like Zinedine Zidane, I know he does so much charity work that no-one knows about. Much of his sponsorship money goes toward building houses for poor people, helping sick children or other charities. He is such a genuine bloke off the pitch it's incredible. And that's why I have so much time for him.

He mumbled "Merci, Trevor." He was inconsolable. I could see he felt personally responsible for the defeat, even though he wasn't. In Toulouse we don't play the blame game.

Freddy tries so hard. Sometimes he's the darling of the public and the media, as in the 2003 World Cup, but then was blamed more than anyone for the semi-final defeat to England. Some days his tricks work, and everyone loves him; the coaches, the players, the fans, the crowd. Some days they don't, and he's the villain.

I could see that Guy wanted a moment on his own with Freddy. Like me, Freddy probably figured that the longer you hung around, by the time you emerged everybody would be gone. Unfortunately, they weren't.

Head down, I went through the crowds and rang the brother. They were in a typical French bar in St Michelle. On my way to the car, I met Reggie Corrigan's mother and father, Brian O'Driscoll's mother and father, Denis Hickie's mother and father and Girvan Dempsey's mother and father; gave them all a kiss and said hello.

Even in those moments it was lovely seeing them again. I know from my own experience that parents feel the joy and despair of victory or defeat, if not more, than the players. It can take them until the middle of the following week to recover.

I could have done with some consoling myself. Losing that game was a huge disappointment and surprise to me, and one of the hardest to take, because of who it was. It had been a mad week in the bar, but the defeat hurt so much that I couldn't even go near it.

I went to the bar in St Michelle to meet family and friends. I ordered a round of about 50 drinks, not for myself, but for all the people from Leixlip. We tried to drown our sorrows, and half watched Munster make heavy weather of beating Perpignan.

After a rake of beer, we went to Bodega Bodega. We drank until the early hours before finishing in Le Dauphine, where everyone danced to the sounds of AC/DC. I was sitting at the bar when I noticed in the mirror one of the Leixlip lads walking past in his underpants. By that stage I'd forgotten we'd played a match.

There was a good mix of Toulouse and Leinster fans, and there's nothing you can do but adopt a brave face. It's sport. It happens sometimes. They came over here as the underdogs and won, and more power to them. And there are so many good people involved with Leinster.

Early the next morning I had a phone call from Shane Horgan's father, John. He commiserated with me for the defeat, congratulated me on all I'd achieved in Toulouse, and thanked me for the way I'd helped to look after his son when Shaggy first broke into the Leinster squad. It was a hell of a nice gesture.

That day, I invited family and friends to a barbecue at my house. Later we drove to the bar, which looked like a war zone. It was still hopping. Flights had been cancelled. A few favours had to be called in as about 150 kegs, that's 10,000 pints, had been drunk in the previous three days, and the bar needed re-stocking.

I may have said it was 'just another game', as players do, and as is always the case, that was all bollox.

I was playing against friends, against a province who'd let me go from a country which wouldn't pick me – despite playing for the best club side in the world for four years.

I'd played with Leinster since I was 17 with under-age teams right through to senior; ten years altogether. And it all just caved in massively on me.

And whatever about my own performance, it was the worst performance by Toulouse in my time here. We were shite. You have to give credit to Leinster. They scored some cracking tries. The one Denis Hickie finished off in the corner after Contepomi had run turnover ball from under his own posts, was vintage Leinster. As good a try as any visiting side has scored in Toulouse.

But for me, what Leinster did that day against us was a once-off. It was partly luck, because three weeks later they were exposed by Munster. Toulouse definitely under-performed hugely in that quarter-final. People will say I'm being bitter, but I'm not. That defeat rankled for a long time.

For years, Toulouse had been trail-blazers in the way they ran their club and played the game. But if you stand still, you actually go backwards, because everybody else is progressing.

More and more teams began to emulate the Toulouse style of play. And perhaps, they too could learn from other clubs without sacrificing what it is that makes Toulouse unique. It wouldn't be selling Toulouse's soul to bring in a defensive coach.

If there was any silver lining, it gave us our best chance to concentrate on the French Championship. In previous years, we'd had the excuse of prolonged European Cup campaigns. So even though some of the French media immediately wrote us off as a team over the hill, within the club we saw this as our best chance to win Le Bouclier in my time at the club.

We didn't have much time to recover from our defeat to Leinster. Typical of the French treadmill, we had to play Biarritz away the following Wednesday. Another loss. After that, it was make or break for the club. One more defeat would mean we would drop out of the top four. Next up were Stade Français.

A cousin, Terry McMahon, an actor and now a scriptwriter with Fair City, came over with his wife for the weekend. I met him on the Thursday and the Friday, and we had dinner in the bar. He's not terribly interested in rugby but that was all the better. And he lightened my mood in the build-up to this match.

It was another sell-out in Le Stadium. We played in a thunderstorm, and it was one of the best games I've ever played in. In other games against them we seemed to freeze, but even coming into the ground you sensed something special in the air. The place was electric in more ways than one.

As usual, we'd been told of the need for discipline, but after our warm-up in the pouring rain, Yannick Bru called us into a huddle. There were no coaches within earshot, and he said he was fed up of losing to these f****** and fed up of being bullied around by these f******. If there was any fighting we were all in. Anybody who didn't, he'd thump the head off him himself.

I started in the second-row and played the first 65 minutes. We won 15-0. Five kicks to nil. Not a try in sight. It was a dog-eat-dog match, like a Munster Senior Cup final in the '60s. I loved it.

About 20 minutes from the end Yannick Bru and Dimitri Szarzewski clashed heads at a 'hit' for a scrum. The two of them came up fighting, and everyone piled in. Florian Fritz came in from mid-field, picked up David Auradou and turned him upside down.

Romain Millochlusky, who is normally quite passive, came in swinging and punching. It was literally 15 against 15. That set a marker. The video of the match the following Monday showed fellas like Clément Poitrenaud and Vincent Clerc throwing punches. I was thinking "Ah no, this is not right. These aren't the same fellas I've been playing with the last few years."

After the game, I had a few beers in the sponsors' tent and headed off to the bar with Terry and a bottle of Jack Daniels. We drank whiskeys and coke into the early hours, him smoking away. I wasn't surrounded by friends and rugby players, and I woke up the next day feeling so fresh. The pain of the Leinster and Biarritz defeats had eased.

We qualified for the French semi-finals comfortably. As usual, we were given the short straw, playing Stade Francais in the second semi-final on a hot Saturday afternoon in Lyon. It was an absolutely incredible game. The ground was like a sea of red and black. It seemed about 90% of the crowd were Stade Toulouse supporters. They attacked our line solidly for about 20 minutes and we just defended, defended and defended.

On two occasions, they went through more than 15 phases of play inside our 22. I made 20-something tackles that day. Jeff Dubois came on with 20 minutes to go and kicked a late drop goal to win another dogfight 12-9, the same score line when Biarritz had beaten Perpignan the night before. That's how tough these play-off games can be.

The final was the following Saturday against Biarritz in Paris and so, as bloody usual, we had the shorter straw in that we had a day less to recover from our semi-final. It had been too much like a final for us and I felt increasingly drained during the week. By the day of the match I felt sick, and by Sunday it all made sense. I had the flu.

Against Biarritz we didn't play as a team, we didn't play the rugby that we're known for; offloading and throwing the ball around. We don't have any game plan, we never have had in my four years at the club. We don't have any defence coach, we don't have any real defensive pattern, we just play off the cuff and we defend off the cuff. That's the way Toulouse have played for years. We don't have a kicking coach, we don't have a scrummaging expert like Roly Meates. We don't have a line-out coach as such, we more or less come up with our own as players. But it just all fell apart that day, especially our defence. Individual errors cost us again.

It was incredible, really. We were only 9-6 down at half-time. They caught a ball from the kick-off, attacked up the wing, got into our 22 and did about six phases of pick and go before spreading the ball wide. Damien Traille came in between Michalak and Yannick Jauzion. They both simply looked at him before Michalak scragged him, and regrouping under the posts for the conversion they looked accusingly at each other.

"You said you had him?"

"You said you had him!"

We had the ball from the next kick-off. It went to Éllisalde, who tried to box kick from a ruck, but Bobo caught it. He ran 20 metres, chipped ahead and, in a race with Heymans and Vincent Clerc, won the touchdown. Within minutes of the restart we were 17 points down. Game over. You couldn't get the boys to lift their heads at all. In fairness, I could see why. The heat was incredible, and again in our last game of the season we faded away in the second half.

Biarritz played open, free-running rugby and our heads had dropped. They'd obviously done their homework as well. We put up three pods on their line-out. To counter this, they threw a short ball to the prop at the front, who gave it back to their hooker. He ran 20 metres to score a try untouched. There was an argument for starting Izzy Maka in his last match, but by the time he was brought on, the game was up.

I know he was very disappointed not to start, even though they picked his brother Finau ahead of him. Four weeks previously he had played his last game at Le Stadium against Brive, and he must have sent two fellas off on stretchers. Scored two tries. Just so determined. Then he was carried around on a lap of honour. "Goodbye Izzy" and "Thanks Izzy" were two of the banners amongst the crowd.

It was a crushing disappointment. Some supporters made the point afterwards that maybe it was better to be beaten that way than to lose a game by one or two points. I thought that was bull. Others talked about fatigue. Again, bull. We shouldn't suffer from fatigue.

No-one had expected us to beat the big men of Stade Francais in the semi-final. Everyone had built them up as having the bigger pack and that just fired up our lot. The problem with winning that semi-final was that heads went skyward, with the final of the French Championship only six days away. We'd played 34 competitive games to reach this final match of the season and then we blew it.

After losing that final, we were obliged to come back to Toulouse for a mayoral reception. It was so hard coming out on the balcony as our names were called out one by one. Instead of the 10,000 that might have been there had we won, there were just the 3-400 loyal souls.

At 5.00pm I asked everyone to come to De Danu where I'd put on a free bar for Guy, the coaching staff and the playing squad. "Let's have a bit of a blow-out at the end of the season, before the French internationals head off to South Africa."

We set up the tables at the back of the bar. As it was a Sunday, it was fairly quiet. We played drinking games like Fizz Buzz, had a bit a of craic, while others played poker. That night we went to the St Tropez for an end-of-season meal. It was also Isitolo Maka's last hurrah before going back to New Zealand, and then Japan. I got the boys going by singing *Today Is Going To Be The Day,* by Oasis. Guy was breaking his sides laughing at the end of the table, along with the president.

Then I asked Maka up to do the haka and he got Slade McFarland and his brother to whack it out with him. They looked ready for war. I suggested to Guy that we should learn that haka. It would be a good way to build up the boys. Guy laughed at the idea. And that was it. We split up after that night and didn't see each other again for months.

PATRICIO ALBACETE

TOULOUSE AND ARGENTINA LOCK.

"I first watched Trevor in the 1999 World Cup when I was back in Argentina. I thought he was a very good player, with a big heart. He did everything well and was very aggressive. I liked him.

When I first came to France, in Colomiers in 2003, I watched the Toulouse matches and noticed Trevor again. The aggressive way he played. He always gives 100%. Then I have the good luck to meet him and play with him here, and what surprised me was that on the pitch he is very aggressive, but off the pitch he is such a nice person.

He received me very well. And when I played with him in the Heineken Cup, it seemed that he knew everybody and everybody knew him with affection. Even the other players who play against him up front. On the field they might fight with each other or insult each other. But then after the match, everything is okay.

I respect him a lot as a player and there was never any rivalry between us. I never played against him with Colomiers or Pau, but it was an honour to play with him at Toulouse. He was always encouraging his team-mates, and lifting our spirits."

CHAPTER 17

BANNED FOR LIFE

THE DREADED NEWS

"They've banned you for life." he said. Silence followed. Neither of us said a word for a few seconds.

"Is that it?" I asked, still trying to take this in.

"No' he said, adding that they'd fined me €25,000 and ordered me to pay the costs of the hearing as well as a sum of €5,000 to the Ulster spectator. I asked him how I would pay the fine, stupid questions like that. I felt as if I'd been hit by a bus.

"Sit tight." he added. "We're going to appeal this. They can't do this."

"Okay, I'll wait till I hear from you."

"Okay, right." he said, and I hung up.

I put the kettle on and made a cup of tea. I felt okay because I'd had time to prepare myself for this moment. A few minutes later, Paula returned from collecting the boys from school. I told her the news.

Saturday, January 27th, 2007

MY LAST EVER GAME. I TRAVELLED WITH THE SQUAD TO PARIS AS 23RD MAN for a Saturday night match against Stade Francais in front of a full house of 80,000. On the morning of the game, we went for a light work-out by the pool with our forwards coach Serge Lairle. I asked him whether or not I'd be on the bench.

"No, you're the 23rd man," he said. But Gregory (Lamboley) had a dodgy back, so there was still a chance I might make the bench. I said fair enough, that was no problem. That had happened to me plenty of times during my career, whether with Leinster, Toulouse or Ireland. Ironically, it had happened to me once with Ireland at the very same ground.

Around lunch time, the president, René Bouscatel, coach Guy Novès and I had coffee in the hotel lobby. They spoke about the seriousness of the case pending against me. That they'd back me in every way they could. They would be as good as their word and for that I'll be forever grateful.

Six days before the Paris match had been that fateful game against Ulster during which – to my profound and deep regret – I hit an Ulster fan. An action that would ultimately – if briefly – see me stigmatised as a player who was 'banned for life'.

When I look back at the events of that day, they seem to unfold almost as if in slow motion. Both teams had been knocked out of the Heineken Cup. Even though the game was of no consequence, we were keen to avenge a pretty humiliating defeat to Ulster at Ravenhill, earlier in the season.

There was nothing special about the day at all – a normal, routine match day that will forever haunt me.

The sun was shining and the atmosphere was nice and relaxed. I didn't start the match, and after 20 minutes or so went for a warm-up behind the Ulster posts with half-a-dozen team-mates. There was a bit of banter from the Ulster supporters – nothing unusual in that.

Not long after the second half began, I was told to warm up. I went back down behind the Ulster posts to do my stretches. There was more banter, but maybe because I was on my own I took more exception to it than I ought to. I said to the supporters "Steady on lads."

And then I *thought* I heard something that simply turned a switch on in my head. I jumped over the wall and went for a supporter in what was without doubt the most reckless and stupid act I have ever committed.

After that moment of madness I returned to the team dug out and was almost immediately called into action on the field by Guy Novès – who was totally ignorant of what had just occurred.

Still fired up and seeing red, I shocked just about everyone by immediately getting stuck into Ulster's Justin Harrison. I was sin-binned for my troubles. As was Harrison who – not unreasonably – had a go at me.

Guy then discovered that there had been an incident involving supporters and decided not to put me back onto the pitch after my ten minute sin-binning was up.

I immediately realised the enormity of what had happened. In the dressing room, Guy told me the president wanted to see me. I went to the president's office along with Guy. He wanted me to explain what had happened, because the press were asking questions. They told me to wait there until they'd dealt with the media. I was escorted to my car by Fabien Pelous, William Servat, Guy and a few others, who kept some angry fans away from me.

I went for a pizza with Alfie (Gareth Thomas) in Pizza Hut and a pint in a pub near the airport. I dropped him off outside the airport, as he was flying to Cardiff to link up with the Welsh squad for the Six Nations. Then I went home.

For days and weeks afterwards, I fell into a complete depression. I hardly wanted to leave the house. Except for training sessions, I didn't.

I'd turn off my mobile only to discover "You have 44 new voice messages," when I turned it back on. Everyone wanted to talk to me – and I wanted to talk to no-one. I felt physically sick and depressed and kept going over the events in my mind.

Slowly, though, I began to get myself together. I'd love to turn back the clock – but I can't. I've done it. I have to live with it. I have to make other choices in life. I've three kids. I have to put bread and butter on the table for them.

It was a grim time – no doubt about it – and there was a heap more trouble waiting for me further down the road.

The day after the Ulster game, the ERC opened an investigation. By the Thursday, the ERC announced misconduct complaints against both myself and Gareth Thomas; Gareth had gone to the end of the ground where I'd had my alter-cation and gestured to some of the Ulster supporters.

On the morning of the match against Stade in Paris, the ERC summoned both of us to a Disciplinary Committee hearing for the following Thursday.

I went to the game in my suit. I was one of the last on the coach, and was very relaxed. But in the dressing-room beforehand, Guy said to me "Get togged out in case – Greg is doing a fitness test." No sooner had I put on my gear than Guy said Greg wouldn't be playing. I was on the bench.

Guy called me to one side in the shower room and spoke to me as a father would to his son when telling him something really important.

"Trevor this is your chance, this is for you, this could be your last time to put on the jersey. Wear it with the pride and the passion like you always have. Enjoy it and enjoy the moment. And thank you for everything."

Whatever is meant to be is meant to be, he added, followed by some words that brought tears to my eyes.

"Trevor the doors are always open in my house for you. Always. Today. Tomorrow. Always." He hugged me and kissed me on the head, then walked away.

It was a beautiful moment. Let's just say you had to be in my shoes to under-stand how it felt.

I did the warm up in the huge Stade de France training area adjacent to the dressing rooms. I sensed that everybody was aware this might be my last game. Taking my place on the bench before kick-off, I looked around at that beautiful stadium, full to capacity, and thought "What a nice way to finish your career, in front of 80,000 people."

The usual pre-match entertainment at a Stade Francais game in this ground was just finishing; inflatable dolls, cheerleaders, acrobats... It was like the opening ceremony for the Special Olympics in Croke Park.

You wouldn't see anything like it for an Ireland v France game. I was blown away by it. Then the tears began to well up. I could feel them. Then I saw the cameras zooming in on me. I picked up one of the towels in the dug-out and put it over my head. Willie Servat put his arm around me and said "Don't worry."

When I went with the subs for a stretch at the Toulouse supporters end of the ground, I could hear my name being chanted. I kept my eyes focused on the ground.

About ten minutes from the end Guy gave me the nod to go on as blindside flanker. I hadn't played blindside flanker in over a year.

Their number eight, Pierre Rabadan picked and bang; I tackled him. I got up, one of their second rows picked off a ruck and bang, I tackled him. I made about four tackles, one after another. I wanted to give everything I had in my body for those few minutes.

After the game the lads who had been watching from the sidelines commented on my seven tackles in five minutes. I just had that gut feeling that this could be my last game, especially after my earlier conversation with the club president and Guy. I could sense something big was going to tumble down on me.

We spent the night in a Parisian hotel and most of the lads hit the big smoke. I just stayed in my room and had some drinks from the mini bar. I was going through a down-in-the-dumps period.

Later, I went downstairs and had a couple of drinks with a few stragglers. The coaches were there, the doc, the physio.

I spoke for a little while with Guy. He wasn't happy that we'd lost the match by two points, but he was happy that I'd had a run.

He said "I think this is it now. I think you are going to get 18 months, two years." And that was the talk from journalists and others.

We spoke a bit about the route my career had taken, coming to Stade Toulouse and the manner of its ending. But what he'd said to me in the dressing-room before the game amazed me, because while I'd always respected him, there was always a fear factor – a distance – with Guy. Ever since, for the remainder of the season, when I went to the club to train with the boys, he kept me involved and always kissed me the way you would a best friend. Ever since that 'incident' Guy has given me the 'bisou'. It was almost embarrassing.

Wednesday, January 31st.

Jean-Michel Rancoule, the Toulouse scout who initiated my move to the club, accompanied me to Dublin the day before my first, scheduled ERC hearing. My solicitor Donal Spring and my barrister Jim O'Callaghan were to seek an adjournment of the hearing in the High Court. We were met by my brother Ronnie at the airport. We headed to the Hole in the Wall, Ronnie's local, for something to eat.

Sean Boylan, the former Meath manager, joined us and we had a good long chat. I'd helped organise a training camp for the Irish International Rules squad in Toulouse, and he told Jean-Michel how much they had enjoyed the trip. That the club couldn't have done more for them; giving them use of all the facilities.

When I told Sean that Jean-Michel had won Le Bouclier twice as a player with Toulouse in '85 and '86 and that he was originally from Lourdes, that got them talking. Sean had been to Lourdes a few times. We said our farewells and later that evening, as a way of settling the nerves and showing Jean-Michel a bit of Dublin, I took him to the Brazen Head, where we listened to some traditional music.

Ronnie's brother in-law, Maurice, joined us and from there we crossed the road to O'Shea's. Jean-Michel ended the night dancing jigs and reels, the whole lot, and we had to practically carry him back to our hotel.

The following day, when Jean-Michel and I met Donal in the Four Courts, we went to the coffee shop downstairs. Donal and Jean-Michel exchanged a few stories about the old days, when Donal played for Bagnérais and Jean-Michel for Lourdes, which would have been a local derby. I was a bit taken aback to discover that Donal is still fairly fluent in French.

Jim Glennon had helped me to engage Donal and Jim, but I'd only spoken to Donal over the phone before this day. We exchanged a few funny stories from our playing days and he really put me at ease.

Donal advised me that we would seek an adjournment on the grounds that the ERC case should not proceed while there was a criminal trial pending in France.

Springer and Jim O'Callaghan briefed me not to say anything, just to sit at the back of the court and listen. Myself and Jean-Michel went into the courtroom, where I met Derek McGrath, the ERC chief executive, and shook his hand. "How's it going Derek?" I've known Derek for years and was hardly going to ignore him now.

Gareth Thomas had his ERC hearing scheduled for the next day. He had been cited for attempting to follow me into the crowd and making a two-fingered gesture towards some of the Ulster fans. He'd had to leave the Welsh Six Nations camp and I went to his hotel and wished him well. He rang me after his ERC hearing to tell me he'd received a four-match ban and a €7,500 fine. I thought to myself "He didn't even get over the f****** wall! What are they going to do to me?"

My hearing in the Four Courts attracted quite a few journalists, though the only one I recognised was John O'Sullivan from *The Irish Times*. He asked me for a few words but I told him I had been advised not to comment. "Sorry about that John."

He said "No worries Trev, sorry about your bit of trouble and to be meeting you in these circumstances."

St Valentine's Day.

One of the worst aspects of this whole episode was that Paula was eight and a half months' pregnant. I didn't want to upset her too much but, of course, she already was. She's always been very emotionally attached to my rugby career. She feels all the things I feel. I've been going out with her since I was 16. We've shared half our lives. She's been through so much with me; the death of my brother and all the ups and downs of my rugby career.

She didn't jump on a bandwagon. She was with me when I was a milkman, and a breadman; she's seen it all. When Toulouse first made their offer, Paula had a very good job, but it was never a question of "Ah no I'm staying here, I can't give up my job." She regarded the whole thing as a great adventure which she probably thought would last just a couple of years.

If she'd said "I want to stay in Ireland" would I have stayed in Ireland for her? I don't know and I'll never know, because when I said that I wanted to go to France, she said "Yes, no problem."

I woke up on Valentine's Day and had a bowl of cornflakes, while Paula, as usual, turned on the television.

"Trev, I feel something. I don't know if it's going to happen today." Paula wasn't due for another two weeks but said "I can feel something going on here."

"What do you want to do? Maybe a cup of tea?"

"Oh Jaysus Trev, I really do feel something now!"

"Well, what will we do? Do you want to go into hospital?"

"I think we'd better just in case."

The boys were at school and we arrived at the Clinique de Sarrus in St Cyprien. I rang ahead and told them we were coming. When we arrived, there was no messing around. They took the details and Paula was quickly assigned a room on the second floor.

Within minutes, a midwife arrived to take Paula's blood pressure and told her "Yes, you'll be having a baby today Mrs Brennan." I rang a neighbour, Crystal, who said she'd collect the boys from school and give them dinner. I think it was around

4.00pm when Paula gave birth to our third boy; a healthy bouncing baby boy, and a great source of joy in a difficult time. That's what Paula said, "There's a silver lining behind every cloud."

An awful lot of people expressed similar sentiments to me in the hours and days that followed. "That's what's important: the birth of a new child who's healthy." "That's what life is all about."

Saturday, February 24th.

The day Ireland played England. This wasn't just any game. This was history. England in Croke Park. But, thanks to the powers that be, I was in Paris for a disciplinary hearing with the French Federation. On a Saturday. Offices aren't normally open for business in France on a Saturday.

As the High Court and ERC hearings dragged on, I was still eligible to play. Clearly unhappy with this, the International Rugby Board (IRB) entered the fray. They sent a letter to the French Federation, citing special circumstances, asking that I be banned until the ERC had sorted out my suspension.

The IRB letter was signed by Dr Syd Millar, chairman of the IRB.

Mark McParland, President of my old club Bective, had asked me to speak at their 125th anniversary dinner on the Friday night. I was raging that I couldn't attend, not least because there was a match ticket thrown in to go to Croke Park with some of the Bective lads.

So, following the demand from the IRB, the French Federation set their hearing for Saturday, February 24th and instead of going to Dublin, I flew to Paris the night before the hearing. The Toulouse president, René Bouscatel, represented me.

This was on a Saturday! Nobody works on a Saturday. "Saturday?" said my solicitor Donal Spring. "I'm in Leitrim on Saturday and Croke Park on Sunday." Fair play to him, Donal was willing to come to Paris. But he and René agreed there was no need for him to travel over.

René trained as a professional lawyer before he became President of Stade Toulouse. He flew up on the Saturday morning.

As well as the Ireland-England game, France were to play Wales that night in the Stade de France.

Okay, picture this: I'm in the lobby of the French Federation at 8.30am. The place is buzzing, people coming in and out getting tickets. I was asked by a gentleman if I'd like a coffee. "Oui merci." I drank it. Fabien Pelous had booked two tickets for myself and Donal, and I went upstairs to a ticket office to pay for the them. I'd initially bought one for Donal before it was decided he needn't attend. So there

I was with two tickets and lots of 'bonjours' and friendly faces. People shook my hand and wished me luck. I watched some of the greats of French rugby come in and out of the building; Serge Blanco, Jean-Claude Skrela, Bernard Lapasset, the president of the French Federation, and many more.

René arrived just after 9.00am and told me "When we go in here today you don't speak."

"Why?" I said.

He said "You just don't speak." He was defending my right to silence pending any civil case. We were summoned into a conference room where there were about 35 people sitting around a conference table.

Bernard Lapasset spoke briefly, explaining that they had been asked to examine this case by the IRB and, as they worked under the IRB regulations, were obliged to suspend me. He spoke about the letter from Syd Millar and how this hearing was seen as "special circumstances".

René wasn't happy about any of this, and immediately let it be known. He seemed to be doing a great job. He stopped the proceedings on three occasions. He said this was not a French problem. This was an ERC problem and now the IRB had become involved.

"Qu'est-ce-que c'est?" "What is this?" He mentioned other cases. "Pourquoi est-ce-que ceci se passe?" "Why is this happening? Why is this man being discriminated against? Tell me why? You don't have to work, you don't have to do their job," he said, ie play rugby for a living. I'd never seen René like this; I'd never seen him in action.

When Lapasset asked me to speak, René grabbed me and declared "Non, il ne parle pas," and dragged me from the room. I kind of gestured apologetically and, as I was going out the door, saw Blanco smiling as if he'd seen this before.

Outside I asked René "Qu'est-ce-qui se passe?" What's happening?

"Je suis pas d'accord," said René.

"What do you mean you don't agrée?" I asked.

"No, let them come to us," he explained. "I've given them the terms now."

Ten minutes later someone came out and said "We're ready for you now Mr Bouscatel."

The hearing had resumed for two minutes when René declared "Trevor on s'en va." Let's go. And we walked out again in protest.

We stood in the hall. "René what's the f****** story? Just let me speak, let me tell my story."

"No, you're saying nothing."

We went back inside and I looked at a picture of the Irish team that had played France in 1956 – the little pennant the referee had given his touch judge. And all the memorabilia decorating the French Federation head office. To me it was like a mini tour of a museum. I'm sure there aren't too many players who've seen the inside of that room.

Meanwhile, René was still going mad and we walked out in protest once more. The third stand-off was the longest; we remained outside about forty minutes. Inside the 35 who had gathered were going to the France-Wales match that evening, with a dinner or other engagements to attend beforehand.

Skrela was amongst those outside waiting for this hearing to finish. People were glancing at me, clearly becoming a little agitated.

Eventually Blanco himself came out and said "Trevor it looks like it's good, a lot of people are for you."

Serge Simone of the Players Union then emerged and said "Trevor, a lot of people are voting for you."

We were called back in to be told they'd given me a three-week suspension. They said they had to give me three weeks. But this covered the remaining weeks of the Six Nations, when the French Championship was closed down anyway.

In other words, I was free to play Toulouse's next match. I was hugely relieved. Outside Bouscatel said this was good news. In other words, they'd supported me.

Myself and René went for lunch. We chatted about many things, and when we were finished I paid the bill. I walked with René to a taxi rank as he was flying back to Toulouse that day. I thanked him again.

He said "You are my friend," and off he went. I walked back to my hotel for a nap because, with an 8.30pm kick-off, it was going to be a rather long night.

I tossed and turned for an hour; too many things were going on in my head. I got up, had a shower and went to Notre Dame. I became a tourist for the afternoon and took in some of the main sights. I had a few hours to spare before the game, so after a quick bite in McDonalds, I tried the Paris metro system for the first time. And the last time. I should have taken a taxi.

The underground was like another world. The heat was unbearable. No indication of a match anywhere. It certainly wasn't like Dublin on match day; on the Dart, say, from Dun Laoghaire to Lansdowne, you follow the flags, the scarves, the hats. This was another world. Not a blue jersey in sight. Not even a Welsh one.

Four trains later I arrived at my destination sweating and smelly. I made my way to an Irish bar near the ground and watched the Ireland v England game with hundreds of Welsh fans, who kept singing *Ireland's Call*.

French supporters who recognised me, asked what had happened at my hearing with the Federation. Most were saying "tres bon" when I told them I was banned for the remaining three weeks of the Six Nations. I still spent most of the match wishing I was in Croke Park. Regular communication from brothers and friends who were at the match – relaying how brilliant the whole day was, and the atmosphere and the game itself – didn't help my mood.

Before the game, I met up with William Servat and ten of his family and friends outside the stadium. I'd a spare ticket for the match, which cost me €250. I'd said to Fabien "get me the best tickets in the house" because I wanted to look after Springer. Instead, one of William's friends was ticketless so I gave it to him.

Willie's friend spent the whole match on his mobile phone. "I'm in Stade de France, and guess who I'm sitting beside? Unbelievable. He gave me a ticket. We're in the presidential suite."

"What are you doing?" I asked him.

"Oh, I'm telling my friends I'm at the match!"

"You feckin' eejit; watch the match!"

After the game we all met up outside the ground and made our way to the metro. The rain poured down and the police only permitted a couple of hundred at a time through their barriers. We queued for nearly two hours just to get on the metro. "What a hole," I thought. It's as if they picked it up and stuck it in the middle of nowhere; no bars, no taxis, no buses. You can't get out of it.

Willie and his brother took us to a night club, the Crème de Pousse, beside the Eden Park bar. It's a little like Temple Bar. It's where many of the French rugby players go. I'd been to the same place after France's Grand Slam win over England two years before. Most of the French team and their coach Bernard Laporte were also there.

One of Willie's mates at the match worked as a barman in Crème de Pousse, and occasionally myself and Willie went behind the counter to pull pints. When Bernard Laporte turned up at the club, I made eye contact and waved to him. He made his way over to our corner, put his hand out and said

"Bonjour Trevor."

"Bonjour Bernard."

"Je suis désolé; désolé," he said, commiserating over my ban.

"Merci Bernard."

He repeated his commiserations, and Willie and the others in my company were all taken aback that Bernard had made his way through the crowd to express his sympathy for me. I felt he'd like to have stayed and had a beer with me but there were people all around him.

I offered him a drink, but there was one fellow, completely drunk, who was in his ear constantly. "Non Trevor, merci. Une autre fois," and he went on his way. Everybody was fairly taken aback and spoke about it for a while.

"Ca, c'est incroyable," said Willie. It's unbelievable.

"Ca, c'est gentil," said Julie, Willie's girlfriend. That's nice.

However two days later – Monday, February 26th – the ERC independent disciplinary committee dismissed my application for a further adjournment pending any civil case. They reset my hearing for three weeks' later; Friday March 16th in England. This was the same day my three week suspension by the French Federation expired. Things didn't look good.

Friday, March 16th

We didn't attend the ERC hearing in London. My lawyers maintained that to do so would contravene my right to silence pending my criminal trial. He rang me when word reached him of the disciplinary committee's decision to say he had the verdict. I was at home.

"Okay, Donal."

He said "Are you sitting down?"

I said no; I was leaning against the kitchen counter at that moment, but said don't worry about it. I'd stay standing.

"They've banned you for life." he said.

Silence followed. Neither of us said a word for a few seconds.

"Is that it?" I asked, still trying to take this in.

"No" he said, adding that they'd fined me €25,000 and ordered me to pay the costs of the hearing as well as a sum of €5,000 to the Ulster spectator. I asked him how I would pay the fine, stupid questions like that. I felt as if I'd been hit by a bus.

"Sit tight." he added. "We're going to appeal this. They can't do this."

"Okay, I'll wait till I hear from you."

"Okay, right." he said, and I hung up.

I put the kettle on and made a cup of tea. I felt okay because I'd had time to prepare myself for this moment. A few minutes later, Paula returned from collecting the boys from school. I told her the news.

Paula is a very honest woman, very straight, very well-educated, who believes that no-one is completely wrong; everyone deserves a chance no matter how bad they are. She's not a judgemental person.

When I told her the news she went ballistic.

I'd never heard her speak that way before.

"Don't worry, calm down, calm down, don't be worrying," I said.

She was a bit taken aback that I was so calm about it but. I explained that I had prepared myself for something like this. She was waiting for the fireworks, she was waiting for me to explode. But I didn't. I told myself, 'I'm gonna move on now and turn over that chapter in my life.'

In the build-up to that hearing, I had asked for my right to silence, as had my legal representatives, but I was refused it. A criminal case was pending against me in France and I wasn't sure what the consequences would have been as a result of taking part in a hearing.

Any evidence I gave in a rugby disciplinary hearing, and the ensuing verdict, might have been prejudicial towards me in a French court of law.

So, partly in protest, I had announced my retirement from the game of rugby four days before the hearing in England.

Obviously that was a hard decision. It didn't hit me until it was pointed out as an option to me by my legal team.

"What? You want me to do what? Retire?"

I hadn't planned on retiring. I was hoping to play with Toulouse for another six months and then I was considering signing for Montauban for one year, with an option on a second year. The reality of retirement was tough.

By retiring, I felt I gave the ERC the option of adjourning the case until after my criminal trial was finished.

I wasn't obliged to attend the hearing in London, although as it transpired if I'd refused to pay any fine, the ERC would have been entitled to take it out of Toulouse's participation fee. It's not what I'd planned to do. It certainly was not the circumstances I'd expected to retire under.

It was the suddenness of it all. Sure I'd worked, and I'd held down more jobs than most professional rugby players. But in the previous 11 years rugby was all I'd known, and all of a sudden it was gone. Now what would I do? Sure, the bar is there but, Jaysus, you don't make the kind of money a professional rugby player with Toulouse earns out of a small bar in France. You have busy weekends, football and rugby matches, etc... but it's not comparable. What was I going to do?

I found the official response by the rugby hierarchy – by the IRB, the ERC, the FFR – and that whole process, very daunting. I was out of my depth and drowning fast. I found the system worked on the basis, 'guilty until proven otherwise.' To me the system appeared unfair.

I had the impression from day one that they were not interested in hearing my side of the story. It was like going down a fast flowing river with a heavy current – but without a canoe, never mind a paddle.

I know better than anyone that what I did was wrong.

But a life ban?

What was their point? Did they want my punishment to be a deterrent? No player is likely to ever repeat what I did. And if one did, in the heat of the moment, he'd hardly start flicking mentally through the history of cases such as mine before making a clinical decision to jump a wall and go after a spectator.

What I didn't expect was the reaction over the next few days and weeks. E-mails came flying in from all over the world. Barnhall started a petition; phone calls, handwritten letters, people outside the club ground on match days signing petitions. Irish clubs and players signed petitions or wrote letters or e-mails in support of my case, and against the severity of the ERC sentence. Provale, the players union in France, became involved; with every professional club in France signing a petition.

The story became big news in France. Comparisons were made with other sports and other suspensions, notably Eric Cantona's nine-month ban for his attack on a Crystal Palace fan. I sat in front of the computer at nights reading some of them. Or I'd be in the sitting room watching TV and Paula would call me. I'd hear her crying. "Read this one, it's amazing."

It was an astonishing time for the both of us, and we were deeply moved and encouraged by both the nature and volume of the support we received. It lifted our spirits hugely and gave us hope that the future was not as bleak as we had previously feared.

Friday, May 10th.

Our last home game of the season was against Agen, but again, I wouldn't be playing. A load of people had travelled over from Leixlip, Lucan and Celbridge. Friends, uncles, aunts, friends of friends, lads from the GAA and soccer clubs in Leixlip, as well as from Barnhall, had travelled over for what should have been my farewell match in Stade Ernest-Wallon.

Keith Brennan, whom I had played with in Barnhall, was having his stag, which accounted for about 20 of the invasion. Most had booked their flights four or five months prior to my suspension in the expectation that this would be my grand finale. I'd let it be known that Stade Toulouse always gives a memorable send-off to players who are retiring or moving on, and ten players were finishing up with the club at the end of this season. But they said, what the hell, they'd come over anyway.

They landed in Blagnac Airport at 10.00am and the phone began to hop; they wanted me to meet them in De Danu. But first I had to take the new addition, Bobby Valentine, to the doc at 11.00am for some injections,. As well as carry out some cleaning duties Paula had lined up for me: take in the clothes, clean around the pool, sweep the driveway so as to have the house looking spic and span. All part of my new life of blissful domesticity. Although no-one was staying with us, we were going to host a barbecue on the Sunday.

At about 2.00pm myself, Paula and Bobby – the other two boys were in school – headed in to meet the crew. It was a beautiful sunny day. As I came over the bridge at Pont Guillenery, several of the lads were spilling onto the street.

The stag group wore Borat look-alike black wigs and moustaches; but whereas the lads wore pink t-shirts with 'Keith Brennan's Stag' emblazoned on them, Keith himself was dressed in nothing but a bright green crotch-sling.

He looked the real deal as he cycled up and down the footpath on an old postman's bike. We'd brought it over that weekend and now it hangs in the window of the bar. The locals looked on in astonishment.

I spent three hours talking to them all before dropping Paula and Bobby home. Then I got ready for the match, which had an 8.30pm kick-off. Driving towards the ground I felt as excited as if I were playing.

There was that pre-match buzz in the air leading to the ground, with everyone wearing the colours for a Friday night 19,500 sell-out. Cars were being abandoned on the roadside two miles from the stadium. As the motorway was blocked, I chose a back route. I reached a roundabout where the police waved me through so I could park in the club. I wondered how long that perk would last?

I'd bought tickets for my friends amongst Le Huit, the hard core supporters with the drummers and flags. The president of the supporters club had asked me to sit amongst them. This is the place to be if you want to soak up the atmosphere.

As I came up the steps the crowd began to cheer 'Brenn-an, Brenn-an, Brenn-an!' The hairs on my head – the few that I have left – stood up. And everywhere else on my body. A cameraman following me told me this was their way to show support and say thanks. The game kicked off. I let off some of the crackers with the rest of the supporters.

The atmosphere was magical. I'd never watched a match from this angle behind the goalposts, or been this close to what I call the real supporters. They're not sponsors of the club, they pay €150 for season tickets which give them seats to all the home games and first preference for away games. They're just ordinary Joe

Soaps; working-class fans.

To their right is the Kop for the kids, which was full with about 2,000 youngsters. They jumped up and down, and sang, for the duration of the match. The flags were unfurled before the kick-off, and when the crowd quietened down, the 80 or so Paddies in front of me sang *The Fields of Athenry*. The French loved it. They'd brought about fifty flags, the green white and gold mixed in amongst the red and black. Including an enormous one that read "Best of luck Trev, thanks for all the memories".

Looking down on them, I felt so proud to be Irish and one of their family and friends. I felt pride in our flag, in our madness, our poetry and songs. That is literally what was going through my mind.

At half time I made my way down to the subs bench and watched the rest of the game with Emile Ntamack between the two dug-outs, as there were no seats available. Christian Labit and David Gerard, who had also come over from Northampton, joined us and the four us chatted together as we watched the second half.

The boys played champagne rugby, winning their eighth match in a row, 47-0, and Guy Novès threw on all the subs. When the final whistle sounded, I walked to the dug-out and shook hands with the coaches and the players who had been substituted.

Guy grabbed me and said "Go on the pitch with the players". They always do a final lap around the pitch after the last home game.

I didn't want to but he said "Go on or I'll kill you." So I walked on with a few other players, such as Yannick Nyanga, who was injured and wearing a suit, and I think, Benoît Baby, and joined the rest of the players behind the goalposts. We formed a huddle and Fabien Pelous and Yannick Bru said a few words. "We're in the top four now, destiny is in our own hands."

Frédéric Michalak and Jean-Baptiste Elissalde started singing some rap song for about ten seconds before we broke up the huddle. Freddy, in his last match before going to South Africa to play for a year with the Natal Sharks, was picked up and then Yannick Jauzion came up behind me, stuck his head in between my legs and lifted me onto his shoulders.

He carried me half way around the pitch. I felt embarrassed. "Jaysus lads, let me down." I was the only one in civvies; jeans and a black t-shirt.

They said "No, you deserve it, stay up there."

I continued pleading "Lads let me down." But they wouldn't relent, so I began to give the royal wave and clap the crowd as they chanted "Brenn-an, Brenn-an," along with "Fred-dy, Fred-dy". I could feel myself welling up inside. It took a huge effort not to start crying. And I was sweating as much as if I'd played the match.

Finau Maka took over from Yannick in hoisting me into the air, before letting me down when we reached the other end of the pitch – where I'd watched the first half, in front of all the tricolours and noires et rouges. Conrad Burke climbed out from the throng of Irish supporters and tried to hand me a tricolour, but was immediately surrounded by several security guards who wouldn't allow him onto the pitch.

"Il est avec moi, Il est avec moi," I explained, and Conrad handed me the tricolour. I waved it over my head and could hear my name being chanted again. In my entire career I'd never known moments like these.

The only other time I'd ever held an Irish flag on a rugby pitch was after Toulouse beat Stade Francais in the 2005 Heineken Cup final in Murrayfield. I draped this one around my shoulder and walked with the rest of the players along the side of the pitch to the dressing-room.

Once there, I sat down and looked around, and took it all in; what had just happened. Guy enjoyed making the point, as he did again in the papers the next day, that normally it's Freddy who is the darling of the crowd. But on that night the biggest cheers had been for me. He said he was impressed.

Everyone was on a bit of a high. We'd had a great win. As it was the last home game of the season, I was kind of sad. Not just for myself, but because of all the other lads. Ten players were leaving. There is a strong possibility that Michalak would be back, but the others probably wouldn't be. Jeff Dubois, a great character on and off the pitch, was heading to Racing Club Paris. And you do lose contact with these players.

You always say "Ah yeah, we'll stay in touch," but the reality is different. I've realised that since I left Leinster. You don't stay in touch, not as much as you'd like to. It's too hard. I didn't feel it would be the last I'd see of this dressing-room or this club. I intend to keep involved in coaching the under-19's next year; I intend to keep involved with the club, in some capacity. I'll still go and watch matches.

These guys have become my friends as well as my team-mates over the last five years. Jeff likes a party. Typically, he had organised a farewell barbecue for the next day and he was usually the first to arrange a night out, maybe with a fancy dress theme. For his going away do, we all had to wear some sort of headgear, be it an army hat, a woolly hat, a baseball hat ... he's a real character.

Yannick Bru is probably one of the most genuine people I've ever met in all the years I've played rugby. He helps everybody. He helps all the foreigners who come into the club get settled and find houses. He helps people with their taxes. I still haven't a clue about the French system, but he helps me out. He explains when, or if, I have to pay. He does all the tax returns for the players and never asks for payment.

I've never heard him raise his voice. Off the pitch he's just so genuine but on the pitch, of course, he can be a hard man. There's no doubt about it. He's played for France, and he's the new forwards coach of Toulouse, which shows how highly the club regards him.

Jean-Baptiste Élissalde is always joking. A bundle of energy, flying around like a little Duracell Bunny. He's a lovely fella, though he can be serious when required. He's hot-headed on the pitch and the boys constantly slag him.

Yannick Jauzion is the quietest in the dressing-room; says bloody nothing! It's weird, a six foot five, 17 stone centre, who says nothing. But a pure gentleman. Everything is so straight, by the book. You'd never see him in a fight.

I met up with the family, who were outside the sponsors' tent behind the stand. They were amongst the mobile Heineken bars and thousands of Le Huit supporters. The place was a sea of red and black. And green, white and orange. Before long, we were singing to about 2,000 supporters from the steps above them.

The Barnhall boys launched into the club anthem, *Blue Is The Rose*, which prompted a sing-off. The beer was flowing and at one point, I orchestrated the sing-song – smiling from ear to ear, like a kid. Because of the noise, people actually left the sponsors' tent to look on or take part. I was down amongst the mix of French and Irish supporters, when the club president René Bouscatel approached me and commented "Maintenant je sais pourquoi tu es le Roi." Now I know why they call you The King.

An hour or so later, I said "Come on lads we'll be here all night, these guys have a lot of songs!" The president of the supporters club asked me to call into their clubhouse about a mile away, as they wanted to make a presentation to me. I made sure all the Irish contingent had boarded their bus into De Danu and then headed off.

There were 300 to 400 people in the supporters' clubhouse, and after a little while in walked Warwick Bowden and a few of the Barnhall lads. They'd missed their bus and when given a lift by one of the Toulouse supporters had asked for "Brennan's Bar."

He said "No, Brennan is not in there, he's down in this club."

I was presented with a hamper of wine, foie gras and bits and pieces, along with a portrait of myself. Their president said a few words, as did about half a dozen of the players who came along, including Freddy, Clement and Jeff. I said I'd never seen supporters like them and that they are possibly the best in the world. I thanked them for everything they'd done for me.

"J'aimerais bien chanter quelque chose pour vous; chanson Irlandais. C'est une chanson que j'aime bien." I said that I'd love to sing something for them; an Irish song. It's a song that I love. It was the same song that I'd recently sung at a boules competition in my village, and I broke into the first verse of *Ordinary Man*. I didn't realise at the time that the Toulouse television station, TLP, was filming all of this and would show me singing at the supporters' club on TV that Monday night.

It was hard to cram everything I wanted to do into this one night. After heading into my own bar for a few hours, I sneaked away to meet most of the Stade players. They were having a party in a local night club that Yannick Bru had hired for the night. There were a few hundred there, invitation only, with doormen, food and a free bar. It was full of former and current Toulouse players that Yannick would have played with.

I asked him how much it had cost him?

"You only get to do this once in your life," he said.

I was glad too that I got to show a bit of respect for Yannick. He knew there was a massive Irish contingent in town and he hadn't expected me. I spent the next four or five hours there with the Toulouse lads. We sang, had dance-offs and I spoke to former players. It must have been quite emotional for Yannick. I watched him work the room, and seemingly talk to everybody.

The next day was tough. There were end-of-season parties all over town. Jeff Dubois asked William Servat for the use of his house, because it has plenty of land and a large swimming pool. Whereas his was a three-bedroom house in Colomiers. The place was filled with food and beer.

A few of the lads, coaches and sponsors were amongst the 100 or so people present. 'Ricard' had set up a bar in Willie's garden; Heineken contributed five kegs of beer; Didier Lacroix's father, Jean, provided all the meats, and there was champagne, wine and a DJ. The sun shone all day.

I had Danny and Josh with me, and I slipped away quietly and early, although later that night some of the boys rang me and started singing *Connemara* down the phone. It's a brilliant French song, called *le lac de Connemara*, about a Frenchman who goes to Connemara and falls in love with a red-haired girl.

About 30 of the Irish gang stayed on until the Monday and had their private bus bring them to my house for the barbecue that day. Everyone was taking it easy, chilling out and chatting in the back garden, when one of the lads, Shane, jumped into the pool fully-clothed. That got the party going.

Some sunbathed, most drank, while I panicked over the BBQ – burning sausages and burgers. Luckily, Tom Halpin came to my rescue. He looked like a veteran barbecuer. The sun was splitting the stones, and standing over a BBQ in such heat is not the place to spend the guts of two hours. I eventually got down to some drinking with Ronnie and the lads in the front of the house, where it was quieter.

The soccer boys said that they'd followed Ireland all over the world, yet had never experienced an atmosphere like the previous Friday night. I agreed with them that Stade Ernest-Wallon, when it's full on a Friday night, takes some beating. But not every home game is like that. Not by a long way.

Tuesday, May 22nd.

In court yet again; this time a French court for a criminal case brought against me by the French authorities. It was a small court. I had to be there for 2.00pm. There were several cases before mine, some funny, some sad. One involved a father and son who had started fighting with each other in a bar after a liquid lunch. They'd been asked to leave, whereupon they attacked the barman and thrashed the place. They had to pay for all the damage to the bar and €3,000 compensation to the owner.

A motorcyclist had the book thrown at him for knocking down a woman. Then there were some speeding cases. Throughout the hearings, in between witnesses giving evidence, solicitors converged at the back of the court and were regularly told by the judge to be quiet . Eventually, my solicitor, Olivier Thevenot, nodded to me from the front of the court.

I walked to the stand and stood in front of the judge.

"Bonjour."

"Bonjour, madame."

She asked for my name and address.

She repeated my name and address. "C'est ca?"

"Oui," I said.

Then as my solicitor spoke, I could hear one or two voices whispering "C'est Brennan?" "C'est Brennan?" "Oui, c'est Brennan, c'est lui, oui." "Oui? Qu'est-ce-qui se passe? Qu'est-ce qu'il fait ici?"

It's Brennan. Yes, it's him. What's happening? What's he doing here?

Several gendarmes were amongst the 60 or 70 people in the room, to give evidence in various cases. There'd been noise and chatter throughout the morning, but suddenly you could hear a pin drop.

Earlier, when I'd taken a toilet break, I'd been asked to sign a few autographs.

"C'est pour Jerome."

"Cest pour Jean Luis."

"C'est pour…" Alright, grand. "Bonne chance."

"Nous sommes avec toi." We are with you.

The courtroom was silent, everyone was listening to my solicitor. The judge seemed curious; she was smiling slightly. I picked a spot on the wall and just focused on it.

Then she asked me if I'd ever been sent off or been in trouble before in France.

I said "Oui. Oui madame, une fois, contre Agen." I explained that I'd received a red card against Agen in 2003 for fighting with Luc Lafforgue, their captain, and that I had been suspended for two weeks.

She laughed and said that because it had been a local derby against Agen it didn't count. That put a smile on my face. She asked me how long my suspension was for this time.

"Vie."

"Quoi?" she said.

"Vie," I repeated.

"Quoi?" she repeated, widening her eyes in surprise.

At that stage, more talking in the courtroom prompted the judge to bang her gavel on the table and demand silence in the court.

"What do you do now for a living?" she asked.

I said I had a bar but my wife had found a few jobs for me to do, trying to make it a bit humorous. Obviously you have to take courts seriously, but at this point, it seemed like the right thing to do. I felt fairly relaxed anyway, I'd been given my life suspension, so I felt this day couldn't be any worse. Going in that day, I'd told my solicitor that whatever I was fined, I'd pay it.

In the end I was fined €820 euro.

But just as that chapter was coming to a close, another was opening.

Friday, June 1st.

Back to Dublin for my appeal against my lifetime suspension. It's funny, I was quite relaxed about the whole thing. I'd watched a programme a couple of nights before entitled Sports' 100 Maddest Moments. It showed mass brawls, players from the same team beating each other up, Cantona's moment of madness, the Zinedine Zidane incident, Mike Tyson biting Evander Holyfield's ear and spitting it out on the canvas – as a result of which they took away his licence to box... I was half expecting to see myself pop up on the screen.

I came home two days before my appeal and stayed in my parents' house. On June 1st, I caught the early bird train from Leixlip to Dublin, arriving in Connolly Station at 7.00am. Then I took a taxi to Donal Spring's offices in Fitzwilliam Square. We weren't due at the hearing until 9.00am, so I headed down the road for a walk to kill time.

Several people stopped to wish me well and good luck. I wondered how so many people rushing to work knew what was happening that day. I figured there must have been something in the morning papers. Outside the café I met Jack and his son Joe Looby; the current and incoming presidents of Barnhall.

Sitting at the window of the café, a taxi driver pulled up, beeped his horn and gave me the thumbs up. Then he held up *The Irish Independent* back page with a picture of me coming out of the Four Courts back on January 31st. I smiled and returned the thumbs up.

We headed to Donal's office at about 8.50am, into the reception area. My Barrister, Jim O'Callaghan, arrived, and then another character witness, Jim Glennon.

There was some discussion in the reception area and Jim and Donal agreed that the Disciplinary Committee probably wouldn't allow everybody to speak.

We discussed strategy until an apprentice solicitor, Avalon Everett, came in with a suitcase on wheels.

"What's that?" I asked.

"It's all the paperwork on your case."

We had to wheel it down Pembroke Street, turn left onto Baggot Street and then to the ERC offices on Stephen's Green. There were ten of us; Donal Spring, Jim O'Callaghan, his devil (assistant Barrister) Hugh O'Flaherty, Jim Glennon, Jack Looby, Joe Looby, Avalon Everett, myself and Seamus Given, an employment lawyer from Arthur Cox Solicitors.

Some TV cameras and photographers were waiting outside the ERC offices. I tried to look serious but a smile appeared. I was relaxed. We went up to the third floor.

While everyone was chatting, I walked around, looking at some of the memorabilia on the walls, the signed jerseys, balls, old programmes from matches dating back years. All I could think was that some of that stuff would look great on the wall in my bar. I hadn't realised, until that point, that the ERC and the IRB actually share the same building in Huguenot House. The ERC are on the third floor and they sometimes use the IRB conference room on the second floor.

I spotted a door with Syd Millar's name in bronze. I looked around for any sign of a camera and wondered would it be cheeky to pull it off the door? 'No Trevor. Leave the sign on the door. You're in enough trouble.'

We were called into a room for the hearing and I sat down and looked at a cabinet about ten feet away from me with the William Webb Ellis trophy inside and wondered if it was the real thing. I looked at the three judges – Justice Wyn Williams QC, chairman of the WRU, Robert Horner of the RFU and Sheriff W. Dunlop of the Scottish Union – and tried to form an impression of them. In their 50s or 60s, they seemed to be likeable lads.

Jim O'Callaghan asked that witnesses speak on my behalf. They said yes to Jim and Jack Looby, but no to Seamus Given, the employment expert.

Jack was articulate in recounting how I'd started playing for Barnhall in 1982 and how I moved on when I was 18 but that I had come back to the club regularly for coaching and charity work.

Then Jim Glennon came in and spoke about his time as manager of Leinster and that he had taken a chance picking me because of the route I'd come through. He described how I settled into the Leinster squad, how honest I was – honest to a fault in some of the interviews I'd given – and how rugby had changed. Nowadays, when people are asked to do things their first response is "How much?" but, he said, in my case it's never "How much?" It's "Where and when?"

I was a little taken aback by what he said about me.

After a short break it was my turn. Jim O'Callaghan asked where I'd started playing, what school and college I'd gone to; he was demonstrating that I hadn't come through the normal rugby route, that myself, and the rest of my family, all worked hard, before I charted my rugby career.

He then asked why, on that day, why did I hit the Ulster fan? I gave my reasons.

He asked me if I regretted it?

I said of course I did, and I could honestly put my hand on my heart there and then, and say of course I regretted it. If I could go around Dublin on an open top bus with a microphone and tell the world how sorry I was, and if I could tell the man who I hit how sorry I was, I would do so. If I could turn back the clock I would. I said I couldn't, I'd done it, that's why I was there in that room. I knew that my actions had to be punished, but that the punishment handed out was – in my view, and the view of others – unjust.

I was asked whether I wanted to stay involved in rugby, and to coach and I said yes. I felt relaxed and delighted to get it all of my chest.

When Jim had finished, the ERC's senior counsel, Paul Burns, cross-examined me. During that time I responded to a series of questions as best I possibly could. Once or twice I could feel the emotion and strain of the experience getting to me, and I could sense Donal and Jim urging me to answer the questions without emotion.

It was difficult, though, and I found the experience hard going. When I had concluded giving my evidence, the ERC legal team made their submissions. I was astonished to hear them say the penalty given to Eric Cantona should not be considered as standards in soccer were not the same as they were in rugby.

They also claimed that the offence I had committed was far more serious than match-rigging or taking performance-enhancing drugs. I found this astonishing to say the least.

When the hearing concluded, we were informed that the decision would be given in ten days.

We headed off. Jack and Joe Looby, Jim Glennon and Seamus had left as there was no need for them to hang around. So myself, Donal, Jim O'Callaghan, Avalon and Hugh O'Flaherty went to a restaurant just off Fitzwilliam Square called Dax. It's owned by Olivier Meisonnave, a huge rugby fan from the French town of Dax.

We talked about the case. How we'd given it our best shot and we'd just have to wait and see. After lunch, I rang Jack and along with two of his workmates, he met me in Kehoe's off Grafton Street.

The sun was shining and everyone was milling onto the street. Fellas asked me how the appeal had gone. The phone started to hop, but I ignored it. Peter Clohessy's name was coming up. The Claw had been on to me during the week because he was looking for a couple of English-speaking French chefs for a new restaurant he was opening and suggested I visit him that weekend. But I had a wedding to go to the next day; my ex-Leinster and Toulouse team-mate Aidan McCullen, who was joining London Irish, was marrying Niamh Redmond. So I ignored it. My brother's name came up. I ignored it. My ma and da's number came up. I ignored it. Then The Claw's name kept coming up, and eventually I answered.

"How'd it go today bud? How'd it go?"

"I don't know Claw. The decision will come in the next ten days."

He asked if I'd come down to Limerick, but I explained that I couldn't as I had a wedding to attend the next day and an early flight on Monday morning.

"Oh, you're a bollix; you're a bollix," he said.

So I said "Right. I'll be down in a couple of hours."

"Are you coming down? Are you serious?"

I said "I'm gonna get a taxi now and go to the train station." I told Jack what I intended to do and he said "You're mad. Stay in my place in Drumcondra."

"Jack, I promised him. I promised him."

I didn't want to go to Leixlip. I felt I needed some space. I needed to get out of town. If I went to Leixlip, I'd have been talking about nothing else all night except the hearing. That's all anyone would have wanted to talk about.

I dashed into Timberland off Grafton St, bought myself a pair of jeans and a t-shirt, and a toothbrush and deodorant in a chemist's, and hopped into a taxi. It really was a spur of the moment decision.

At Heuston Station the ticket clerk told me the time of the next train to Limerick, asked for my autograph for his son, and guided me to the front of the queue. Then into a first class carriage for €11 extra. He said "Look after this man, it's Trevor Brennan. He's going down to Limerick."

I was wrecked. The last thing I remember is the train stopping in Kildare before I fell asleep. I was woken by an announcement about Limerick and asked the attendant "Will you give me a shout when we get to Limerick?"

"Oh jaysus, we just pulled out of Limerick Junction. You have to change at Limerick Junction for Limerick."

"What?"

"We just pulled out of it boy."

"You are f****** joking!"

He said the next stop was in Mallow.

"Mallow? Where the f*** is Mallow?" I'd never heard of Mallow. "How far is that from Limerick?"

"Oh Jaysus," he said. "You won't get a taxi from Mallow to Limerick, there's very few lads that'll take you." He suggested the best thing to do was stay in a B&B that night and catch the 5.30am train the next morning.

"I'm going down to meet my friend in Limerick tonight for a few drinks. I'm going back to Dublin tomorrow for a wedding."

"Well, why didn't you tell me boy?"

I said "Why didn't you wake me?"

"You never told me you were getting off at Limerick junction."

I was giving out to this fella because he hadn't woken me up.

He said "Hold on boy, hold on boy."

"Oh my god this is terrible," I said, and then the phone rang.

"Where are you?" asks Claw.

"I'm on the way to Mallow."

"You're on the way to Mallow?" He said he was waiting outside Limerick Junction.

"This is a nightmare, my worst nightmare Claw. I just woke up, I'm smelly, I'm stinky." I told him I'd try to hail a taxi from Mallow.

There was one taxi driver outside the station.

"Will you take me to Limerick?"

"What?" He said he'd take me into a taxi rank in town for a fiver. He had no interest in driving to Limerick Junction.

The first three or four taxi drivers at the rank in Mallow said no before an older driver agreed to take me there for €120; cash up front.

Half an hour down the road Claw rang. "Where are you?"

"I'm on the way."

He said that they'd meet me in Patrickswell, and there he was there with Anna in his jeep at 11.10pm.

Himself and Anna were laughing. "You feckin' eejit. You feckin' eejit."

I presumed we'd head straight in to his club, the Sin Bin.

"So where are we off to Claw?"

"A classy joint," he said.

"Anywhere Claw," I said. "All I want is a few pints now." I had sobered up on the train, especially after the extra, unscheduled stop in Mallow.

"The best place in Limerick, Austin Quinlivan's, beside the train Station. The Munsters' supporters bar." In we went and fellas greeted us.

"How's it goin Claw?"

"Howya Brennan? How's it going?"

"Howya Anna?"

We took some seats at the bar and I thought to myself "There's something wrong here." It's a real spit-and-sawdust pub. A couple of aul ones were sitting in the corner drinking pints. I looked at a newspaper cutting on the wall from 1993, when Young Munster beat St. Mary's in the AIL decider, with Ger Earls scoring the winning try. And it was literally just a newspaper cutting, sellotaped to the wall.

Although the rivalry between 'the Cookies' and St Mary's was fierce, especially between players like Ger Earls and Steve Jameson, I actually think they are two of the unluckiest people never to have played for Ireland. Jemo was a workhorse of a second-row and, I believe, better than some of the second-rows who were picked ahead of him.

Ger Earls was hard as nails. He was a natural born rugby player; he was fast, he could tackle, he could carry a ball as well as being an enforcer. And you can see it in his son on the Irish under-21s. I had a few run ins with him, but I respected him as a player. Besides, I had run ins with everybody – Quinny, Gaillimh, Claw – but you respected them because they never took a back seat; they challenged you.

A bit like me, Ger Earls' face didn't fit because he came from Young Munster and had a hard man reputation. My face didn't fit either, so I felt lucky in getting 13 caps.

There were also some pictures of Claw playing under-12s at Young Munster, and newspaper clippings of Paul O'Connell.

I had about seven or eight pints of Beamish, or whatever they were serving to Claw, before we headed to the Sin Bin. There I had a feed of toasted ham and cheese sandwiches, and a few more pints, before Anna drove us back to their house. It wasn't a house so much as Fort Knox. Big electric gates opened into a laneway, which we seemed to drive along for about five minutes.

I said "So where's your gaff?"

"Oh up at the top of the road."

"That's not a house," I said, as it came into view. "That's a hotel."

They had 80 acres of land, and inside 'Fort Knox' were pictures of Claw horse-riding and fox-hunting.

"You've changed," I said to him.

Anna showed me to my bedroom – over in the east wing! – and I had a deep sleep; one of the most comfortable sleeps of my life in fact. Claw had wanted to show me around his place but I woke up at 10.00am – in the back of my mind I remembered I had Aidan's wedding to go to. Their babysitter was leaving and when I asked her if she was heading anywhere near Limerick train station, she dropped me off there.

The father picked me up at Heuston, drove me to my aunt's in Blanchardstown; I had a shower, she pressed the suit I'd worn the day before, and went to the wedding in Mullingar. A fantastic time at Lard's wedding. And I'm glad I didn't sleep in and miss it.

The next day I returned to Toulouse. It had been a good laugh, as impromptu nights often are, meeting the characters in the Charles St George; the stories, the picture of Brent Pope hitting one of their players. They have it in five frames; showing Brent lining up his punch, landing it and Francis Brosnan falling to the ground. Brent was sent off and Munsters won. I thought it was the best thing ever. I wanted to take it off the wall and bring it back to De Danu.

Monday June 11th.

A life ban was a terrible way to end my career; that's what everybody said to me and that is why I appealed it and why I felt so strongly about an appeal. I also think that's why I received so much support.

On June 11th, the Appeal Committee announced their findings. My lifetime suspension from playing rugby of any kind, or of coaching in an ERC competition, had been reduced to five years. All the original fines were re-imposed.

At least a five year ban removed the stigma of a life ban, but ultimately it was the same thing. They didn't change the fine, the money part of it. They could have reduced that too, but they didn't.

It seemed to me as if they were aware a life ban wouldn't stand up in a European court, and reducing it to five years was a way around that. As well as reducing the heat from the rugby-going public.

Plenty of people rang me to say "Ah, it's great, that's a victory'. A victory? No way. A very small victory at best. I'm glad to have that whole stigma of a life ban off my head, and off my children's heads; the sons of the player banned for life.

Now that I've had time to fully realise my rugby career is over, I think that maybe this happened for a reason. My body is wrecked. I sit here now with a terrible pain in my lower back which I've had for two months. Sometimes I wonder "Could I have continued playing professional rugby at the top, week in week out, for another forty games?"

I believe I've been lucky in a sense; I've come away from this game pretty much unscathed. I didn't come away with a broken neck. I've been knocked out in games, and I suppose the worst case was against Castres. I was like a timber tree falling, and who's to say that wouldn't happen again if I continued playing?

Or maybe something was about to happen and somebody up there likes me. You've got to believe that everything happens for a reason. What's for you won't pass you by. Paula always says "If it's meant to be it's meant to be."

It's what she said in reference to the move to Toulouse, and to getting more Irish caps. I can't be negative about it.

It's been a good career. I'm often asked "What was the most memorable moment in your career; winning the European Cup?" Perhaps some Munster players would say that. But for me, because it was a dream to climb that Everest, playing for Ireland was the pinnacle.

Like most kids, I had pictures on my wall of soccer players, rugby players and American Football posters or other sports pictures. I went for runs before school at 6.00am, I did weights sessions in Motions gym before work and bought my first set of weights at 16. I lived in my own world. I used to set goals; I'd write them on my wardrobe. I'd set myself targets and if I hadn't played for Leinster youths, the Irish

21's, or Leinster by such and such a date, I'd have travelled the world for a year.

But all the time it was my goal to try. It was never easy for me. I had to make people notice me and start talking about me. "Who's this fella, Trevor Brennan?"

And when I'd reached my mountain top, I never, ever wanted to be just a one cap wonder. That happened to so many players. So when I made the tour to South Africa and then made my debut, I was over the moon. Over the next three years I managed to pick up 12 more caps. Thirteen caps isn't an awful lot over a three year period, but it's there; it's on paper. No-one can ever take that away from me.

I'd never really planned a future beyond rugby. I don't know if we'll stay in France, I don't know if the bar will be there forever. At the moment, I'm comfortable.

I'll turn my hand to anything. That's one thing about me, I'm a trier.

I've been a breadman, a milkman, a barman. I've been a builder, I've tiled... I'll give anything a go. Thanks to rugby, I've become used to a good way of life.

It's time to move on, it's time now to get something better for myself and my family. I want to be able to go on holidays, not have to worry about where my next few quid will come from, and to pay the electricity bill.

Myself and Yannick Bru intend to go into business together, selling French properties on the Irish market. I like the idea and hope that I can learn that business and make it work.

I have some punditry lined up with TV3 during the World Cup due to my knowledge of French, Argentine and Irish players. Rugby gave me a diary in *The Irish Times,* and that has opened doors for me.

I'm not 18 anymore, with £200 in my pocket from working in the Ryevale Tavern. I've a mortgage to pay and kids to educate. I have to think about their future as well as mine. I worry about the future. I am a worrier; a big worrier. I probably shouldn't be, but I worry about everything. When I was playing for Leinster, I'd worry what the coach would think of me. I'd worry whether I'd make the team. I'd worry if I was going to be ten minutes late for training. I'd worry if I was selling packaging for Ray McKenna, got stuck in traffic and couldn't get to a job. I've tried to teach myself not to be a worrier, not to be that person, but I'm a natural worrier.

I worry about the bar, about paying the rent, paying the bank loan, and paying the staff wages. If I still had my wages every month from Toulouse it mightn't be too bad, but all of a sudden that was taken away in mid-season, and replaced with a hefty fine.

But then in another sense it doesn't matter how much money you have, or what you have or what you don't have; because we're all here on borrowed time. That's what I believe. I could walk out this door, God forbid it doesn't happen, and be run over by a bus. I've seen things in my life, I've seen friends die of natural causes. I've known friends who took their own lives. I've lost family; grannies, granddads and a brother.

I wouldn't change too much. I want my kids to appreciate the value of money and of hard work, and I think we're achieving that. I believe all kids should go to school for as long as they can. If I could do one thing differently, I'd have worked harder in school. It wasn't that I didn't want to, it was because I was just too busy working outside school.

But rugby has been good to me. I haven't done too badly. I've even written a book. And the last five years have been the most enjoyable of my life. It wasn't just a great adventure. It wasn't just winning Heineken Cups, playing in French Championship finals, earning more money than I ever earned in Ireland, learning a new culture and a new language, and winning the respect of the coaches, the players and the public... As much as anything, it was simply the game time.

I was just 'Trevor Brennan, rugby player'. Guy Novès picked purely on merit. I never felt that I was above or below anyone while I was playing for Toulouse. Whether it be Fabien Pelous, Frédéric Michalak, William Servat, David Gerard or any of the others. And whether I started or was on the bench.

I felt everyone was given a fair opportunity, we all had to prove ourselves. The summer before I came to France I trained hard. When I arrived, I really knuckled down and trained harder. I looked around; most of the squad were French internationals, so I knew that I'd be playing against French internationals week in and week out.

I had to learn the Toulouse style of play, the running, passing and offloading game. The training sessions were different. The weights sessions were different. The video sessions were different. Everything was just different. It was like going back to school – but in my case it was learning how to play rugby again. And I did.

My reward was that I played in practically every key game for Toulouse in the five years that I was there. Certainly up until the second half of the fifth season.

I played in every semi final; three in the Heineken Cup and four in the French Championship. And every final; three in the Heienken Cup and two in the championship. I started them all. All 12. Not one of them as a sub. There might have been a rotational basis in the early part of the season, to give players rest and recovery, but any time there was a big game, I played.

That's something I'm proud of. When I reflect on my time at Leinster, by the end, most of my games were off the bench, as was the case with my Irish caps. Those games I started, like against Italy – I got Man of the Match – and I had a good game against Argentina. Playing for eighty minutes, or even the first hour, allows you to build your way gradually into a game.

It's better than five or ten minutes at the end of a game because you can't really make an impact. Some players can. Some can do something special. Subs have come on and scored three points in a GAA match, or kicked a free to win it. It has happened. It happens in football, it happens in Gaelic football, it happens in hurling. Substitutes come on and turn games.

I've seen it with Toulouse as well. But for me at Leinster, it was a case of having to learn to be an impact sub and always trying to do something in twenty or thirty minutes. Because I knew that was all I had.

In Toulouse, I learned to do it both ways, but more often when making an impact for the first 60 or 80 minutes. Guy always left you on the pitch for eighty minutes if it was a tight game. If we were leading well, and he felt you needed a rest, he'd substitute you and give someone else 15 or 20 minutes. I felt very strong, I felt very fit, I felt aerobically fit. I felt I could run faster. I don't know what it was, but I found a new lease of life.

A whole new lease of life.

That's what my entire experience has been, here in Toulouse. A new culture, a new language... Something profoundly different and unique which I was determined to make work for my wife and my family.

I am immensely proud that we all did it. That we made wonderful new friends, immersed ourselves in this culture and became part of the life of the city we now call home. And part of a remarkable club that has gifted me the most memorable of times in my career.

It is a gift and a privilege that I can never repay, but one which I, my family, friends and supporters shall cherish always.

Merci.

CHAPTER 18

A BACKWARD GLANCE

ON THE COACHES HE HAS WORKED WITH

Guy Novès is definitely the best coach I've ever had. When he walks into a room he has an aura about him. When he talks everybody listens. What sets him apart is not what he actually does on the playing pitch, it's the respect he commands from players. He demands that they think of nothing else but rugby and Stade Toulousain. He also demands, at the start of every season, that we win something.

ON SUBSTANCE ABUSE IN RUGBY

I can't make any accusations. I've seen lads take protein shakes, and I've seen them take creatine. I took creatine. But I haven't touched it in years. We were the guinea pig generation. Even schools teams were given creatine.

WHEN I FIRST BROKE INTO THE LEINSTER SQUAD IN 1996, CIARAN CALLAN, Jim Glennon and Paul Dean were the coaching ticket. Rugby was not yet professional and I can't really say whether they were good or bad coaches as I spent most of my time back then on the fringes; a few training sessions here and there, and then warming the bench a few times.

The back-rowers were Chris Pim, Dean Oswald, Stephen Rooney and Colin McEntee, while the second rows included Neil Francis, Brian Rigney and Steve Jameson. I was on the bench for one particular match against Connacht in Galway. The game was just a few minutes old and Connacht were all over us when Franno went down with a leg injury and was stretchered off the pitch to hospital. A few others departed early with knocks that day, but Pim, being Pim, played with an ice pack strapped to his leg for half an hour rather than give The Horsebox a run.

From what I could tell, the lads pretty much coached themselves. Jim helped with the line-outs, while Cally, along with Paul Dean, oversaw the backs. And Roly Meates took scrummaging sessions.

Some drills still stand out. I recall Deano forming the backs into a circle. They'd pass the ball through the hands as one player circled them in a race between him and the ball. It may have been inventive for its time, and the rugby was just as tough, but like I said, it was the amateur era.

Then again, when Mike Ruddock came in as Leinster coach in 1997-98, he did virtually everything on his own. He even took the fitness sessions. Although Jim Glennon brought Paul Dean back in again to help out with the backs, it wasn't until Mike brought Matt Williams in as his assistant coach, in his third and final year taking the backs, that things became a bit more professional.

He was definitely better with forwards than backs, and I personally thought he was very good. He had some clever line-out options, was knowledgeable technically with scrums and analysed the opposition shrewdly. He identified their strengths and weaknesses, be it attack the loose-head, or different ways to defend the opposition back-row, because their number eight does this, or their number six does that. I'd never really been exposed to this before.

He also assembled a relatively new squad. And as Mike was an unknown quantity, there was a fear factor there as well. He had the respect of the players.

He trained us harder than we'd ever trained, and made us fitter than we'd ever been before. Initially, we all thought Mike was mad. During punishing sessions, especially the morning after a defeat, he shouted terrible abuse at players, and some lads couldn't take it. I've seen lads break down crying in training.

As a bloke, I couldn't fault him. A great party man. He loved nothing more than throwing his guitar in the bag and having a sing-song. When Gary Halpin came along they were like Beavis & Butthead, the two of them playing the guitar.

Gary was like Christy Moore, and Mike tagged along; he loved his Tom Jones tunes. I suppose it's no wonder that since his sacking by the Welsh Union he's gigged around Wales in a band called Mid Life Crisis.

He was very down to earth, just like his wife Bernie. He could be hard too, but fair and honest. When I came in, he said he'd pick me if I deserved it. He told me he wanted the best possible team for Leinster. The team was picked on merit.

I wouldn't say a bad word about him. Even when my good mate Gareth Thomas led the player revolt to oust Mike from the Wales job the season after the

Grand Slam. He'd claimed that Mike would get back in his car if the weather was cold and leave all the work to Scott Johnson. I said "Not a chance." I told Alfie that they stabbed Mike in the back by going to the Union and having him fired. I fundamentally disagreed with what they did, and particularly the manner of it.

Mike came into that job when Welsh rugby was on a downer, and helped turn it around. I firmly believe that if you're not happy with the coach, you have to be up front about it. At the end of the day, Mike was the head coach and the buck stopped with him. But he must have done something right for them to win the Grand Slam for the first time in 27 years.

The Matt Williams, Alan Gaffney, Willie Anderson trio were a good coaching team. Matt brought a bit of overdue discipline to Leinster and developed a good support staff around him. Brett Igoe was introduced as video analyst, and Roly was brought back from the wilderness for the scrummaging. Williams also arranged for two masseurs to come in twice a week, which was kind of unheard of then. He even had the branch subsidise it, which was probably an achievement in itself.

After matches in Donnybrook he organised trips to Riverview for hot and cold baths to aid recovery, whereas before we used to hit the showers and proceed to Kielys as quickly as possible for pints and cocktails. Riverview was a gym less than one kilometre from Donnybrook where he made us do lengths of the outdoor pool in all weather – hail, rain or snow. Professionalism or stupidity? I don't know.

Riverview replaced our 'gym' in Old Belvedere, which was actually more of a tin shed; Matt arranging full-time memberships for all the players. I don't know whether he got this through sponsorship or through the branch, but to his credit he did it. This was typical of the new, more professional mindset he introduced in Leinster.

He didn't stop the trips up to Kielys; he just denied us the first two hours' drinking time! Drinking was a huge part of Leinster's culture. After matches anyway. If more for some than for others. Williams liked a drink himself, as did Al and Willie, but he knew how to keep the lads in line.

He did everything to try and make Leinster a professional outfit, but in my opinion, he overdid it at times.

Yoga classes were a typical example. These were usually on a Monday. A female instructor took over the function room in Belvo. Some guys suffered more from the night before than others and found it easier to drift into a deep sleep. However, asking Reggie Corrigan, Trevor Brennan, Victor Costello, Bob Casey and others, too many to name, to lie on the floor, take deep breaths and fall into a deep sleep, wasn't our scene. Even so, we had to do it.

Dave Fagan knew plenty about weights and to his credit, imparted good advice to all the boys.

Jason Cowan was the other fitness trainer. He knew his stuff, he knew the lads, and if you felt you needed less, he'd cut back on your workload. If you needed more, Jayo always gave you extra time.

We had Arthur Tanner as the team doc. Leinster rugby owes this man so much. Any problems on or off the pitch, Arthur was the man to see. Whether it was your knee, your back or personal problems, he was always available for guys and their families. A guy who would go out of his way to do anything for you, or for anyone else who asked. Arthur always gave you the best medical advice. Such was Matt's attention to medical detail that Dr Harry Beacham, another excellent doctor, was sometimes on hand as well.

Johnny O'Hagen, the bagman, did everything. From fixing lights and plugs, plumbing, a bit of chippy work (he was an electrician by trade, I think), laundry etc. He was a general handyman who loved the pints and the craic with the lads and has never in his life been short of a word.

Ken Ging. The Manager. Kinger. Well-known on the pre and post-match dinner circuit. He always had a joke and could put a smile on anyone's face.

I think it's important to name the crew, because nowadays behind every good coach there is a good team, and to his credit Matt wasn't paranoid about having good people around him, including specialist coaches. Alan Gaffney, his assistant and backs' coach, was probably the best of them. In my opinion he kept the ship afloat. Most players respected him hugely. He was like a father figure.

Willie Anderson was, for me, excellent technically at line-outs and scrums, and knew how to bring out the aggression in players. To get them wound up and tackling hard. I think his approach to coaching mirrored the way he played, if you know what I mean.

Sometimes we would have preferred shorter training sessions. He liked a bit of 'opposition'. For both teams to get physical. He didn't seem to object too strongly when a fight broke out in training. Which happened often. To some he seemed rather too intense at times, but not to me.

In one Leinster session myself and Eric Miller started one of our fights. We rolled around on the ground before we were separated.

"I need to have a word with ye boy," said Willie, putting his arm around me and dragging me over to the side of the pitch. I was expecting a lecture.

"That's f****** great. That's the f****** stuff I like to see in this team. That's the kind of men I want."

I think it's a shame that he's not at least with a province because he has so much know-how and experience to offer.

Matt was a good technical coach too, but I still wonder: why, with all these other coaches and excellent back-up staff, not to mention the squad of players he had at his disposal, did Leinster not achieve more? I don't believe any coach should be held fully responsible when the shit hits the fan.

Matt brought many good things to Leinster but made mistakes too. He rejuvenated and prolonged many careers, Reggie Corrigan, Victor Costello, Shane Byrne, myself and others. He got the best from us. Victor Costello was one of the most naturally gifted players I've ever encountered; natural strength, speed and power.

Matt was on his back 24/7, and had all the staff on his back too; about his weight, about doing weights, about his physical fitness. He even insisted Victor run from his house in Donnybrook to training sessions in UCD or Belvo. I think it's fair to say that Matt's persistence was responsible for Victor's recall to the Irish team.

The same goes for Reggie, who was stuck on ten caps until Gatty got the chop. Then picked up another 30 or so under Eddie. He was brought back because he was fitter and playing better for Leinster. And the same was true of Shane Byrne.

Matt was also very insistent on daily skills sessions. We did defensive drills, we did line-outs, rucks and mauls under Willie Anderson. We scrummaged with Roly Meates. Matt and Gaff improved the skills of a gifted back-line. Matt fine-tuned our defensive system beyond recognition and gave our game attacking shape and inventive moves. All this was rewarded with plenty of wins.

In my last season there, 2001-02, we won our first 15 games of the season and weren't beaten until February. But despite the excellent coaches and professionalism, in the European Cup we came up short. Why? I have my theories.

There was an 'Us and Them'. He had his first XV, or first 22. The rest of the squad were just cannon fodder. When there were injuries they were slotted in, but no matter how well they played they were never considered for the big games.

I think myself, and a few others on the fringes of the team, struggled to believe we could make the team. In saying all that, he was technically a brilliant coach. One of the best I've ever had. When he left, Matt took both Willie and Brett with him – as head coaches do – to Scotland.

Rugby is also about having a bit of fun. When you take that away, you may as well hang up the boots. That's what I would have done if I'd stayed in Leinster.

Matt maintained that I would have had another five years' in me if I was used primarily as an impact replacement. I appreciated his honesty, and it did help me make up my mind about leaving. Although I think my five years in Toulouse showed that I was more than a good substitute.

He made quite an impression on me in many ways. And in all of this, I have to confess that my view of Matt was probably based on whether I was in the team or not. In this way, all players are the same. If we are in the team, we love the coach. If we're not, we complain about him. It's often as simple as that.

Overall, Matt Williams was just what Leinster needed. Although I'm sure he must still feel he could have taken the team a little further. I'm surprised he didn't enjoy more success at Scotland, and he's a loss to the game now.

I first came across Warren Gatland at Irish training sessions in the ALSAA complex when he was with Connacht. Brian Ashton, Irish coach at the time, had asked him in to assist. I thought we hit it off well from the start. At the end of the sessions we would sometimes play a bit of a match, and Gatty always took charge of the lads who were on the fringes, or were there to make up the numbers. He used to wind us up very cleverly. He'd tell us that "This is your chance to show what you are made of. Don't hold back." When the tackles went in, I don't think I let him down.

He always encouraged lads when they did well; rarely criticised them when they didn't and he never blamed players for mistakes, which I liked. He had some novel coaching techniques and innovations. And excellent line-out options. The most famous of which was the 15-man line-out that he had perfected with Connacht.

Typical of any New Zealand coach, he had some excellent rucking drills. He used to tie a rope from one goalpost to the other, which he lowered gradually until you were hitting ruck bags from about two feet off the ground. He introduced a really effective rucking game to Irish rugby, something that Irish rugby was not renowned for. Ultimately his results with Connacht, Ireland, Wasps and Waikato speak for themselves.

He gave me my first cap, for which I'll always be very grateful, as will many others whom he discovered. He also did some weird shit. Early in my first tour with Ireland to South Africa in 1998, during which I won my first cap, we played against South West Districts in a place called George. At a team meeting he suggested that the South Africans seemed bigger and stronger partly because they had great skin colour.

So, he sent Rala, our bag man, to buy false tan and asked all of us to apply it for the next game. Now try to picture this: Mick Galwey, Peter Clohessy, Victor

Costello and the others "doing a Gavin Henson" in front of the mirror in the team room, lashing on the cream. What a sight!

I collected my bottle from Rala and went to my room about an hour before line-out practice in the hotel grounds. I spent most of that time smearing the false tan on my legs, arms and face. I already had a bit of a colour as it had been quite warm during our time in South Africa. I looked in the mirror and was happy with my work. I threw on the shorts, socks, boots and top, and went down to do the line-outs. I could see in the distance the lads comparing their tans. They turned around, looked at me, and ... collapsed in a heap.

Let's just say I overdid it on the cream. I looked like yer man out of the "You've Been Tangoed" ad. My skin was orange.

I had won my third cap as a replacement in the 10-9 defeat to France in 1999 but the following week I was sent off playing for St Mary's against Shannon when a scuffle with Anthony Foley earned me a second yellow card. That ruled me out of the Wembley game against Wales seven days later.

Gatty summoned me to his room and told me he had been at the Shannon match. Though he didn't think I really deserved my sending off, it had cost me my place on the team. He added that Ireland would win the following Saturday against Wales. As I would miss out on the £4,000 win bonus, it would be an expensive lesson. They did win and it was a great occasion.

He recalled me to the squad for the 2001 game against France in Paris. We were based in the Glenview and trained in Greystones. I was named on the bench on the Tuesday morning, but later that day Kieron Dawson picked up an injury and as a precaution Andy Ward was called in as cover. Andy trained with us for the rest of the week and travelled with us to Paris on the Thursday.

We stayed out in Versailles and had two training sessions there. Donal Lenihan, then the Irish manager, called me aside as we were getting off the bus for the second one.

"Listen Trev, Kieron Dawson is alright but we've made a decision that we're going for Wardie on the bench."

I asked him "If Kieron is okay, why are you changing the bench at the last minute?"

Donal explained that because of the slight doubt about Kieron, they needed a specialist open-side on the bench. I argued that Easterby could move to open-side, and I'd come on at blind-side. But they'd made their decision and I was hardly going to change their minds.

I thought it was bad form for a coach to have the manager give a player such news 24 hours before a game. It obviously didn't help my mood that I had been building myself up to play. I'd have had more respect if he'd been man enough to tell me in person, which was always the case with Gatty. Sure enough, when he saw me in the lobby, Gatty came over to me, put his arm around me, and said "Sorry, Trevor."

To no-one's surprise, I suppose, I didn't sit in my hotel room and sulk about it. I found the nearest Irish bar and spent an enjoyable night with a few French people and let off some steam. To make it worse, we won the game. Drico's famous three tries. Another win bonus gone by the board, although at the time that was the last thing on my mind.

Gatty selected me for my last three caps when Gary Longwell broke a finger at the start of the 2001-02 season. I came on as a replacement in the wins against Wales, England and Samoa. The week after the Samoan game, Ireland played the All Blacks in a thriller at Lansdowne Road, leading 21-7 at the break before losing 40-29. Again, I wasn't involved.

Then Gatty got the sack, and that was the last of my caps. Had Ireland beaten New Zealand they could never have fired Warren Gatland. They were clearly just looking for an excuse.

I definitely felt that Gatty had belief and faith in me, and I possibly let him down as a player on a few occasions; before the Wembley game and especially the 1999 World Cup game when I had a fight with Toutai Kefu and was given the two-match suspension which put me out of the Lens game. I hold myself responsible for those incidents. He used to tell me that he had to fight for me, with other coaches and with the IRFU hierarchy, and I believed him.

Overall, I have to say I liked Gatty very much, even though you didn't always know where you stood. He was a typically reserved and quiet New Zealander, and I cannot recall him once raising his voice in a training session, or even in the dressing-room.

And for that one bad example in Paris, I could cite a hundred good ones. When Danny was born, he and Trudy sent flowers to Paula and myself. When he was removed as coach I wrote him a letter thanking him for my few caps and a week later he wrote me a lovely letter back telling me the respect he had for me as a player.

Eddie O'Sullivan, who had been assistant coach to Gatty for almost two years, took over an Irish team that Warren Gatland had built. Gatty had brought in Peter Stringer, Ronan O'Gara, Simon Easterby, Shane Horgan and John Hayes, as well as recalling Mick Galwey, Denis Hickie and Girvan Dempsey for the 44-22 win over Scotland in 2000 that had turned Ireland's fortunes around.

I can't really say anything one way or the other about O'Sullivan as a coach, because he never coached me.

Noel McQuilkin coached Bective when I arrived there. I heard Noel before I saw him. He was giving some lad an earful on the back pitch about a drill the player was doing wrongly.

He gave me my debut in senior rugby in a friendly in Glasgow on an international weekend. He also converted me into a number six, having joined the Rangers as a number eight. He said "You've got the speed and you're a good ball carrier."

Noel also arranged my trip to Taumarunui in New Zealand in the summer of 1993 because he believed it would make me a better player. He was right; it did. I ate, slept and drank rugby for four months.

He also coached King Country, as did his son Kurt more recently. Kurt was an excellent player for us, who was also capped for Ireland. He's now working with the Leinster team. I stayed in Noel's house in 1993 when he introduced me to the legendary All Blacks second row Colin Meads.

Harry Williams arrived when Noel McQuilkin moved on to Greystones before returning to New Zealand. Harry was a very softly-spoken man. As well as coaching the team, he was very good at picking out players individually and working on their strengths and weaknesses. He worked on my lines of running, speed and tackling, and he used me as a line-out option.

What I remember most about him was his practice of calling me aside for a chat before games. I used to love those few minutes. If we were playing away, he'd sit me down in the team hotel before we got on the team bus, sometimes over a cup of tea and a few biscuits. It usually helped me to relax and focus on what I had to do, and what not to do. I'm not sure whether it was the tea and the biscuits or the chat I loved more, but it was good for me.

He also told me that I had the potential to play for Leinster and Ireland, and wished me the best of luck when I moved on to St Mary's. I was delighted to see him coach Ulster to their European Cup victory. Leinster played Ulster in Ravenhill during his time as coach there. When we arrived at the ground, we had our walk around the pitch. Long before the crowd started to fill the stands.

"Hello, how's it going Harry?"

"Fine. How's it going yourself, Trevor?"

The usual stuff. As we said good luck and maybe we'd meet up later, he tapped me on the back and said "Go easy on my lads today Trevor. Don't hurt any of them." We both laughed, and off I went.

Steve Hennessy and Hugh Maguire coached me in my first two years at St Mary's. They were true Mary's men, really genuine, honest men who were very good coaches in their own right. They led us to two semi-finals in a row, and we scored plenty of tries before we came up short.

Brent Pope had something different. He had that hard edge, and he made the provincial/international players work harder and give more to the club. He knew the team's strengths and weaknesses. He loved the trips to Limerick and Cork. And the battles that came with them.

Brent told fellas to stand up and fight, not to back down. To give as good as they got. He talked about pride in the jersey and the history of the club. About how we had to have self-belief if we truly wanted to win the league.

"What's the difference," he'd ask, "between us and them? Nothing. It's just in the top four inches," he'd say.

His training sessions were quite similar to Gatland's. There was a big emphasis on the setpieces, and on rucks and mauls. He brought that New Zealand influence, and sessions became much more physical. He had the respect of everyone, on and off the pitch.

Brent led St Mary's to the All-Ireland League in his first year with the club, when I was captain, and remains the only coach to have guided a Leinster team to the title. He coached the way he played; hard and no nonsense.

Guy Novès is definitely the best coach I've ever had. When he walks into a room he has an aura about him. When he talks, everybody listens. What sets him apart is not what he actually does on the playing pitch, it's the respect he commands from players. He demands that they think of nothing else but rugby and Stade Toulousain. He also demands, at the start of every season, that we win something.

He brings the best out of you. If I'm injured, he comes to me. As he did before the Heineken Cup quarter-final against Northampton in my first year at Toulouse. He said "Irishman, you're soft. You're not able to play. You're afraid of the English." He knows this is guaranteed to wind me up, and nearly always chooses the right words to do so. He'll tell you before matches that the opposing team has a player who's going to do this or that to you.

Like that example I've highlighted before the semi-final in 2004-05 against Leicester in the Walkers Stadium . When he predicted that I would be "like caviar" to someone like Martin Johnson while pushing and shoving me to provoke a reaction.

After we'd won, he asked me "What was it like to play in a game where you didn't get involved in any controversy or fights or didn't get a yellow card?"

I said "It was great Guy. It was fantastic."

So he said "You see, I told you, it can be done. It can be done."

He asked me if there was any aggro. "A few niggles, a bit of rucking and a bit of gouging and whatever in the rucks and mauls. At one stage I had a few words with Martin Johnson."

"And why didn't you react?"

I told him I'd just said "Look at the score Martin." Which I did, late in the second half when we were winning 27-12, before they got their last try. He had been yapping at the referee, demanding yellow cards, that we were cheating. Guy was delighted. He knows I have a temper and an aggressive streak. He loves it, but tries to channel it correctly.

He sometimes says, "Listen lads, why's it always Trevor in there fighting the corner? Why can't somebody else do it?" He respects that bit of fighting spirit, that Irish thing.

But there's more to Guy than man-management. He buys the right players. I joined the club when Stade Toulousain were coming to the end of an era. They'd won six French Championships (1994, 95, 96, 97, 99 and 2001) and a European Cup (1996). Players such as Didier Lacroix (only 30), Franck Belot (30), Jerome Cazalbou (31), Hugues Miorin (34), Franck Tournaire (30); it didn't matter a damn. Gone! Past achievements, or even friendships didn't count. He just scrapped them all. And these were guys who'd been there for most, or even all, of those six Championships, and that European Cup.

Many people, inside or outside the club, might think "What a bastard". But he just wanted the best team for Stade Toulousain, and felt these lads were past their best. He brought in new blood; Trevor Brennan, Vincent Clerc (21), Jean-Baptiste Élissalde (24), Yannick Jauzion (24), Patrice Collazo (28), and Jean-Baptiste Poux (22). That year, 2002, was a bigger turnover than usual. But they were invariably good signings who each brought something different to the club. As have nearly all his subsequent additions.

Undoubtedly, some players hated him for being so ruthless when they still had a year or two's rugby in them. For example, he refused Yann Delaigue's request for a two-year contract in 2004 when Yann was 31, offering him only one year. So he moved to Castres for a little more security.

But that's Novès. Guy thinks 'What's the point in keeping a player in the comfort zone just because that player wants a bit of stability?' Again, he simply believes this is serving Toulouse's best interests.

I respect him for that. And, more to the point, for being the coach who consistently brought the best out of me. We're not best buddies; I've never had a drink with the man in my five years here. At Leinster it was commonplace for the coaches to have a few beers in Kielys with the players. Guy Novès? No.

Perhaps he keeps his distance to retain that respect. After home matches we eat together as a team, but he might socialise with the players only two or three times a year. Even then, he sits at the far end of the restaurant with the club president and observes everything. He won't mix with the players and share the joys of putting 50 points on, say, Mautauban. Whereas back in Ireland, I would have been more used to hearing a coach say "C'mon lads, let's get another one in."

He treats every player as an adult. I have played under coaches who regard players as kids; locking them in hotels, watching what they drink, what they eat, monitoring everything. And that's not, in my opinion, the way to bring the best out of players.

On a Saturday night Guy says "Right, go out, drink, have a good time. I'll be there in Calicéo (leisure centre) at 10.00am tomorrow morning when you come in for your recovery session. I don't care what sort of state you turn up in, as long as you turn up at 10.00am for that recovery session." That's his attitude.

When we played Northampton in the 2002-03 Heineken Cup quarter-finals, I suffered a six centimetre tear in my leg. Normally a three-week lay-off. We were due to play Munster in the semis a fortnight later. I didn't train until the team run on the Friday before the semi-final, after an X-ray that morning. It felt bad but I could run.

In the dressing room before the Munster game he talked about "Munster, vos amis", Munster, your friends. "Was I going to play against my friends today, was I going to let my friends win today. Was I going to be French today, or was I going to be Irish, and who's side was I on?"

"I don't know, I'm wearing the f****** Toulouse jersey, what do you think?"

But that is his way. He tests you and tests you, though when it suits him or his Toulouse agenda, he might not. For example, an obvious red rag to wave at me (and Alfie) before the semi-final against Leicester in 2005 would have been to mention they had eight Lions in their ranks.

But the Lions' squad to tour New Zealand was soon to be named. He knew there was speculation about me being selected. Though it would have been the highlight of my career, he didn't want me to play for the Lions.

I've no doubt that he was quietly pleased I wasn't involved in the Irish set-up.

Indeed for that reason, from his point of view, I was probably the perfect signing.

He said he was delighted for me when I was called into the Irish squad for a couple days of training before facing England in 2004. "It's what you deserve. It's what you worked hard for." I'd say he was no more thrilled than the man on the moon.

Similarly, I'd say Guy hated it when Gareth Thomas was made captain of Wales and was away on international duty the whole time. It's a headache for him. The French squad is different. It's not like Ireland. When the lads play for France, and there's no international the following weekend, they're usually back in Toulouse on Monday morning for a recovery session with us and preparing to play Auch, Castres or whoever the following week.

Before this year's one-off agreement between the clubs and the French Federation – when the Top 14 closed down for seven weeks – our French internationals even played for us on the two 'free' weekends in the Six Nations.

That said, if he sees one of his players is struggling with the demands of playing for club and country, he works around that. He's very good that way. But playing for your country is a bonus. The priority, the first loyalty is Stade Toulousain.

DRUGS IN SPORT

People often ask: Are drugs widespread in sport? I can only say from my own experiences in rugby that the answer is a big Yes. I'm not talking about recreational or performance-enhancing drugs such as steroids. I mean the things I've taken to dull pain or get through games, to bring down swelling, to get you through training sessions or a match. Painkillers, anti-inflammatories or anything else my mother could acquire from the doctor. And boy have I taken my fair share.

Never, in my career, did I see anyone take performance enhancing drugs. But of course that doesn't mean that they didn't. Injuries are a major part of any contact sport, rugby being no exception, and I've had my fair share of them. I was only 16 when I sustained a cracked vertabra. The Barnhall Under-18s had finished their campaign and I was called up to their first team.

Whatever about my natural strength, I doubt my body was sufficiently developed to play first team rugby at 16, even though Barnhall were playing in division three of the junior league.

So begins my tale of woe, for that was only one of the vertebrae over my career:

Cracked the L4.

Cracked the L5.

Slipped discs in my back.

Broken ribs – most of them. Possibly all.

Dislocated rib cartlilage.

Dislocated both shoulders (requiring surgery on one).

Broke my nose several times (requiring two operations).

Broken fingers.

Dislocated fingers.

Both ankle ligaments.

Both knee ligaments and cartilages.

Snapped hamstring.

Torn biceps.

Knocked out several times.

And about 200 stitches in all.

They're just the injuries I can remember. But I feel blessed. I had no career threatening injuries, unlike some. I never had anything that put me out of the game for a year, or threatened my career. You look at players such as Ciaran Scally, Conor McGuinness, with his arthritis, or Brian Carey; all talented lads whose careers were cut short. I truly have been fortunate. Even with that catalogue of injuries (and I've probably left out a few) I feel blessed. The only thing I suffer from is my back trouble. I guess I always will. It's just something I have to learn to live with.

Now, to the drugs I've taken or have been given over the years.

Brufen.

Nurofen.

Diclomax.

Voltarol.

Naprosyn.

Cortisone.

Morphine.

These are the ones I remember because they are still fresh in my head or because I've taken them repeatedly since the age of 16. I can't remember the names of others which were prescribed to me by doctors without me knowing exactly what they were.

Maybe, like many other players from my era, I have occasionally, unknown to myself, taken substances which are now deemed illegal. There wasn't much drug testing in the early '90s, and who knows, in one or two of those prescribed pills or medicines, there might have been 0.00001% of something now on a banned list.

Most of the above are used to reduce inflammation or relieve pain. You are advised to take them with or after food but in my case it was usually before and after either training or matches. Stomach pains, vomiting, diaorrhea, headaches etc were among the side effects I've had from these drugs.

You get to a stage where you ask yourself why you do this? Because I love it. I love the feeling of being part of a winning team. Sport is, above all else, about winning and losing; everybody plays sport to win. Luckily enough, from an early age in my career, I've won my fair share.

Aside from the numerous under-age trophies, I've captained an All-Ireland League winning team, won an interprovincial championship (when it was considered worth winning) and a Celtic League with Leinster. And two European Cups with Toulouse. I love the feeling when you're part of a winning team.

Of all those drugs, how or why did I take morphine? Let's just say it was by mistake. I was in the Leinster squad in 1996 for a game in England. I was still breaking into the squad and had been on the bench a few times. On this trip, I was rooming with Niall Hogan, then a medical student and now a doctor. Before leaving home I'd told my mother that my back was giving me terrible pain again. I asked her whether she had anything in the press, as she always had a great stash; brufen, voltoral, diaphin, something along those lines. She was out of stock but said she had something even better. "Take a few of these son and you'll be alright." She also recommended that you take a double dose of whatever was written on the box or bottle.

So I did. Never question the mother, as she always know best. The squad were scheduled to rendezvous in Bective and I remember feeling marvellous as I drove into town. I was as high as a kite driving a car! I don't think you're supposed to drive while on morphine.

On arriving at our hotel I unpacked my bags and put the morphine on top of the tv. I still didn't know what it was.

Hogey said "What the f*** are you doing with them?"

I told him about my back, how my mother had given them to me, and that they must have been something prescribed for her. He emptied the contents down the toilet and told me that I could have been done if I had been tested.

The mother continued to get me painkillers and I suppose that shows how easy it could be for athletes, unknown to themselves, to take a banned substance.

Rugby wasn't professional then and I still had a day job. There weren't as many random tests then as now. I must have had to piss into that bottle about 30 times in my professional career.

Post-match drug testing usually consists of anti-doping agents pulling two names from each team out of a hat. I thought, at times, mine was the only name in the hat, it was picked so often.

In 1999 there was a pre-World Cup tour to Australia, incorporating tests in Brisbane and Perth. I busted the shoulder in an early tour match against New South Wales and was ruled out of the first test, when we were hammered 46-10. I managed to be fit enough to play in the second, when we were narrowly beaten 32-26.

Prior to the World Cup a few months later, Mick Molloy, the IRFU team doctor, examined me and effectively ruled me out of the tournament. "This man cannot play in the World Cup. He has a dislocated shoulder; an A/C joint, grade three." Desperate times require desperate remedies. I went to a doctor whom I know, but whose name I won't mention, and had a cortisone injection in my shoulder to get me through the World Cup.

Warren Gatland, then the Irish coach, had said he'd give me every chance to prove fitness. I hadn't played in either of the warm-up games against Munster or Ulster when he said to me "Trevor, questions are being asked. You're going to have to play against Connacht."

I got through it, with the aid of the cortisone injection and heavy strapping. I'd already had injections while playing for Bective and St Mary's. These were cortisone injections for various injuries, but I knew the risks. When you want to play badly enough, this is what you'll do.

Of course I was in agony the morning after the Connacht game and the World Cup matches I played in, but I was willing to do it. Following the World Cup I had an MRI scan which showed that, because of the injections, part of the collarbone had become infected. I needed an operation to have it open so that the infected part could be shaved off. Again, no regrets. I loved the World Cup, and it's enough to say I've done it.

I've never taken performance enhancing drugs, except that one time with morphine, which was accidental. I've never seen anyone do it either, and I've never been offered any. That's why when Neil Francis, in *The Sunday Tribune*, sparked that whole debate with his claims of drug-taking in rugby, I couldn't believe it. Yet when you see some fellas getting bigger, only to become incredible shrinking men when their playing days are over, you do wonder.

I can't make any accusations. I've seen lads take protein shakes, and I've seen them take creatine. I took creatine. But I haven't touched it in years. We were the guinea pig generation.

Even schools teams were given creatine.

But I stopped taking it because no-one knew the possible side effects, even though we underwent some tests which clearly showed improved performances from taking creatine.

A player would be timed over the course of ten 100 metre runs, before taking creatine for six weeks, then undergo identical tests, and post faster times. Similarly when a player took creatine for six weeks, he benchbased 30 kilos more. You were told, in effect, that you could become faster and stronger. Personally, I didn't buy it.

I don't want to sound naïve either. You can't help but notice that players are becoming bigger and stronger. I'm amongst the last of a generation whose career began in the amateur era. You see 18 and 19-year-olds now who look like Hulk Hogan.

With professionalism, the temptations to take performance-enhancing drugs are greater. There are also significant discrepancies in testing procedures. You could go through your whole AIL career and not be tested.

It would be interesting to conduct a survey of players in different countries and find out how many have been tested. There is random testing, especially at inter-national level, rather than regular monthly testing. And there is a sizeable cost factor in testing every player in the world at club, provincial and test level, say, once a month. But at the moment that is clearly not being done.

France is quite unique in that there is blood testing, as well as urine testing. That was rare in Ireland, although I do recall it being introduced in Leinster pre-season. But this was as much a test for HIV and for health assessment in general.

I've been blood tested four or five times a year in France. This also tells us what areas of our diet need balancing, be it water or iron levels or whatever. But testing procedures do seem to be more advanced in France than most countries. That's why Bernard Laporte had a point when he raised the matter before the 2007 World Cup.

Rugby has to be more careful than most sports, because it doesn't want to end up like cycling. In my opinion, cycling has become a complete joke. I don't see the point in following that sport. I have similar views about athletics, which seem to be as much about how good your doctor is as anything else. In modern profes-sional sport you have to work and train harder than ever, and drugs can help an athlete with that workload.

It's time for rugby to get real.

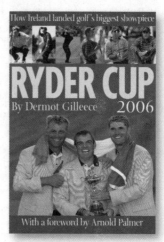
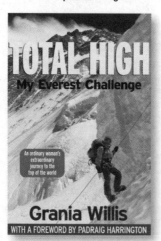
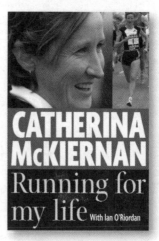